TOUCHED BY GRACE

LGBT STORIES IN COMMUNITY OF CHRIST

Co-published by John Whitmer Books and GALA.

Printed in the United States.

John Whitmer Books is a trademark of JWHA.

ISBN 978-1-934-90136-6

View our complete catalog online at *www.JohnWhitmerBooks.com.*

Learn more about JWHA at *www.JWHA.info.*

Learn more about GALA at *www.GALAweb.org.*

Cover design and typesetting by John Hamer.

TOUCHED BY GRACE

LGBT STORIES IN COMMUNITY OF CHRIST

compiled by david howard

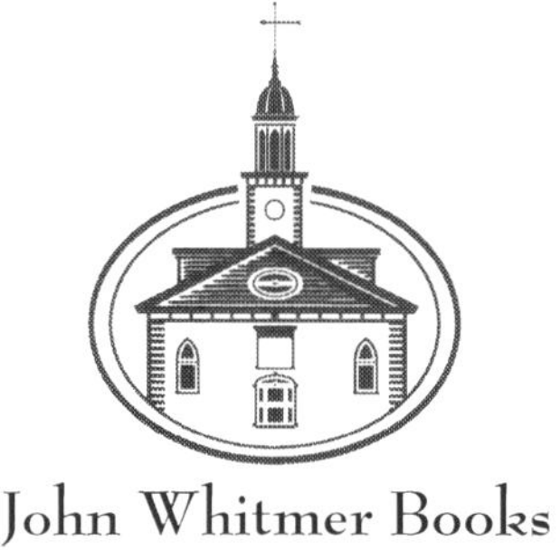

Independence, Missouri
2012

Dedication

To all of the lesbian, gay, bisexual, and transgender members of Community of Christ and their families and allies who, for their own reasons, could not wait for change to happen. We miss you and love you, and encourage you to listen to the Spirit that calls you into community and wholeness.

CONTENTS

Acknowledgements

GALA would like to recognize the following groups and individuals that made contributions to the effort of producing another book, realizing how many people were involved in this effort, how much time and creative talents were donated, and the importance of each contribution.

GALA BOARD, 2010–2011

David Howard, president, for his vision of a book that would highlight the stories of those who have remained to change Community of Christ from within; his organizational and taskmaster skills which enabled the book to be completed within a year, and an understanding of how this piece can instruct the conversation on the key issues of the 2013 US Conference.

Clyde Phillips-Frey, secretary, for his creativity and vision of book layout and flow, countless hours of editing and formatting, perseverance with rewrites, and daily support to keeping the project moving.

Allan Fiscus, past president, for his early relationship with John Whitmer Books, which paved the way for its support for the publication of this book, teamwork in working out details for the publication, compiling photos, and committing both books to Kindle.

Also, David Woosley, undersecretary for publications; Pat Danielson, treasurer; Chuck Hewitt, member-at-large; Erin Cavanaugh, member-at-large; Saundra Merth, member-at-large; Melba Jean Dixon, member-at-large; and Charlie Robison, chaplain—for risking the telling of their stories and revisiting the sometimes painful experiences; acting as the content editors in determining which stories to include; making the financial sacrifice of time and travel; recruiting additional stories for the book; and for their support for making this project of grace happen.

Our thanks go to Mary Kohlman, copy editor of the manuscript, for her generous financial contribution to this effort and her skills in making the book a better product; John Hamer for the cover design and typesetting; John Whitmer Books for its willingness and enthusiasm in publishing the second book and the gracious offer to co-publish with GALA; Vickie Speek for her work with the manuscript as editor of John Whitmer Books; Erin Jennings as copy editor of the typeset galleys; and Bill Russell, for his encouragement and guidance during the process and his "first read" of submissions to make sure we were on the right track.

We are indebted to members of the world church community who encouraged us to print this book, who see the potential for transformative power of the book, and who will use this as part of the tools to construct safe places of dialogue and spiritual conversation and transformation in the life of the community.

Our special thanks go out to each of the contributors—who revealed a sacred part of themselves, partly cathartic, partly realizing the power of the story and its part in the journey. During the weekend GALA board retreat, individuals left the table in tears because of the power of these stories to change the lives of those who had gone through similar experiences. Without exception, each of the stories in this volume carries the positive power of witness. Thank you for being part of our sacred journey!

Last, but most importantly, our hearts are full of thankfulness to the Holy Spirit, who graces us with creativity, understanding, and courage in transformative ways that we all fully don't understand, but we strive to follow.

In Memoriam

David Alan Howard

September 22, 1948 – January 12, 2012
GALA President-elect, October 2007
GALA President, October 2008 – January 2012

The world lost a man that was nothing short of incredible! He has done so much work for God in his life. While I struggle to understand you being called home, I know I can rest on the friendship you shared with us. I know I will continue to learn from your leadership in GALA for years to come. I will carry your laughter, smiles, and joy for life with me as I struggle with the loss of your friendship.

—Erin Cavanaugh
GALA Board Member at Large

For God so loved the world that he gave his only begotten Son, that whosoever believeth in Him should not perish, but have everlasting life.

—John 3:16

David believed this profound statement and recognized that every person is a "whosoever," without regard to gender, race, sexual orientation, or religious affiliation; people loved by our Creator, promised everlasting life, and designed to love each other. His life was lived in leading, encouraging, and supporting those in his family, church, profession, and community to live up to their potential as they shared their stories.

The October 2010 GALA board meeting minutes include these words attributed to David, "Perhaps now is the time to publish a companion volume (to *Homosexual Saints*) or volume two." And from this point forward, it was only a couple of months until the annual board retreat meeting at which the plans for this book were put into motion. Bill Russell, the editor of *Homosexual Saints*, attended the January 2011 meeting and provided insight into what would need to occur up to and including publication. There was much work to be done. People needed to be contacted about writing and sharing their stories; GALA board members were at the top of the list. Potential storytellers were listed and the work load divided for contact and follow-up. A special board retreat was held in Ohio at David's home during late May where the manuscripts that had been received were reviewed and assessed. The sharing of stories at the retreat was, in a word, awesome! David was the driving force of this book with the vision of how our stories could benefit those seeking a broader relationship with their God, Community of Christ, and each other. The movement of the Good Spirit has been recognized through this project.

Stories are passed down from generation to generation, told over and over, because they have special meaning, teach a lesson, or provide courage and support in their telling, as well as in their hearing. David's story is included in this volume. In it, he provided valuable insight into the life of David Alan Howard when he stated:

> But through all this turmoil of growing up cluelessly gay, I found stability and safety in the large RLDS congregation where I was raised. That congregation loved me and my family. They encouraged me, challenged me, and gave me opportunity to find my gifts and develop them. They taught me about God and gave me experiences with the Spirit that continually reside in me and guide me even through the dark times I have experienced. They helped me build my foundation on a rock, not knowing what storms would confront me.

In these sentiments is the heart of this volume, as the authors bear their souls about the struggles that surround their journey along with the return, of many, to the foundational church in which they were raised and upon which their hopes for full recognition and participation reside.

Unfortunately, David didn't get the chance to see the published copy of this volume or the full recognition and participation of LGBT members of Community of Christ. From our perspective, he passed from us much too quickly. We give thanks and celebrate the passionate life of David Alan Howard. He touched our souls and shall have a place therein forever. David shall be remembered with fondness each and every time we share our stories. His spirit lives in these pages.

—Clyde Phillips-Frey
GALA Secretary

Introduction

In 2008, John Whitmer Books published a collection of personal stories edited by William D. Russell and Lavina Fielding Anderson titled *Homosexual Saints: The Community of Christ Experience.* This volume met an important need for personal stories of gay and lesbian people in Community of Christ and has sold very well.[1] It seemed to the board of the church-related Gay and Lesbian Acceptance organization (GALA) that a second volume of stories was still needed. In this introduction, we are presenting a short summary of the fifty-seven-page history that Russell wrote for the earlier volume. A new, more diverse collection of stories completes the book.

As far as we can tell, the issue of homosexuality was not confronted by the Reorganized Church of Jesus Christ of Latter Day Saints (RLDS, now known as Community of Christ) until 1954, when C. George Mesley, a popular and highly valued member of the church's council of twelve apostles, was pressured to resign due to allegations from people in his native Australia that Mesley was homosexual. This case was, apparently, the reason that, in 1961, the First Presidency asked the church's Standing High Council to review the

[1] Russell's volume contained four historic documents on the issue: The Standing High Council statements of 1962 and 1982; World Conference Resolution 1226 on human diversity (1992); and the World Church Leadership Council's statement in 2002. Appendix B incorrectly dated the 1982 statement as March 18, when it was actually October 18.

issue of homosexuality. The result was the statement, dated October 18, 1962, "Re: Homosexuality and Other Sexual Perversions."[2]

By 1978, when Wallace B. Smith, a medical doctor, became the church's president, it seemed time to reconsider the church's position. In the 1970s, several professional associations revised earlier policy positions that had seen homosexuality as abnormal or as a mental disease. Various committees of the church worked on the issue between 1978 and 1982, with the result being a new position statement by the Standing High Council dated October 18, 1982, "Standing High Council Statement on Homosexuality."[3] This statement altered the very conservative 1962 policy by declaring that a homosexual could be in the priesthood if he was not involved in homosexual conduct.[4] A distinction was made between a "condition" and a "sex act," based on that statement. Some members saw this as a giant step forward, while others regarded it as an inadequate baby step.

In 1992, the world conference adopted resolution number 1226, prepared by a world church committee, chaired by Gwendolyn Hawks Blue, titled "Human Diversity." It remains the church's clearest and most progressive statement on the importance of avoiding prejudice and discrimination against the wide range of categories of people who are marginalized in the world.[5]

Finally, in 2002, after considerable backlash caused by President W. Grant McMurray's lengthy discussion of homosexuality in his world conference sermon, the World Church Leadership Council issued a statement, "Community, Common Consent, and the Issue of Homosexuality." This statement affirmed that the 1982 standing high council policy was still in effect, although ordinations conducted in violation of that policy would be respected. This backtracking

[2] *Homosexual Saints,* 238–242. The 1962 statement was not made public until the September 1971 *Saints' Herald* when World Church Secretary Fred Young published the last ten paragraphs in a "Question Time" column.

[3] *Homosexual Saints*, 243–248. Portions of the statement were published by W. B. (Pat) Spillman in a "Question Time" column in the March 1985 *Saints' Herald.*

[4] Members of the RLDS priesthood were all male until November 17, 1985.

[5] *Homosexual Saints*, 249–250.

greatly distressed the LGBT community and their supporters within the church.

The Gay And Lesbian Acceptance Organization (GALA)

In 1984, several unofficial meetings of gay and lesbian church members were held during the week of world conference. The result was the organization of GALA, which quickly became an important organization for both advocacy and mutual support for the lesbian, gay, bisexual, and transgender (LGBT) community in the church. By the end of the 1980s, GALA was allowed to have a booth at world conference, as well as a worship service which addressed the issue of AIDS. Over the years, GALA's involvement at world conference has expanded.

The annual GALA international retreat, held at a variety of locations throughout the United States and Canada, has served as a significant opportunity for fellowship and encouragement. LGBT people, and their family, and friends can share their testimonies—often heartbreaking—and gain much-needed support. A significant number of world church leaders have attended GALA retreats, including the current president, Steve Veazey, and past president Grant McMurray.

Meanwhile, at church-sponsored Graceland College (now known as Graceland University), prompted by Robert Mesle, a philosophy professor, and other professors and students, a nondiscriminatory policy was adopted regarding sexual orientation. A domestic partnership policy was later adopted which allowed LGBT employees to declare a same-sex partner as occupying the same kind of committed monogamous relationship as is the norm for opposite-sex, married couples.

By 1995, Graceland students began forming an organization, now called the Gay Straight Alliance. It started, in secret, with quiet meetings and soon blossomed into a fairly large organization that became public. Advertised meetings often drew more than thirty attendees. In April 2003, the student organization planned a street protest when a notorious anti-gay scholar gave a series of lectures in

Lamoni over a period of two days. On both evenings, students and faculty engaged in a street protest on Main Street, outside the buildings where the lectures were presented. About ninety people in all, protested on those two nights. This scholar's research methodology has since been denounced by several professional organizations, and one judge in Texas instructed a jury to ignore the scholar's testimony as it was not up to professional standards.[6]

Since the 2002 statement by the World Church Leadership Council, world church leaders have worked at promoting a continuing civil dialogue between church members, in hopes that greater understanding among members can be achieved and social change can occur without disrupting the church—like the ordination of women did in the 1980s. At that time, there seemed to be some recognition that the 1980s division was not handled skillfully by the leadership. Dissenters were driven from the church. They might have been retained, in many cases, if a more pastoral approach had been used.

A number of events took place over the next several years, leading the GALA movement to where it is now. Church leadership abruptly changed, which threw the progress on LGBT issues into a period of uncertainty. GALA began an initiative of working with congregations to explore what it meant to welcome all people—not just LGBT. The desire was to help congregations become an ensign of safety and community. A grant was secured, and a formal, separate organization called the Welcoming Community Network (WCN), was formed. WCN began to develop resources and a process to move congregations toward inclusion.[7]

Under the initiative of its president-elect, David Howard, GALA began direct advocacy and education with the new church leadership. Their first meeting was held in January 2008. It was GALA's desire

---

[6] The preceding paragraphs are a very brief summary of Russell's essay "Homosexuals and the Community of Christ: A Continuing Tension," *Homosexual Saints: The Community of Christ Experience* (Independence, MO: John Whitmer Books, 2008), 1–57.

[7] See *welcomingcommunitynetwork.org* for a listing of member welcoming congregations and *galaweb.org* for a listing of congregations who welcome LGBT persons without going through a formal welcoming process.

that one of the First Presidency would be available to attend. To the surprise of Howard and GALA president Allan Fiscus, all three First Presidency members were present. For the next ninety minutes, the five of them shared their stories and listened to each other's hopes as the journey toward giftedness and self-worth was explored. The meeting ended in a circle, with a prayer offered by President Steve Veazey. From this moment, all realized this relationship could blossom—that GALA could be a partner in the journey the church would pursue in creating an environment leading to new understandings of what it means to truly be the body of Christ in a world that is marked by fear and separation.

Over the next several months, additional meetings were held with the First Presidency, Presiding Bishopric, most of the apostles, Presiding Evangelist and his quorum secretary, President of Seventy, High Priest Quorum and its leadership, and other staff. WCN flourished and began to train people in facilitating welcoming congregations. Several congregations became a part of WCN. *Homosexual Saints* was widely distributed throughout world church leadership. LGBT people reengaged in the life of their church community, advocacy training was provided at GALA retreats, and a strategic plan was developed for the 2010 World Conference.

And then along came Chuck Hewitt and Mike Albers-Hewitt! (Their stories are included in this book.) Several states had already passed the right for same-sex couples to marry. But, in 2009, much to everyone's surprise, Iowa became the first midwestern state to approve marriage for same-sex couples. For the tenth anniversary of their commitment ceremony, Chuck and Mike traveled to Graceland University to sanctify their marriage by an elder in their church in a state that recognized it. Needless to say, this caused quite a stir in Community of Christ. Other ceremonies were conducted. Policies on the use of buildings were changed, an investigation was conducted, and some priesthood members were silenced. Community of Christ lost a gifted elder that day, and GALA lost a past-president and advocate for inclusion dating back to the 1980s in San Francisco. That year, GALA also lost another gifted past-president, and an ally and his family. We hope this is only temporary. But how long will people stay if they are not included as persons of worth in the body of the church? Many in the LGBT community have rejected churches due to persecution, condemnation, and hatred directed towards them by people within the organizations.

During this period, GALA and WCN also crafted resolutions to be presented at mission center conferences for inclusion in the 2010 World Conference agenda. These resolutions ranged from formal information coming from world church on the issues, to the ordination of priesthood, and sanctifying of same-sex marriages within the church. The Eastern Great Lakes Mission Center Conference was the first to approve these three measures. Additional resolutions came from Florida, California, and Colorado. Independent resolutions came from Texas, Canada, Australia, and the Polynesian Islands. Opposing resolutions came from Southeastern USA, Africa, and Central America. However, those opposing were more conciliatory in nature, and requested deferral or referral to the First Presidency for a decision.

The stage had been set to discuss the issue of homosexuality with the world conference. And while the world church leadership may have wanted to manage this discussion in a different time frame, the cat was out of the bag, and it would be on the agenda.

It soon became evident that a global policy on homosexuality in the church might be extremely disruptive in some countries where homosexuality is taboo. In those societies, the ministry of a homosexual would not be accepted. In some cultures, homosexuals are so deep in the closet they sometimes give the impression that, by some miracle, there are no homosexuals in that culture. The church might be banned from some countries if a positive, affirming, global church policy existed. This bore heavily on the minds of leadership as preparations were made for conference.

World Conference 2010 began with much anticipation. Twenty-one resolutions dealing with some aspect of the LGBT issue, both pro and con, were on the agenda. Over two thousand buttons inscribed with rainbow colors and the words "unity in diversity" (from the document that was to become section 164 of the Doctrine and Covenants) were distributed. Rainbow lanyards were worn throughout the delegations. For months in advance, prayers requesting spiritual direction had been offered on behalf of the leadership. Resolution discussion was civil and balanced. The document was presented and was approved as section 164, which allowed cultural issues, like this one, to be resolved on a national level, through a national conference. All issues of substance on the resolutions that referred to the LGBT community were referred to a future national conference.

National conferences will be held in the future, with the US conference following the 2013 World Conference. It is hoped that these conferences will inform church leadership as to the level of acceptance of LGBT persons into full fellowship, including marriage and ordination, so that national policies can be appropriately established.

After conference, the First Presidency, in consultation with the Standing High Council and the World Church Leadership Council, reaffirmed the 1982/2002 policy that LGBT persons in relationships would not be eligible for ordination until the world church leadership approves changes based on the consent of the national conferences. This, in practice, has also been applied to LGBT persons in general. So, while we wait, silencing of priesthood may go on, priesthood status can be challenged and reviewed, giftedness lost, and the patience of LGBT members tested again. While this policy is harsh and discriminatory, it is necessary for the integrity and trust of the process. Let's get it changed!

It is hoped that the personal stories in this book will help readers become better informed about this important issue that faces Community of Christ and many other churches. We owe a debt of gratitude to the people who have graciously contributed their stories.

1

Welcoming Community Network

Welcome one another, therefore, just as Christ has welcomed you, for the glory of God.
—Romans 15:7 NRSV

Meredith Bishoff

Beginning in 2003, the Welcoming Community Network (WCN), as a program that was originally part of GALA, has grown to become an international, grassroots organization committed to seeing full participation of persons of all sexual orientations and gender identities in the life and ministry of Community of Christ congregations.

WCN is composed of members and friends of the church, and a coalition of congregations who have chosen to publicly express the extravagant welcome and inclusive ministry modeled by Jesus. Before the establishment of WCN, five congregations independently declared themselves to be intentionally welcoming and affirming to all—including lesbian, gay, bisexual, and transgender persons. Those congregations were Basileia: An Open Door Community of Christ (Southern California); Lakeview Community of Christ (Chicago, Illinois); St. Paul Community of Christ (St. Paul, Minnesota); Berkley Peace Chapel (Berkley, California); and Open Door Ministry (Mount Pleasant, New South Wales, Australia).

The number of welcoming and affirming Community of Christ congregations and ministries has grown to twelve, located in California, Florida, Colorado, New York, Illinois, and Missouri. Another ten congregations are currently in the process of exploring the decision to become publicly welcoming and affirming.

In January 2007, WCN received news that it, in collaboration with three other organizations, was approved to receive a $150,000 grant from the Arcus Foundation of Kalamazoo, Michigan. Sharing the three-year grant were the Association of Welcoming and Affirming Baptists, Gay and Lesbian Affirming Disciples (Christian Church, Disciples of Christ), and the Brethren Mennonite Council for LGBT Interests—all are members of the interfaith Welcoming Church Movement. The grant was used to hire a full-time, faith-based community organizer who worked out of Minneapolis with all four programs—individually, as well as collaboratively—to develop regional ecumenical workshops. The focus of the workshops was to help individuals from each denomination acquire the training, resources, and support necessary to assist congregations that desire to become more welcoming of lesbian, gay, bisexual, and transgender persons.

During the Community of Christ's 2007 World Conference, WCN worked collaboratively with GALA in presenting a worship service. The theme "Christ Is Our Host: There Is Room for Us All," was taken from the words in a beautiful hymn written by Ruth Duck. During the service, three individuals shared their sacred stories. They also expressed the need for welcoming and affirming congregations, since there are those, who, even today, do not feel fully welcome to live authentically, and at times, fear rejection from their own families and, often, from their congregations and the church.

In April 2007, WCN responded to a report submitted by the Committee on Homosexuality and the Church, Community of Christ. Although no recommendations were offered in the report, which was presented at world conference, the Welcoming Community Network applauded the call to uphold the inestimable worth of persons of all sexual orientations and gender identities in Community of Christ. WCN called for the Committee on Homosexuality and the Church to develop strategies that would assist congregations in becoming welcoming and affirming of LGBT persons, and encourage congregations to explore the possibility of becoming intentionally welcoming and affirming of LGBT persons on their own. The process included study, discussion, prayer, discernment, education, and the development and adoption of a welcoming covenant made public by the congregation. WCN has a cadre of volunteers trained to assist congregations in this process.

In 2010, WCN collaborated again with GALA and shared a booth, reception, and worship service during that year's world conference.

Further information about WCN, faith-based organization training opportunities, how congregations may become intentionally welcoming and affirming, and a list of affiliated congregations may be found on WCN's website at *www.WelcomingCommunityNetwork.org.*

2

Our Transforming Journey

Sam and Pat Marmoy

Before Pat Marmoy returned to college to study for a master's degree in counseling, she gave little thought to homosexuality. She had little awareness of it, and when the subject came up in her studies and in conversation, she commented that she thought homosexuality was a way that teens could embarrass their parents and get attention. She was emphatically told that she was absolutely wrong.

She remembered Thomas—a delightful, openly gay young man in her practicum class. She recalled stating that he was the first person she knew who was gay. However, she later remembered that, many years before, she had come to understand that one of her relatives was gay, and, then, she realized she had tried to bury that memory.

Thus, her journey began. Pat first wondered why she had let herself forget, and then she asked other questions. One of these was: What causes homosexuality? Her human sexuality class had not given her any definitive answers. Then, one day when she was pondering this question, she had an experience of understanding. The words were not audible but were very clear and definite: Why do you need to know? As she puzzled over this question, she realized she wanted to know so she could pass judgment. Since Pat believed it was wrong to judge others, the message became clear: She did *not* need to know.

Shortly after that experience, the church released two new Temple School courses: Human Sexuality, and Homosexuality and the Church. In conversation with other Community of Christ mental health professionals, Pat shared her desire to teach those courses and was advised to "get the other side of the story" by attending an upcoming GALA retreat.

Pat was afraid her presence at the retreat might make those attending feel uncomfortable, but she was reassured that she wouldn't be the only straight person there. The accepting, loving fellowship she experienced, and the stories she heard there of rejection and fear changed her life. Besides that, the closing communion service was the most spiritual she had ever experienced.

When Pat returned home, she shared her experience with her husband, Sam, and they both began attending GALA activities in Independence, where they lived. They have attended several GALA retreats together and now have a huge community of friends they love and respect, and who are blessings to their lives.

As Pat shared her experiences, and growing understanding of homosexuality and its issues, opportunities opened for her to support others, including people close to her, as they struggled with loved ones coming out. She taught the Temple School courses at the Mesa, Arizona, congregation where she and Sam attend in the winter (with Sam as one of the students). She and Sam later teamed up to teach the classes at the Chandler, Arizona, congregation, as well as at several other congregations.

Pat and Sam Marmoy's involvement in GALA led to GALA's growing participation in the national welcoming church movement. As they became aware of the need for changing the culture in congregations, the Marmoys took several trainings with this movement, and started doing what they could to promote their work.

Eventually, the decision was made to separate the welcoming church activity from GALA, and the Welcoming Community Network became an entity of its own. Sam, a WCN board member, works to change materials prepared for liturgical churches with language applicable to our own denomination. He also prepares resource listings and provides ways of accessing these materials. While not a board member, Pat works in the background, in as many ways as she can, to promote the sharing of stories. They both work to promote the welcoming and affirming of lesbian, gay, bisexual, transgender, and questioning persons in Community of Christ congregations.

Their conviction is: "Advancing the understanding, acceptance, and love of LGBTQ persons is the focus of our lives. The heart of the ministry and message of Jesus was the absolute worth of every single person, particularly the marginalized. We cannot imagine that it is possible to be genuinely Christian and still reject anyone for any reason."

3

Fort Collins, Colorado, Congregation Weaves a Tapestry of Welcome

Fort Collins WEAVERS Committee

In April 2008, three members of the Fort Collins, Colorado, Community of Christ congregation went to their congregation's leadership council with a proposal. They proposed to start a one- or two-year process of study, discussion, and prayer to determine if the congregation would be receptive to becoming a welcoming congregation. One of the three members served on the board of Welcoming Community Network—an international, grassroots organization that exists to enable full participation of persons of all sexual orientations and gender identities in the life and ministry of Community of Christ, both in policy and practice.

With the leadership council's support, this WCN group used a variety of methods to educate and stimulate discussion in the congregation about how the LGBT community is often excluded from participation in faith communities. Films, such as *For the Bible Tells Me So* and *Coming Out—Coming In: Faith, Identity, and Belonging*, were used as discussion starters. The 2008 summer adult Sunday school class used Bill Russell's book, *Homosexual Saints: The Community of Christ Experience,* as a text. Panel discussions, articles in the congregation's newsletter, and worship services focusing on radical welcome were all a part of the nearly two-year process in which the congregation participated.

In November 2009, the Fort Collins congregation voted to become an official WCN congregation with the adoption of the following *Covenant of Welcome*:

> We welcome ALL to our congregation and uphold the dignity and worth of all persons. We extend the love of Jesus Christ to everyone including those who are marginalized for any reason such as: age, race, gender, education, marital status, sexual orientation, socioeconomic status, political viewpoint, immigration status, gender identity, disability, national origin, or religious belief.

As reflected in the Covenant of Welcome, displayed prominently through the church building, the congregation desired to celebrate diversity in even broader ways than just the LGBT community. Following the adoption of the covenant, a committee called WEAVERS replaced the WCN group. The name WEAVERS was chosen to represent the congregation's desire to be like a tapestry or cloth, unified in its inclusive diversity. The committee's responsibility is to help the congregation more fully live out, or flesh out, the Covenant of Welcome within the community of Fort Collins.

In addition to participating in Spirit in the Park, Pride in the Park, and other LGBT events, the congregation is involved in giving ministry to the homeless, sponsoring a senior meal site, making lap robes for nursing home residents, collecting food for the local food bank, and many other community outreach activities.

In 2010, when WEAVERS had a booth at the local Spirit in the Park (the spiritual part of Pride in the Park), it was realized that northern Colorado's welcoming faith communities, including Christian and Jewish congregations, didn't really know much about each other. Early in 2011, WEAVERS represented Fort Collins Community of Christ in initiating a meeting with representatives from twelve other faith communities. After several months, they created the Northern Colorado Coalition of Welcoming Faith Communities. The desire was to have people of faith, who celebrate the dignity and worth of all persons, be more visible. This is, of course, one of Community of Christ's core spiritual principles. This is one way we can put action steps to our Covenant of Welcome. Too often, people who are marginalized believe there are no churches, synagogues, or mosques that will embrace them. The first activity of this new interfaith coalition was to help welcome students back to Colorado State University on a day designated as Finding Your Faith Community!

As a welcoming congregation, it is our hope that the 2013 USA National Conference will lead the broader denomination to live out that core value of the worth of all persons.

4

Only a Snapshot

Stacie Wittenmyer

I knew I was different early in my life, but I didn't have a word for it until I was a teenager. I told a few of my high school friends about it and then went off to college. Eventually, there was no one in my life who knew.

While I was a student, I was baptized into Community of Christ. At that time, I understood that being gay was a sin, and I accepted that to be true. I dated a few men and, eventually, just stopped trying to date men or women. My inner turmoil was more than I wanted to deal with.

During the next twenty years, my theology evolved from literalism to something less rigid, and I was able to release myself from the idea that being gay was condemned by God. However, I still kept it all to myself.

In 2006, I received a priesthood call. I only knew of about a dozen people in all of Community of Christ who were LGBT affirming. I didn't want to accept the call and have the congregation feel deceived. I also didn't want to come out publicly because of the turmoil it might bring to my niece and parents. I decided I would ask someone to help me make this decision. A man from my mission center was coming to Toledo to teach a weekend Temple School class, and I planned to ask him to be a sounding board for my fears, thoughts, and questions.

To this day, coming out to someone brings with it a great amount of anxiety and fear. With my heart in my throat, I went to a lesbian bookstore, and looked for a book that might help me in coming out to the man from my mission center. As I left the store, I noticed a man getting into an SUV across the parking lot. He stopped, looked at the store I had just come out of, came over to me, and wouldn't let me get into my car. He never spoke. He just looked at me with hate and jockeyed back and forth, blocking my path so I couldn't leave. I didn't want the situation to escalate into something more violent, so I pulled out a pad and pen to write down his license number. The pen didn't work, but it did the trick. The man suddenly looked alarmed and went back to his vehicle. He didn't leave; he just watched me get into my truck.

I rushed to the church, five minutes away, hoping I wasn't being followed. When I got there, people were waiting in the parking lot for someone to unlock the door. I let them in, and busied myself helping them set up and find the supplies they might need for the weekend class. I felt so lost. If I had just experienced road rage or other violence, I would have been able to tell them about it. At that point, I didn't feel comfortable sharing information about this apparent gay rage. However, before the weekend was over, I had come out to the teacher of the Temple School class—the first person I had told in twenty years. I was drained. I felt fear, relief, and a new freedom. That weekend began my truer life.

I am a longtime member of Community of Christ's online community called the Cyber Congregation. At the same time I was struggling with my role in the church, an unidentified young man there was struggling with his own sexuality and identity. He was having a rough time. Many people encouraged him to renounce homosexuality and gave him their full support in that endeavor. A few people encouraged him to accept himself first and then make his life decisions. The LGBT folk of the Cyber Congregation erupted in anguish and told their own heartbreaking stories of condemnation, rejection, and, sometimes, violence from their families, friends, and church.

In the midst of all this pain, anger, and condemnation, I found myself spontaneously telling my own story. To my surprise, I was not condemned—perhaps because I am a woman. People asked genuine questions and held me in their prayers as I came out there, even though most were completely against homosexuality. It was then I realized that sharing my truth could help people get close enough to see the issues, to feel compassion, and to begin to rethink what they had always believed to be true.

I eventually decided not to accept the priesthood call in my congregation. It seemed to me that asking the congregation to consider a call for an LGBT sister would be too stretching for all of us. Later, I came out to them after a prayer service; since then, I have never doubted their love for me.

The following paragraphs are taken from my journal, written on the eve of the prayer service. I realized I was taking a turn that would change my life and ministry forever. I tried to capture a snapshot of my feelings and explain to myself why it felt important to live openly in the church. I had been reading Luke, chapter 15—the stories of the lost coin, lost sheep, and prodigal son:

> For now, my silence buys me a place in the safety of the 99, but as I begin to speak my truth, I step into the vulnerability of that 100th sheep. The shepherds of our church are not really going to come looking for me, though. They say they will support me, but only until that point where they have to take a stand. Then, they will look away, pretend not to see, and say a shamed prayer of petition that I will quietly leave.
>
> I am not the coin of great worth. As this prodigal is walking up the road to her spiritual home, there are no servants of my God running to greet me, to welcome the authentic me home. I will be worshipping in the same house with the family of God, but, too many, will no longer be known as a sister. I don't know what grace will be afforded me. I don't know who will be able to accept my reality, my presence, my servanthood.
>
> I do believe that our leaders long to be true to the call and obligations of the kingdom, but the poverty of our spiritual lives limits that

response. In the economy of our church today, it is the 99 sheep, not the Good Shepherd, who calculate the worth of the one. The cost of accepting the truth of the outcast is too high to attempt. We will lose our illusion of unity; we will lose our ignorance of the boundaries we place on God's love; we will lose our status among the competing kingdoms in Christianity.

My shame is that I support this economy as well. I am not willing to endanger the body of Christ to save the outcast, even when it's me. I am painfully aware that my actions and inactions are prolonging the estrangement of my gay brothers and sisters, and I knowingly compromise their worth for the nonconfronted comfort of my congregation and denomination.

My prayer is that by becoming visible, I will help the church to better see Christ's redeeming love in this world. In a way, I am the found, seeking to draw the 99 more fully into the light of God's grace.

Since that time, I have processed my thoughts a bit more. These reflections remain true for me, but more like I'm looking through a wide-angle lens. When I zoom in on individual relationships and encounters, I can see that the larger picture is indeed moving—sometimes painfully slow—in the direction of compassion and grace.

5

Exactly Where I Am Supposed to Be

David Woosley

After reading the stories in *Homosexual Saints: The Community of Christ Experience*, and being asked to provide my story for the second edition, I wasn't sure what I had to contribute that would be of interest for others to read. Most of my experiences with Community of Christ have been positive, as opposed to many of the negative experiences depicted in the first book. So, after a lot of thought, I realized that a positive story is what many people need these days, much like what is shared in the *It Gets Better Project* started by Dan Savage.

I didn't grow up in Community of Christ, but was raised in the Christian Church (Disciples of Christ). I converted after graduating from college and moving away from home—but, more about that later. I know, for sure, that I am exactly where I am supposed to be, and I am doing exactly what I am supposed to be doing. It hasn't been a *straight* line from there to here (pardon the pun). In fact, God has had to step in and take action, on numerous occasions, to get me where I am today (what some people may call coincidences). I don't believe that the events in my life were coincidences any more than I believe that this world and all the intricacies of life are coincidences.

Perhaps, the best way to tell my story is to list some of the events that occurred when God took action in my life. The first one that comes to mind was shortly after I graduated from college. I had been in ROTC and had a commitment to the US Army, including at least ninety days of active duty in the summer to attend Infantry Officers Basic Training. Because of that, I was not actively looking for a permanent job. As it turned out, God stepped in, and I received a call from the City of Moline, Illinois, asking me if I was interested in interviewing for their vacant position of civil engineer. I accepted the interview and was offered the job, but I had to advise them of my military commitment. Since most construction takes place in the summer, my active duty was a conflict; however, the city engineer was a former military officer and knew the right people to contact in order to delay my active duty until the following winter.

It was very important in the grand scheme of things that I move to Moline because that was where I was introduced to what was then the RLDS church. Just before I moved, I found out that a former college housemate of mine had, just a few months earlier, obtained a job with Deere and Company in Moline. I contacted Rick upon my arrival, and we ended up becoming roommates. To get to the point, let me just say that Rick was a member of the RLDS church. I started going to church with him and eventually joined.

I now need to fast forward about twenty years. I married and had two wonderful daughters. I changed jobs three times, divorced, and ended up in Lubbock, Texas. I was active in the RLDS church in Lubbock, and Lubbock is where I met my partner. We have now been together twenty-one years. However, the last I heard, Lubbock County is the second most conservative county in the United States (although I'm told they are still striving for first place). So, there was no way I could serve God, and my brothers and sisters in Lubbock, the way God had in mind.

Events then took place that resulted in me changing jobs again and moving to Lawrence, Kansas, where I situated in the only truly "blue" county in the state of Kansas. I started attending church in Lawrence immediately and, several months later, received a call from one of the members inviting me to weekly, contemporary, small group worship. This small group evolved into a mission and eventually into a separate congregation.

About this time, God stepped in again, and my partner and I separated for several months. It was during this period of time that I was called to the office of priest and was ordained. Our separation was necessary in order to not violate the Standing High Council Statement on Homosexuality (March 18, 1982). I became a part of the leadership team of my congregation and continue in that role today, as the congregation's financial officer.

One Sunday, I was asked by one of our congregation's small group leaders to fill in for her and lead the discussion, as she was going to be out of town. Looking back, I believe this, too, was God stepping in. The group was studying Rick Warren's book, *The Purpose Driven Life*. This was another important point in time for me, because the discussion that day led me to understand that God wanted me to do whatever I could to minister to the LGBT community. At that point, events in my life began to move fast and furious.

I started attending monthly GALA get-togethers in Kansas City, after George, a member of our congregation, invited me. Sometime later, George was supposed to attend a meeting of some type in Independence, Missouri, with Sharon Troyer; however, he had also committed to singing in the choir at a Billy Graham service that same night in Kansas City. God stepped in again, and George asked me to attend the meeting in his place. I agreed to, and the meeting turned out to be the beginning of the Welcoming Community Network, which GALA was instrumental in initiating.

I became very active in both GALA and WCN and, eventually, ended up on the executive board of both organizations. I currently serve as a director for WCN. And, after serving as a director for GALA, I am currently serving as the under-secretary for publications. In addition, as a result of training sponsored by WCN at the temple a number of years ago, I became involved with a multidenominational group in Kansas City that adopted the name Kansas City Coalition for Welcoming Ministries (KCCWM), and I currently serve as their treasurer.

When asked why I am involved with all of these organizations, I reply that God has called me to minister to the LGBT community. He stepped into my life on numerous occasions to make sure I had the opportunity to do so. I quote Doctrine and Covenants 151:9: "You who are my disciples must be found continuing in the forefront of those organizations and movements which are recognizing the worth of persons and are committed to bringing the ministry of my Son to bear on their lives."

So, I am exactly where I am supposed to be, doing exactly what I am supposed to be doing. I'm here, not because I planned it this way, but because—I believe—*God* planned it this way.

This is a very exciting time for Community of Christ, a historic time. As Doctrine and Covenants 164:5 states, "Through the gospel of Christ a new community of tolerance, reconciliation, unity in diversity, and love is being born as a visible sign of the coming reign of God." I am very grateful to be a part of Community of Christ doing, to the best of my ability, what I believe God has called me to do—to minister to the LGBT community.

6

Two Persistent Wahines

Rowena "Holly" Holloway and Joyce Bullion

ROWENA "HOLLY" HOLLOWAY, a fourth-generation member of the RLDS church, loves her church and her God. She was born sixty-four years ago and was reborn thirty-six years ago. Basically, Holly came out as being gay in her mid-twenties. Joyce Bullion, a convert to the RLDS church almost twenty years ago, was born sixty-six years ago and was reborn thirty-eight years ago. They met each other through a twelve-step program and were united in holy matrimony (not legally) by a Methodist minister at 8 p.m. on 8-8-88 (August 8, 1988) beside a swimming pool in the Dallas, Texas, gay community of Oak Lawn—and the temperature was 108 degrees. (Holly and Joyce believe that the number eight is a number of prosperity.)

Both attended a relationship workshop in the Oak Lawn area and believe the event set them on a firmer foundation with their own relationship. Joyce had been a member of Unity Church and had grown up in what is now the United Church of Christ. Even though they were active members of a twelve-step program, Holly and Joyce both felt they needed something more inspirational in their relationship, so they could give greater service to their Lord and Savior.

In 1992, they attended a Community of Christ congregation in Oklahoma. Joyce realized that Holly would only be happy in the church where she grew up, so Joyce decided to join her in membership through the sacrament of baptism and confirmation. Before being baptized, Joyce felt she should tell the pastor that she was a lesbian and ask if that made a difference. The pastor contacted church headquarters and received approval.

In time, some of the church members expressed fear and disapproval with Joyce and Holly. Finally, the pastor's wife called and asked them to leave the church. These fearful members suffered with the misconception that gays molested children and were afraid when Joyce and Holly approached their children. Joyce and Holly were devastated, and deeply hurt and angry. Holly was angry at the congregation, but Joyce was so angry she considered leaving the church entirely. They had done nothing wrong. Both knew that Christ would not approve of what this congregation was doing in his name.

After receiving extensive counseling, Joyce came out of the closet at the age of forty-two. The happiest day of her life was when she chose to be who God created her to be, because then she could be transparent. When she was eighteen years old, she knew she was gay, and had gone to a Methodist minister for counseling. The minister told her to ignore her desire of wanting a same-sex relationship, and to date men and marry. She married twice and tried to be normal, but both relationships ended in divorce. She was terrified of rejection, and the incident at the Oklahoma Community of Christ congregation was the very thing she feared the most. Not only did Joyce want to turn in her membership to Community of Christ, she considered quitting *all* churches. It was clear to her that too many Christians were hypocrites; it was inconceivable that people who said they loved everyone could act so badly. She felt they did not speak on *behalf* of Christ, but spoke *instead* of Christ.

Joyce and Holly continued to attend their twelve-step group and prayed for direction about their church attendance. They both had a deep faith, and loved God and Christ with all their hearts. They later moved to a small Texas town where there was a chapter of the Ku Klux Klan. There, they were the targets of police bullying, and were threatened and told to "leave town or else."

They prayed with every fiber of their being for protection and direction, and in 1997, they received a call from a Community of Christ member in Texas who invited them to be a part of a home group connected with their church. The policeman who had told them to leave town actually quit the police force and became a pastor of a church, and the neighbor who also threatened them brought them vegetables from his garden. Prayer was a most powerful force and helped them overcome their difficulties.

Eventually, the home group became so large that the group moved to the community center in McKinney, Texas. These people were civil, but Joyce and Holly were not asked to participate in their worship services, except to read a scripture now and then. Their talents were not in demand there, even though they traveled fifty minutes to attend.

Joyce and Holly had a dream to move to Hawaii one day and had actually set a goal to move by the year 2001. They saved their money for ten years and prayed that if it was God's will, they would go. In 2001, both were laid off from their jobs at Texas Instruments and, after receiving a wonderful separation package, they decided "to make delicious lemonade with the lemons."

After praying the *Prayer of Jabez* that year, everything seemed to fall into place. Their house sold off the Internet, unseen by the buyer, in sixty days. Joyce's father had passed away in July of that year, and she received part of her inheritance two days before they left. On December 28, they put their car on a ship and flew to Hawaii.

In many ways, living in Hawaii was like living in paradise. Not only were they led to the most beautiful place on earth, but they were overcome with joy by the unconditional, loving "aloha spirit" of the people. They cried often with tears of joy. Every time they were asked to read a scripture, give the invocation, assist with the Disciples' Generous Response, or offer a benediction in a worship service, they were joyful. It was clear that their talents were not only in demand, but they were also appreciated. It was the first time that Joyce felt accepted by Christians since she came out of the closet.

Joyce told Ron, a new friend at church, that Holly had a talent for speaking. Holly delivered her first sermon in March 2003 and has done so many times since then. Appropriately, the topic of her first sermon was "God's Grace." In 2006, Holly was told that she had a priesthood call to the office of elder, and in September 2007 she was ordained. Her father came to Hawaii in support of her ordination.

However, a family member later called the first presidency's office at Community of Christ headquarters telling them what a terrible person Holly was, and that she was gay. It was then that Joyce and Holly were asked by headquarters to sign a paper saying they would be celibate in their relationship—and that was after almost twenty years of union. Both signed the paper out of love for God and with a strong desire for both to serve God on a higher level. That was over three years ago. This year Joyce and Holly will celebrate twenty-three years of union.

Joyce and Holly feel positive that the Community of Christ Standing High Council Statement (1982) and, specifically, the policy that was developed around it, needs to be rescinded as soon as possible. Twenty-nine years of asking gays, lesbians, and transgender members who are called to the priesthood to be celibate in their relationships, not only discriminates, but also serves as bullying. They feel it is not pleasing to God or to his Son, Jesus Christ. However, they realize that when changing levels of consciousness, progress is three steps forward and two back.

Holly and Joyce believe that Community of Christ congregations in the Hawaiian Islands are a living testimony of Christ's teachings, but they have been pulled backward by outdated, biased rulings. The majority of the church *ohana* (family) in Hawaii lives Christ's teachings of unconditional, nonjudgmental love. Joyce could go back to the church she was raised in, the United Church of Christ, and has considered it. But, she feels that God wants her to continue to speak out and stay with Community of Christ in hope that, one day, it will become a completely welcoming church. If she were to go to the UCC church, so would her voice, and discrimination would continue on and on. It is their heartfelt *kuleana* (responsibility and privilege) to stay with Community of Christ, to exercise unconditional love to all those who both dislike them and love them, and to serve their Creator.

Joyce and Holly will be so happy when no one asks if a person is black or white, male or female, gay or heterosexual. None of this should ever be an issue. When God calls, we should act on his behalf and not respond with questions directed toward gender, color of skin, or sexual preference. God loves each and every one of us unconditionally, and it is for us to do the same with each other. We are told in Galatians 3:27–29: "As many of you as were baptized into Christ have clothed yourselves with Christ. There is no longer Jew or Greek, there is no longer slave or free, there is no longer male and female; for all of you are one in Christ Jesus. And if you belong to Christ, then you are Abraham's offspring, heirs according to the promise."

Joyce and Holly pray that Community of Christ will stop discriminating—that members and friends who are gay, lesbian, or transgender will be patient with the slow progress for new procedures, and that we will truly become a community of Christ.

7

Connecting the Dots

David Howard

WHERE DID IT BEGIN? I grew up on a dairy farm in eastern Iowa. Every Saturday, my Dad would load milk in our pickup, and we would drive eight miles to the dairy to deliver it to be processed. Then, we would do errands in town. I always enjoyed the first warm days of spring, because there would be men with their shirts off, and I would frantically look for them. And when I found them, my neck would turn to rubber as I strained to capture every glimpse—remembering their physiques for days to come, remembering their images in my fantasies.

But I made no connections. You see, this was the 1950s and I was only four or five years old. At that time, there were no media reports on gay pride or coming out. Male models—in any amount of clothing—didn't grace the newspapers or magazines. And I lived a sheltered life, probably more so than most midwestern kids in the fifties and sixties. The word homosexual was never uttered in my home. There were no national role models, because it would have been the kiss of death—much more than it still is today. It was all underground—so far underground that this sheltered midwestern kid would never find it.

I was precocious and talkative, and way too pretty for a boy. My mom, in her more intimate moments, would counsel me that I was special. (Moms of gay sons always know first.) The women at church would tell her how pretty my hands were and how well behaved I was. The young women, when they got married, always asked me to be their candlelighter or usher, because they knew I was sensitive enough to take it seriously and get it right. I had several encounters with boys my age. I remember one boy who lived across the street and one I met at church. One of these relationships lasted into high school and the other into college. Still, I was clueless. The dots were unconnected.

Junior high hit me like a ton of bricks—damage occurred there that would stick with me for decades to come. I went from being one of the most popular kids in my elementary school to a pariah. Boys and girls began to change. I didn't. I was a late bloomer, partially because I was one of the youngest kids in each grade, having started school when I was four. My voice was high, and I was a choir and drama kid. I was abused and bullied, sometimes physically. But the verbal abuse hurt me the most.

My family was never available for me. My mom worked outside the home, and when she was home, she was tired—and lonely—because my dad was never there. My dad was a man's man, always encouraging me to eat certain foods so I would grow hair on my chest. When I disappointed him, he would ask me when I was going to grow up to be a man. After we moved to town, he spent evenings and Saturdays pursuing his farming and church hobbies. My sister got the prized upstairs bedroom where she would retreat as soon as she got home from school and right after supper. So no one was available to share my pain or help me process it.

The only time anyone said or showed anything negative about homosexuality was when my mother opened, by mistake, an unsolicited advertisement for male pornography that was addressed to me. She gagged and condemned the garbage. Nothing else was ever said—not even the time when the uncle of one of my friends who had moved to Los Angeles visited church one Sunday. He was beautiful. The women fawned over him and asked him why he had not found a woman worthy of him. But the word homosexual or its derivatives were never uttered in association with him in my presence.

High school was not much better, except there was little abuse or bullying. I knew my place by then and made friends within the choir community. I was pretty much disengaged from everyone, especially those outside this community. One of the lessons I learned was that pain hurts—so much so, that I learned to do almost anything to prevent the hurt again. I didn't think about suicide because, for some reason, I really liked most of me. (The tragedy today is that so many LGBT kids are under such intense pressure from bullying that they choose suicide just to relieve the pain.) I made it through high school and on to Graceland College where I found safety and began to blossom. But, still, there were no attached dots.

Through all the turmoil of growing up cluelessly gay, I found stability and safety in the large RLDS congregation where I was raised. That congregation loved me and my family. They encouraged me, challenged me, and gave me opportunity to find my gifts and develop them. They taught me about God and gave me experiences with the Spirit that continually reside within me and guide me, even through the dark times I have experienced. They helped me build my foundation upon a rock, not knowing what storms would confront me.

Postwar babies were given expectations—both written and unwritten. The transcending expectation was that you would graduate high school, go to college (perhaps the first one ever in your family), graduate from college, get married, have two kids, and move to a house in the suburbs with a white picket fence. I boarded that train like so many others who formed the foundation of the middle class.

Linda and I were married in western Canada. I received a job offer in my field in Utah, so off we went. Utah was a hostile place for non-Mormons in the early seventies. It was hard to make friends there. Most Mormons, who we thought liked us, quickly dropped us when we wouldn't convert. Luckily, we became part of a loving RLDS congregation that nurtured us and gave us opportunity to explore our gifts and grow.

Eighteen months later, I got a much better job offer in North Carolina, and we were on our way to the South. Because the area was growing so rapidly, opportunity for career advancement was great. It was nice to be in an area where the abilities of a person were recognized. Linda got a job as a choral music teacher and, because of her abilities, quickly became well known. This eventually led her to a job as a department head at the School for the Arts. I started in an entry-level position, but as my skills and reputation grew, I was eventually promoted to deputy director with a staff of seventeen. We were both well known in the community, so even simple grocery store trips were lengthened by extended conversations with people who knew us.

The congregation in Charlotte was struggling—experiencing difficulty in melding people of diverse education, culture, and geography into a viable unit. Linda and I, being young and full of ideas, I'm sure, became part of the problem. Eventually, things settled and I became pastor, while Linda was involved with the music and teaching. Again, even though the congregation was not unified, Linda and I were given opportunity to serve and develop our gifts, which helped our growth and development in our everyday jobs. During this time, a young man in the congregation came out to me. This was my first interaction with someone I knew who was gay.

During this time, we were also blessed with two wonderful sons. The boys and I were like three peas in a pod and, being immature, I always had someone to play with. How great was that! The boys and I had this strong emotional bond—a closeness that didn't always need to be stated.

But all this recognition and affirmation took its toll. Linda and I were so enmeshed in our jobs, spending so many nights working, that we grew irreparably apart. Also, three of my staff members were in the process of coming out during this time, so I spent hours learning from them and challenging them. And, finally, all the unconnected dots of the past thirty-nine years came together. It was easy to accept myself as gay. It brought clarity to a part of me that was cloudy for so many years.

However, the hard part was about to begin. How was I to navigate through this newfound self with three people who meant so very much to me? I didn't do it very well. In fact, I failed. What complicated the matter was that I was very confused and incapable of making any personal decisions. Linda was more than gracious during this time, especially considering that her world was falling apart, too. Finally, she pressed the issue of talking to the boys. After I struggled through it, my oldest son put his head in my lap and sobbed for an hour. I, along with the entire family, was devastated. I will never forget the pain of that day. I moved out.

I had stopped going to church several months before then, while Linda remained engaged. When our family separated, not one person from church tried to give ministry—not even to Linda. All the years of tireless ministry, literally at all hours of the day and night, came down to nothing at a time when we really needed it. In my mind, the church had left me, and I would not go back.

During this time, I met Stephen. It was love at first sight. This love was something I had never experienced before. It was intense and felt so right. At the age of sixteen, Stephen had left home—or more accurately, been kicked out—for being gay. Over the next ten years or so, he lived in many different cities in the South and West, immersed in gay life. He taught me all about the gay culture, and I gave him a stability that he never had. This was a relationship I had never experienced before, and I loved it.

But the challenges were just beginning. Over a period of twenty-four months, my mom died, my dad died, I left home, I was outed as a homosexual and fired from my job with no legal recourse, my oldest son wanted nothing to do with me, and Stephen was diagnosed HIV positive. I was one broken person. Our mutual friends (Linda's and mine) had deserted me, my friends from work were forbidden to talk to me under threat of being fired, and the church and my friends there were already gone.

Stephen stayed by my side and loved me, and gave me the courage and strength to persevere. As his disease progressed, he turned to alcohol and pills to help relieve his pain. We separated for awhile but, after a year, I moved to Cleveland to be with him. A couple years later, he died in my arms.

I was devastated and alone, except for a few close friends. A year later, I became unemployed for a period that lasted seventeen months. I wallowed on my couch, penniless, in self-pity. I fantasized about walking on the ice of Lake Erie with my dog in the cold of winter, seeing how far I would get before we fell into the ice-cold water. Time passed and friends came to my rescue. I picked up short-term jobs. I saw a little bit of hope.

I also began to feel a yearning in my soul. It began small but grew, until I recognized what it was and where it came from. Prayer had not been on my mind for ten years. I knew this yearning was calling me—but to where? I had looked up the church when I moved to Cleveland, but it was located far away, and I really wasn't interested. On the way to finding the address of a store where I could exchange a gift, I realized it was on the side of town where one of our congregations was located. I made up my mind that I would attend and then drop by the store on the way home. I entered the building, but there was no welcome. I sat in a pew by myself and partook of communion for the first time in years. I cried during the entire service. After the service, only one person—out of the sixty in attendance—bothered to say hi to me. I left in tears and vowed never to go back to church again.

On the way to the mall, I remembered that we had another congregation in the area. I had called the number before and heard a voice that sounded like part of the family—cheery and welcoming. I vowed to give the church one more try. I attended a couple of Sundays later and was greeted warmly by a loving congregation who became my family. Two of the senior sisters loved me, nurtured me, and brought healing into my life. This church family embraced me and gave me opportunity to serve. The Spirit had prompted me to respond and placed me in a situation where I could flourish. We eventually had to close this congregation, and I am now the pastor of another church family who also loves me and allows me to serve. I am reminded of Doctrine and Covenants, section 164, which speaks of a true relationship with God and how this transcends the differences and judgments that afflict us, and melds us into the body of Christ.

The calling of the Spirit in me was undeniable. I also sense that this same Spirit is calling many LGBT people in Community of Christ to come home and take their rightful place as a son and daughter of God, serving in true discipleship. The Spirit is also reaching out to many who have been rebuked by their families and many religious communities to come to a safe place where the Spirit and community can restore them to wholeness. Our challenge is to provide those safe communities without judgment as we fulfill the mission of Jesus Christ in creating communities of joy, hope, love, and peace.

8

Oceans Apart: Together Again

Cindy Howard Campbell

My story is about my relationship with my brother—how it was broken and lost, then found and restored. I first told my story in a sermon using the parable of the lost sheep from the Gospel of Luke. My brother, David Howard, and I grew up in a family where there was a lot of love and a lot of criticism. Our relationship was not close. Both of us went to college, were married, had children, and were active in our respective congregations as priesthood members and pastors—and then, David came out as a gay man. He had waited until both our parents had died and then told me—only when I asked him—so, as a youth, he didn't have family support.

Those were hard times for him and confusing times for me. I tried to keep my relationships with both him and his eventual ex-wife, which was rocky at best, and I lost both of them for about twenty years. We had issues. During those years, it was a one-way relationship—he didn't return my phone calls or answer my e-mails to him. Once, I drove from Florida to North Carolina to see him and his family, but he didn't want to meet. I felt angry, hurt, and rejected. I finally decided to send birthday and Christmas cards anyway, knowing there would be no response. I just wanted David to know I was thinking of him. Now, I look back and realize with more empathy, how much he struggled during those years.

Time passed, and as we got older, I felt an awakening and urgency to do something different about our alienation. I feared we might not make up until one of us was on our deathbed, and I wanted to change that image. I looked about for direction for myself, since by then I saw that I was the only one who I could change, and I settled on forgiveness. Why forgiveness? Because it was a healing theme that kept cropping up as I searched—in scripture stories, in readings, with my therapist, and with my friends. Forgiveness was especially challenging, because it meant I had to start with looking at myself honestly, including my shadow. I had to forgive myself—never an easy task and, in essence, an ongoing one. But it felt urgent to me, and I persisted.

I prayed for some kind of connection between David and me. It didn't happen on my time line. Sometimes, I felt uncertain, as if I was groping in the dark. Sometimes, it seemed like I was the one doing all the work, and it was not reciprocal with him. Sometimes, I felt frustrated, like I had already forgiven him (and myself) many times. So why did I have to keep repeating it? When was enough, enough? Sometimes I felt lost. What was I not understanding, here?

Throughout those years, flashes of insight came from the Spirit now and again that opened my vision and guided me. They came in a variety of forms—in the words of a hymn or a scripture or a book, through counseling with my therapist, in my dreams as I journaled and processed them, and from conversations with good friends also on the journey of reconciliation. In retrospect, perhaps the vessel had to be prepared before it could be filled. Or in other words, the vessel had to grow big enough to hold the blessings in store. I had to find *myself* before I could find *David*.

One more dream confirmed the urgency and clarity of my direction, and I finally felt ready to initiate contact again. In the summer of 2009, I wrote David a card telling him I was planning on attending the 2009 GALA Labor Day retreat. This retreat is a gathering of members and friends of Community of Christ, and my brother was president of GALA at the time. I wrote him so he would know ahead that I was coming and not be blindsided when I registered. I told him in the note that I didn't expect a big powwow between the two of us, as I knew he would be busy. I just wanted to attend. I was very nervous anticipating the weekend, because we hadn't communicated in person or seen each other for several years. My tremendous inner urgency to reconnect gave me the courage to take what felt like a huge risk to me—going there on his territory with his friends, essentially uninvited. I planned to give us both space.

What a pleasant surprise was in store for both of us at the GALA retreat! Tentatively, slowly, and safely we began to reconnect over the weekend in that very accepting and loving retreat environment. I remember feeling acceptance, relief, and then, joy, in this mutual experience of finding each other again. It was a fragile start for us that continued to grow.

After that weekend, the pace of our reconnection picked up. We were brought together several times—at a family member's funeral, a Thanksgiving family reunion (the first since our parents died), the 2010 World Conference, and my Labor Day 2010 visit to his home to help out, because he had just been diagnosed with multiple myeloma cancer. We began catching up on each other's lives and filling in gaps, and, in some ways, it was almost like our past separation hadn't happened, because we found so much in common. Today, I am filled with gratitude for our reconciliation. It is precious to me! During this process I changed, and I also discovered a precious part of myself that I didn't even know was lost. The way things happened turned out to be a better answer to my initial prayers than I had dared hope for. I am so thankful I followed the leadings of my heart and did the work I needed to do instead of putting it off longer. It feels like a God-sized hole inside of me is filling, and I feel deeply connected to my brother as we are now united as family. My cup runs over with joy for our restored relationship. We both rejoice about it.

So the next question begs itself. Why did David get cancer now, after our finding each other? Who knows—stuff happens. But now, we have each other, and we are united and at peace with the future.

In closing, my personal version of this Franciscan benediction seems to fit:

God blessed me with discomfort
at easy answers, half-truths, and superficial relationships,
so that I could live deep within my heart.

God blessed me with anger
at injustice, oppression, and exploitation of people,
so that I could work for justice, freedom, and peace.

God blessed me with tears
to shed for those who suffer from pain, rejection, starvation, and war,
so that I could reach out my hand to comfort them and turn their pain into joy.

And may God bless us all with enough foolishness
to believe that we can make a difference in the world,
so that we can do what others claim cannot be done to bring justice
and kindness to all our children and the poor. Amen.[1]

[1] Original "Franciscan Blessing" quoted by Phillip Yancey in *Prayer: Does It Make Any Difference?* (Grand Rapids, MI: Zondervan, 2006); also, lifebrook.wordpress.com/2008/03/24/a-franciscan-benediction.

9

The Trail of Secrecy

Velton Peabody

In retrospect, the summer of 1954 was a critical juncture in my life journey. After a troublesome start to my school career where I had failed second grade, I turned things around educationally and managed to graduate as valedictorian of my four-member class at tiny Beals High School on Beals Island, off the Maine coast. With the exception of a year during World War II, when both my parents worked at the Bath Iron Works building ships for the US Navy, I had spent my formative years in that close-knit community, surrounded by five hundred or so fellow islanders, most of whom were somehow related to me and all of whom I knew personally. My ancestors had settled Beals Island at the time of the American Revolution, ten generations before me. In the tangled web of island genealogy, as I have since learned, I descended through all four grandparents from settlers Manwarren Beal and John Alley. My three classmates were my cousins.

But in 1954 my face was turned toward the mainland. I had been accepted at the University of Maine in Orono, but it was becoming apparent that I would be unable to enroll for lack of funds. I had earned a little money the previous summer working in the shipping room of a sardine cannery in the nearby mainland town of Jonesport, and I had turned a school reporting job into gainful, part-time employment, contributing news items to the Bangor *Daily News* and the *Maine Coast Fisherman.* I had, in fact, gained some celebrity on the island for my reporting. My byline appeared with some regularity. I still remember the day I was allowed to leave my high school class early to report on the fire that was consuming Uncle Fred Beal's house. But, you don't pay for college on celebrity.

I probably had never heard of Horace Greeley at this point, but this pivotal summer provided my opportunity to follow his "Go West, young man, go West" advice, anyway. While I worked in the sardine cannery, a fellow worker, who belonged to the Reorganized Church of Jesus Christ of Latter Day Saints, befriended me. My friend's mother read church history to me over lunch and invited me to church. A year later, a few days after high school graduation, I was baptized by pastor Chester Gray in the cold Atlantic waters of Moosabec Reach, which lies between Beals Island and Jonesport. Soon after my baptism, three men of the Jonesport church arranged a loan so I could attend Graceland College that fall.

What the good folk of Beals Island and that Jonesport RLDS congregation did not know, was that this young man, who had just joined the church and was headed to Graceland, was hiding what he regarded as a deep, dark secret, not to be shared with anyone. He probably would not have had the vocabulary to describe himself as gay, but he knew he was attracted to men. I had concluded that early on and knew it would not be a good idea to let that attraction become known in church or around town. I knew, by word of mouth, those who were regarded as queer in the community and did not want that term applied to me. Besides—as common wisdom of the day had it—it was a phase that would pass as one entered marriage.

At Graceland, I kept my secret. I dated several girls, took a course on marriage and family, and prayed a lot about my same-sex attraction—but the attraction remained. It was during my tenure at Graceland that the pastor of my home congregation in Maine called me to the office of priest. Without much hesitation, I accepted this calling as the fulfillment of a spiritual experience. Similar experiences validated, for me, my subsequent calls, years later, to elder and high priest, while I was still holding my secret.

Once, during an informal discussion at a reunion at Temple Grove (an RLDS campground), while I was in the early stages of coming out, a friend who did not yet know my orientation asked the group, in general, how a gay person could accept the priesthood, knowing he was gay. I responded before the group on a personal level, citing my own case, and asked: "How could he not?" I would give the same answer today. I believed then, as I believe now, that my calls were divine. God knew I was gay when I was called, and I felt fully accepted by the Divine the way I was.

My journey since Graceland has taken many turns. I eventually earned a journalism degree from the University of Missouri in Columbia, where I served as an assistant to a professor and was voted by the faculty as the outstanding male graduate in 1965. My secret was still intact and protected by the first of my two marriages, both of which ended in divorce. I didn't exactly become another Walter Cronkite, but I found some success in journalism, highlighted by in-depth interviews with Adlai Stevenson and Walter Lippmann, and brief interviews and photo sessions with Eleanor Roosevelt, Ted Williams, Greer Garson, and Ralph Bellamy. I worked on the editorial staffs of the Bangor, Maine, *Daily News*; the Abilene, Kansas, *Reflector-Chronicle;* and the Rochester, New York, *Times-Union* before ending my career as wire editor of the Buffalo, New York, *News,* in charge of national and world news. I also found the time to research and publish two books dealing with "Tall Barney" Beal, a regional folk hero from Beals Island. During retirement, I returned to Beals Island, where I was elected head of the town government, served as a catalyst in construction of the town's only public boat landing, and founded the Beals Historical Society, a two hundred-member organization that constructed a building to preserve the island's heritage—all with my secret largely intact.

On a personal level, I went through two marriages, each lasting about fifteen years, before accepting my sexuality and deciding to live a more authentic life. Coming out has been gradual, on a need to know basis. The process was not complete in any sense until December 2010, when I headed for Rio de Janeiro to visit a male friend. There wasn't much choice. My Brazilian friend prematurely announced our "engagement" on Facebook, and relatives in Maine were asking who this new woman was in my life. It was then that I called the last of my siblings to tell them the real purpose of my visit. Happily, the news was well received, and I wondered why I had not told them earlier.

Over the years, I have been active in GALA and Affirmation (the Latter-day Saint equivalent of GALA). I've also been a member of the board of the Welcoming Community Network. Through these organizations, I have become acquainted with many, who, because of their sexual orientation, have not been privileged, as I have, to serve in the priesthood. My own priesthood, which came while I was still in the closet, has opened the way for me to serve as pastor of one congregation in Rochester, New York, and two in Buffalo. Currently (as of 2011), since my status is grandfathered under church policy, I function as a high priest, serving as a pastor of the Norton Heights Community of Christ congregation in Kansas City, Missouri, where my sexual orientation is well known, but is a non-issue. The congregation, in fact, has established Stonewall Ministry to help meet the needs of gays in the congregation and the larger gay community. Stonewall, and, thus, the Norton Heights congregation, and the larger church, are regularly represented at Kansas City Gay Pride and other gay community events.

My interest in church history (first kindled in a Jonesport kitchen, and in Chester Gray's youth classes, and furthered in courses at Graceland) has found expression in many ways. It has been my privilege to teach several Temple School church history courses. For two years, in early retirement, I was a volunteer guide at Liberty Hall in Lamoni, Iowa, and later, while serving as a volunteer guide at church headquarters in Independence, Missouri, I was hired part time as a supervisor in the guide service.

Community of Christ has been, and still is, the stabilizing force in my life. I have seen the church grow from a very inward-focused body to the outward-looking, inclusive community it is today. My prayer is that, increasingly, young people will be able to live full, open, and authentic lives within the church, without the secrecy that has so marked my own journey.

10

Out and Proud, Queer and Christian

Joy Howard

In 1987, I joined my first gay pride march, and it was a doozy. Official estimates of the attendance at the Second National March on Washington for Lesbian and Gay Rights ranged between two hundred thousand and five hundred thousand. I was marching with my then-partner, Cameron, and a couple dozen of our friends under the politically incorrect banner, "Cute Girls of the Northeast Corridor." Our banner provoked a lot of laughter and applause as we wound our way along the parade route. When we approached the mall, we heard a huge din. It took awhile to register that it was applause—long, sustained, unbroken applause.

I assumed the cacophony was for a famous speaker, like maybe Whoopi Goldberg. When I took a look around, I realized we were bobbing through a sea of thousands of people who lined the entrance to the mall—all laughing, cheering, clapping, and/or weeping. There were queer people, parents of queer people, religious groups in support of queer people, and people of all ages and ethnicities. The whole world was queer that day or so it seemed to me. Everywhere I looked, I saw a part of myself reflected back at me, or I saw tears of joy for who I was. This had never happened to me before.

Being completely engulfed by such an enthusiastic and supportive multitude of people was an extraordinary experience. When we got home that night, I told Cameron I needed to find a church—I may be the only queer person who's had that reaction to my first pride parade. After all, a leisurely Sunday morning with brunch and a newspaper or two is probably a bigger draw for most queer people than Sunday church services—and probably for most nonqueer people, too.

I was born in the late 1950s and was raised a kid of preachers (that's right, *both* my parents are ordained ministers) in Independence, Missouri, the headquarters town of the religious denomination of my birth, with the linguistically challenging name of the Reorganized Church of Jesus Christ of Latter Day Saints (RLDS). And even though my parents were, and still are, among the most progressive religious people I know, this was the early 1970s. When I started getting glimmers of my queerness in my mid-teens, I had no supportive theological or social frameworks for how to be queer, much less to be queer and Christian. Shoot, until I went to college, I had never heard a single positive thing about a queer person.

What happened to me on that sparkling fall day in 1987 was the completely unexpected and transforming feeling of belonging to something vaster than my mind could grasp—not *despite* my queerness but *because* of it. Mind you, I had finally reconciled myself to being queer in 1980. It took another seven years of living into it to work up the nerve to step off the curb and join a pride march, so there was no way I was going back to the curb or the closet, just so I could go to church again.

As near as I can tell, the connection my brain made between that 1987 march on Washington and going to church had to do with an overflowing gratefulness for feeling connected at some deep level with a future that just might be worth living into. The only time I had felt this in church was during congregational singing, but it was powerful stuff—powerful enough to vanquish a lot of oppressive doctrine, biblical literalism, and idiotic or uninspired preaching that too frequently interrupted the singing.

I have always loved the ragged richness of congregational singing where individuals can become a single organism without sacrificing their uniqueness. In congregational singing, you can hear and feel the textures of music, which often—and not coincidentally—reveal the texture of the community. You might hear different octaves or the occasional voice of someone who can't carry a tune and is still brave enough to sing out on a droning single note. You might hear people split off into parts, some folks confidently singing harmonies and others muttering through because they can't read both the words and the notes. There's almost always someone singing the wrong verse. There are snaking *s*'s as people finish a phrase or a word at slightly different times. Puffy *h*'s, *f*'s, and *p*'s. Confident *k*'s. When we join each other in song, we weave our voices together and turn the air into a warm, nubby fabric of sound that we can wrap around ourselves long after the singing is over.

I was a competitive swimmer as a kid, and my experiences of congregational or choral singing have always reminded me of what I loved about being in the water. When we dive in a pool, or when we jump or walk in, or dangle our feet or our fingers, the water opens up as we come in and envelops us. Each of us is equally buoyant in and buoyed up by the water. We can feel both momentum and resistance. We have something to ride and something to push against. We can be lifted up and made to feel almost weightless.

As my group of Cute Girls of the Northeast Corridor waded into the crowded Washington Mall in October 1987, I felt unabashedly and overwhelmingly, loved and cared for by an enormous congregation of complete strangers. I wanted to experience that feeling regularly, not just this one time. Surely, somewhere, there was a church where I could sing (or swim) my way into that feeling on a regular basis, despite my sexuality.

Okay, so I wasn't thinking very clearly about what I was asking of the universe. I'm told by my parents and other people, who have known me since I was a baby, that this is one of my features. After months of trying a variety of churches, a friend of Cameron's recommended First Congregational Church, a United Church of Christ in downtown Washington, DC.

I knew we were on the right track when we learned that in the early 1980s, when the environment was thick with anxiety about AIDS, First Congregational Church was the only DC church that opened its doors to the predominantly queer congregation of Metropolitan Community Church. Metropolitan Community Church had lost its lease due to concerns about transmission of AIDS and had been turned away by numerous other organizations before First Congregational Church welcomed them. Later, in the mid-1980s, First Congregational had been the fourteenth United Church of Christ in the United States (out of almost one thousand to date) to complete the United Church of Christ's discernment process of becoming "open and affirming"—the designation for congregations, campus ministries, and other bodies in the United Church of Christ that "make public statements of welcome into their full life and ministry to persons of all sexual orientations, gender identities, and gender expressions." In short, First Congregational Church was the place I first felt that being queer and Christian didn't have to be an oxymoron.

In 2003, the woman who is now my wife was ordained an Episcopal priest. (Pam and I were legally married in 2004 in our home state of Massachusetts.) After remaining in the United Church of Christ denomination for several years after Pam's ordination, I decided that being active in the parish where Pam was serving was more important to me than avoiding the oppressively (for me) sexist and hierarchical language of Episcopal liturgy. I felt called to show the world that a happily married queer couple can also be actively engaged together in Christian witness. Last May, I was confirmed into the Episcopal Church by the retired bishop Barbara C. Harris, the world's first woman bishop in the Anglican Communion. I have taken a rather unconventional route from being a kid of preachers to becoming a priest's wife.

In sporting terms, the Episcopal Church is the third Christian team that I've played for, after long stints on the RLDS and the United

Church of Christ teams. Each denomination has given me a unique opportunity to wrestle with the conundrum of what it means to be queer and Christian. Like Jacob wrestling with the angel, my journey through church life has both blessed me and marked me forever. My cup overflows.

11

It Was the Best of Times: Isn't That What We All Think?

Pam Robison

It was right after Christmas—the day before our fortieth anniversary. Charlie and I had just finished watching again the video *For the Bible Tells Me So*, and he said we needed to talk. I'm not sure what I was expecting him to say, but I certainly did not expect his next two words: "I'm bisexual."

I felt like I'd been sucker punched. I didn't know what to think or what to say. I felt the word divorce hang in the air. I'm really not sure what I said. The only thing I really remember is asking if he wanted to stay married and hearing him respond with a positive, "Yes."

The next week was a blur. I don't even remember how I felt—mostly numb. I was still in shock that this person I had loved and lived with for forty years had felt it necessary to hide such a huge part of his life. I couldn't wrap my mind around what this was going to mean for us as a couple or to me personally. There were so many questions whirling around in my mind—trying to articulate them was almost impossible. Nor was I sure where to turn. I knew I needed to talk to someone, but who? I did not know.

Eventually, a name came to mind: an acquaintance with a doctorate in human sexuality. I called Matt to see if he had an hour to visit with me—not about business, but as a counselor. He gave me an hour and a half, and that visit was a turning point. Matt listened as I struggled to make sense of all the emotions and thoughts that had been churning the previous week. When I was unable to figure out how to phrase something, he asked probing questions to help me figure out what I needed to know.

I returned home feeling better equipped to deal with these life changes, and I told Charlie, "It's my turn now. We need to talk." I had my list of questions—questions I needed to hear his responses to, questions that dealt with the direction our lives would be taking. It was not an easy discussion, because we had both hidden parts of ourselves from each other, and from ourselves, for so many years.

It wasn't a long talk, but it was probably the most open talk we'd ever had, especially concerning sexual matters. One big concern was answered—he'd been physically faithful to me, and he valued and wanted to continue our marital relationship. I was reminded of the final comment Matt had made during our visit: "I don't know where your journey is going to take you, but hang on for the ride!"

It's been quite a ride! After having worked through a three-year dark night of the soul, I thought I was in good shape for dealing with almost anything life threw my way—but not this. I am grateful that my brother had come out a few years earlier and that we had the opportunity of sharing with him and his husband in their marriage. Seeing how happy he was—happier than I had seen him since a teenager—helped me understand just what a strain Charlie had been under, keeping that part of who he was hidden.

When we shared the news with my family, my brother sent me a book that had helped him in his coming out: *The Other Side of the Closet*. That was the most helpful thing he could have done. It was not a polemic, but instead was an impartial study of what many spouses and children go through when their husband/parent comes out. There were calm, unbiased suggestions of ways to cope with each aspect of the situation, followed by case studies. I devoured it! I don't think I put it down, from the first time I opened it until I finished it.

Then I put it to one side for a while. I went back and reread it after several months had passed, and I could acknowledge that I had gone through several of the stages. I suggested that Charlie read it as well, but he doesn't do a lot of reading, and it took him a while to start it. I don't know if he's finished it yet, but I do remember one comment he made: "I'm glad I hadn't read this before I told you, or I probably never would have!" Some of the families mentioned in the book had come out on the other side in a healthy fashion, but many others split apart.

I'm glad he *did* go ahead and tell me, even though he admitted it took him two years to get the courage to do so. When he did, I began to realize that some of the walls that had been between us for most of our marriage were walls he had built to protect himself, wondering if I would still love him if I knew who he really was. I had often felt like I had to be the initiator of simple gestures of touch, such as holding hands. I had not been able to share intimate thoughts—the one time I had tried early in our marriage, he couldn't respond, and I didn't have enough courage to try again.

It has not always been an easy journey, even though we are now in a good place. My journal—probably the spiritual practice that most helped me get through the initial shock—has some pages that are wet with tears and others sizzling with flames. Sometimes I felt sorry for him; sometimes I felt sorry for myself and angry with him.

Yet, the journey continues as we're exploring an uncharted part of our lives. I'm discovering a new voice, one more willing to speak out for the many marginalized members of the LGBT community. For many years, I have felt that their treatment—both in society and the church—was unfair, but, as is quite often the case, until it touched me directly, through both my brother and husband, I could only think of it as unfair. As we have become more active in that community, though, I now see the ministry and the giftedness that we've lost within the church. I am more aware of the hatred against those who are "other" in society, and I can no longer remain silent.

I'm not sure where the journey is taking me, individually, or for us as a couple. Explorers never are sure. But I do know that even in the midst of that uncertainty, I am more excited and hopeful about possibilities than I have been for many years.

12

God's Persistent, Relentless Pursuit

Charlie Robison

"I am bisexual with strong same-sex attractions." With those words, I stunned Pam, my wife of forty years. It was the day after Christmas 2009, and I had asked her to watch again the DVD *For the Bible Tells Me So*. I wanted to use it as a basis for talking about a secret I had kept all my life and to follow through on a promise I had made to my counselor.

About two years previously, I had reached a point of despair and frustration. I decided I really had no choice but to seek out a few sessions with a counselor. I felt like I could no longer deal with the personal issues that I had struggled with my whole life. When I was about seven-years-old and in the second grade, I had a run-in with a friend on the playground. All of the other kids had gathered around to hear us argue it out. I don't remember what the argument was about, only that everyone sided with *him* and started laughing and making fun of *me*. The emotional pain had sunk in deeply, and I went off to an isolated place by myself and cried until the bell rang. In those moments of solitude, I decided I would never risk myself in front of people again. My foundation for my wall was laid.

After entering puberty, I found myself having attraction to both sexes. This was back during the fifties when sexual issues were not talked about at school, home, or church. Afraid of risking who I was, I was determined to keep it hidden. I had a very difficult time in high school—I had no self-confidence, didn't like myself, didn't know how to deal with my sexual attractions, and I continued to build walls.

In 1966, after college, I joined the US Navy. One of the questions on the application said, "Are you homosexual?" and I checked the "No" box. Because of my same-sex attractions, I had labeled myself homosexual and thought as I checked the box, "Well, that's a lie. I'm living a lie."

While I was in the navy, Pam took my name from a bulletin board at church and wrote me a short letter. That began a two-year courtship that resulted in our marriage in December 1969, shortly after my discharge. However, simmering beneath the surface, were many issues that I still chose to keep walled up.

After experiencing additional family losses and tragedies, things finally came to a head in 2007, and I made arrangements to see a counselor. It was during these sessions of dealing with my sexual identity, as well as other issues, that I made a promise to my counselor that I would tell my wife. I was tired of part of me living in silence and secrecy. However, having told no one for almost sixty years, I found it much easier to make excuses and put it off, rather than taking time to sit down and talk.

In September 2009, GALA arranged to show the video, *For the Bible Tells Me So,* at our congregation, Open Arms. My wife wanted to attend, partly in support of her brother, who had come out several years previously—to better understand him and the issues surrounding his sexuality. I agreed to go with her, though I always felt uncomfortable in LGBT groups, probably because of my unwillingness to face my own sexuality and for fear that someone might find me out. The movie was an emotional experience for me. Through the whole showing, I found myself crying inside, as I related to the emotions and feelings of those dealing with the issues of same-sex attraction in their families.

At one point—after the video had presented the information that the younger son in the birth order of sons is more likely to be homosexual—Pam leaned over to me and said, "Boy, I'm sure glad you escaped that!" and I thought to myself, "If you only knew." It was at that point that I determined, again, that we needed to talk, and I set the date in my own mind as being after Christmas, when she would be off work for a week, we would not have our grandson, and I would be through with my gig as Santa.

After watching the DVD again together, and me coming out to her, she kissed me and held my hand, and we sat together for awhile. But she made no comment, and I thought to myself, "Well, it's out now. So there it is."

About a week later, she said, "Okay, it's my turn to talk." She also is a very private person and finds it difficult to talk about sensitive issues. She told me that when I had shared with her, it felt like a kick in the stomach. She really didn't know how to deal with it or how to support me, and had a lot of questions racing through her mind. She visited with a friend who she remembered had a doctorate in human sexuality. He helped her focus on how she wanted to talk to me and what to expect. The friend's parting comment to her was, "Well, Pam, I don't know where this is all heading, but hang on for the ride!"

After sharing, we both felt like our marriage had opened up, and we began experiencing a new freedom. About a month later, I shared with our grown son, Mark, and he was likewise very supportive. However, as is often the case, while I'd begun to share it with family members, I found that all the walls I had built walled God out. I still did not see myself as lovable or that God could forgive me for some of my failings.

At the end of January 2010, the world church scheduled a weekend gathering for evangelists, spouses, and other interested people. Pam and I registered to attend. During the weekend, one of the suggestions was that all evangelists should have spiritual directors. That was something that I really longed to do, but it also felt threatening. In order to take advantage of spiritual direction, you have to be willing to open up. I finally got up enough nerve to ask one of the trained spiritual directors if she would be willing to work with me in the area of lectio divino (a method of scripture reading practiced by monastics), one of her specialties. I thought, "Well, that's an area that should be pretty nonthreatening! If it goes well, we can go into deeper areas." Little did I know!

We arranged to meet in the middle of February for our first session. The day of our first meeting, I found myself so tired that I decided to take an hour's nap before meeting with her. While napping, I had this dream: I was driving to Kansas City to take care of some personal business when I decided I needed exercise, so I parked the car and got on a bicycle (always handy in a dream). I rode on downtown, took care of whatever the business was, and was returning home during the early evening. As I was riding back, I became aware that I had no clue where I had parked the car. I found myself pedaling through various sections of the inner city in Kansas City—through places that were not safe late in the day. I stopped at an intersection to try to get my bearings, when a young boy—seven or eight years of age and obviously a street urchin and homeless—came up to me and looked at me pleadingly. He asked, "Can I come live with you?" It shocked me. It was obvious that he was not living in a healthy environment and there were bad influences around. I thought to myself, "But what would Pam do with you? She's under a lot of stress at work and dealing with a lot of other issues, and having you around would be unsettling at home." And I didn't know what to do with him either! I finally decided I would just have to tell him that Pam didn't want him to come live with us. That's when I woke up. "Well, that's a weird dream!" I mused.

I met with my director at three o'clock for our first session. We had a nice chitchat, talking about and practicing lectio divino. As we were wrapping up, she mentioned that she was going to be attending a workshop on dream interpretation. She had taken quite a bit of training and felt that dreams had a lot to tell us if we were willing to listen to their issues. I said, "Oh really?" And I told her about my dream. She looked at me and said, "Well, Charles, you know who that boy is, don't you? That boy is you! You have some issue from your childhood that you need to deal with." It stunned me, because she had no sooner said that than I recognized the little boy was that part of me that I had walled off and was now asking to come home.

I left in a state of emotional shock. I didn't really know what to do with it. I felt like it was related to my issue of who I was sexually and my lifelong habit of walling that part of me off—but, I felt like I had already dealt with it. I had talked to Pam; I had talked to Mark. What else was I supposed to do with it?

That night as I was retiring to bed, I picked up a book I had read previously, titled *The Lance and the Shield: The Life and Times of Sitting Bull*. I was about a chapter into the book for the second time, and this was the first paragraph I read as I settled into bed:

> "*Wichasha wakan* were dreamers—men who had experienced dreams with sacred content or who had attained visions of powerful spiritual meaning. Not all dreamers were holy men, but all holy men were dreamers. One function of holy men was to help people interpret dreams, for they imposed obligations as binding as a personal vow, and *to ignore their intent was to invite personal calamity.*"

For the second time that day, I was stunned. I thought to myself, "God, what are you trying to tell me?"

Then, out of the blue, I received an e-mail asking if I would play the role of the father of the prodigal son in a drama at church the following Sunday. Mark would be playing the role of the prodigal. I agreed. Then, I received a separate e-mail asking if I would do the scripture moment. You guessed it—it was the prodigal son! Maybe God was being none too subtle about giving me hints.

As I read over the script the next several days in preparation for the drama, I found myself being emotionally involved, repeatedly, in the story, with a sense of longing to come home, even as the little boy in my dream—but feeling I didn't know how. (The drama turned out to be a powerful experience for both Mark and me, and gave me pause to ponder all that was happening in rapid succession in my life.)

I met again with my spiritual director in March, and we discussed the dreams and the story of the prodigal, but we really didn't sense any light on their possible meaning other than the need to come home. I was still very confused over how to deal with them and their potential significance in my life. She suggested I spend time with Psalm 139. For the next week I read it every day. It was a beautiful psalm, but I couldn't really accept its implications for myself. How could God really love me? My walls stood firm!

It was now drawing close to the 2010 World Conference, and I was feeling the stress of all the things I needed to get done at home. I debated about whether I should continue being a delegate, or resign and use the time more productively. Still feeling overwhelmed by the need to break through the walls around me, I determined that I needed to remain a delegate—I needed to be immersed in conference on the chance that *something* would happen. Emotionally I was desperate.

The first Sunday afternoon of conference was a delegate session on spiritual formation. We went through a series of activities that are outlined in the publication *Yearning for God*. They asked us a series of questions, and we gave our responses:

- How deeply do you want to go in my discipleship? *I long to go deep!*
- Are you willing to be more completely formed into the likeness and life of Jesus Christ? *Yes, that is the yearning of my heart.*
- Practice holy indifference. *I need to focus on divine sharing with me—being indifferent to my own agendas.*
- Shedding—shed barriers, letting go. *Oh, how I need to do that!*
- Doctrine and Covenants 163—pray with body gestures. *I immersed myself in this prayer.*
- "God the Creator weeps." *We cupped our hands to catch his tears, then poured them over our heads.*
- "God yearns to draw you close so that your wounds may be healed." *We circled our arms as if hugging a tree and then brought them to our chests. While doing this, I visualized God drawing me close to heal my pain and woundedness.*
- "Be vulnerable to divine grace." *Many times when we're praying or meditating, our mind wanders, and it was suggested that we pick a word*

to help us refocus. I picked this phrase. I don't remember how long they gave us; I am sure it was not long. But my memory of the time focused on the phrase was a time that was unhurried, immersed in a sense of peace and a yearning to be vulnerable to divine grace, to be able to come home even as the prodigal.

In that moment, my life was turned upside down! I felt affirmed for who I was. I was being immersed in God's love, forgiveness, and grace. I sensed an overwhelming yearning to magnify my calling as an evangelist. Before conference, I could easily have signed my name "Charlie Robison, R.E."—reluctant evangelist—but no more! The Spirit continued to fill me without abatement. I sensed a renewed desire to move to Heritage Plaza across from the temple complex and be available in the immediate area to share with people who might desire an evangelist blessing.

Two years previously, Pam and I had discussed with Lach Mackay, director of Historic Sites for the church, about being guides at the Heritage Plaza in Independence, Missouri. However, difficulties with the heating and air conditioning systems caused us to turn it down, because of Pam's health concerns with MS. But now, sensing a desire to revisit that issue, I looked up Lach at conference to talk about the possibility. Before I had a chance to say anything, Lach said, "Charlie, I'd like to update you on what is happening with Heritage Plaza. We are just finishing up work on installing new heating and air conditioning, so the heating and cooling should no longer be an issue in the house. Does that make any difference?" I could hardly contain my excitement when I said to him, "All the difference in the world!" I went racing off to tell Pam of my excitement. I bumped into her in the hall, as she was madly dashing between events, under a lot of stress with all of her responsibilities at conference. I said, "Guess what? We may be moving to Heritage Plaza!" She threw up her arms and said, "Don't even go there," as she wildly waved me off. "I can't deal with that right now!" and off she tore.

As the week progressed, I sensed an emerging call to reach out specifically to the LGBT community in my ministry as an evangelist, feeling that perhaps there are others who have built walls for similar reasons, who have felt they could not approach God for a blessing. I asked David Howard, president of GALA, this question: "Do you know of any evangelists who are openly lesbian, gay, bisexual, transgendered? Do you know anyone who's dealing with those issues?" Basically his answer was "No, but there are many evangelists who are supportive," which is what I suspected.

In the meantime, Pam was scheduled to play for the conference GALA service at the College Park congregation on Thursday at noon. Originally, I was going to support her. But I now realized that if this was going to be part of my ministry, then I needed to become familiar with gatherings of individuals involved in GALA. It was a beautiful service, and I felt blessed by the ministry of those who shared. At the same time, as I looked around the sanctuary, I sensed many individuals who still had walls—walls like mine that needed to come down. Having avoided dealing with my own sexual identity for so long, I was not sure where all of this would lead, but I was determined to make the effort to become involved.

I left conference transformed, energized, renewed, and saying for the first time in my life two things I'd never been able to say from the heart before—and really mean it: *I'm a beloved child of God. And it is no longer I that live, but Christ that lives in me!*

I have found that for the first time in my life, I am really *seeing people* rather than hiding behind my own concerns and pity parties. I really *see people.* It truly is as the scriptures say: When we become one with Christ, we are transformed and all things become new. Am I still bisexual? Yes. Do I still have same-gender attractions? Yes. I am who I was created from birth. But my life has been transformed. I became vulnerable to divine grace, when the Spirit touched the deep-walled places of my heart with forgiveness, healing, and love, and called me forth into God's light.

It has now been a year since the 2010 conference of my transformation. We have relocated to Heritage Plaza (where I am the site coordinator), and we are both actively involved with GALA. New insights and understandings continue to come as I rejoice each day in the light, and I'm learning to live out what this means: *It is no longer I that live, but Christ that lives in me.* As new opportunities and challenges continue, especially in the body of Community of Christ, Pam and I are frequently saying to each other, "Hang on for the ride!"

I want to emphasize that this testimony is not really about me. My life's journey is simply a vehicle for proclaiming the good news of *God's persistent, relentless pursuit* of each of us, and God will not take "No" for an answer! I would simply plead from the depths of my heart to your heart: Don't wait sixty years like I did! God calls you to come out of the dark places of your soul into the light. Let God bless, heal, forgive, and love you for who you are!

13

BISEXUALITY: MOVING BEYOND LABELS

Sharon Troyer

IN THE 1970S, I HAD a personal experience of "marginalization." I didn't know or use the word then, but in retrospect, I recognized the feelings. Marginalization describes how people are kept "on the margins." To me, it is a well-chosen word, because it describes a state where people perceive their place to be "at the edge." Being marginalized is to remain just barely in. I felt that way. I felt tolerated, especially if I remained somewhat quiet or, better yet, completely silent. Only recently have I more fully realized that the word "tolerance" is likely to be familiar to people living at the margins. To be tolerated is a long way from being embraced or celebrated.

A helpful continuum of language was shared in a recent workshop presented by the Lambda Community Center in Fort Collins, Colorado. Lindsay Melsen, the facilitator, led an experiential exercise which invited us to describe how it felt to be pitied, tolerated, accepted, embraced, and celebrated. It was eye-opening and powerful.

I'm sixty-eight-years-old now, but by the time I was in my middle forties, I had already come to believe that if I had a life path, it might be described as building bridges between people who misunderstand each other. I think it began when I was a young married woman living with my Dutch husband at Michigan State University. It was during the era of the Vietnam conflict, that I first found myself to be an outsider. My husband, studying for his doctorate in history, spoke openly against the war. One day, a neighbor I regarded as a friendly graduate student said to us, "If you don't like what America stands for, you should go back to the socialist country you came from." Instead of feeling like I was part of an otherwise friendly group of inquiring students, I suddenly felt like an outsider. That was very difficult for me because, frankly, my still-being-shaped personality had grown to depend on always being liked. It may have been the first time I felt socially excluded. I tell that story because it wasn't until I was invited to write something for this book that I even remembered that emotionally pivotal event!

Having lived nearly seven decades, I have witnessed numerous changes in thinking about what is just and unjust, both in society at large and, also, within the church I cherish. I am very glad that as a denomination, Community of Christ is preparing for a special conference to take place in the United States in April 2013, and this second volume of stories will be available to help in the discernment process about sexual orientation and gender identity as they pertain to ordination and same-sex marriage.

Why, then, was I so uncomfortable when I was invited to write about *my* experience as a bisexual woman? Were my feelings of fear different from what other marginalized persons might have? I remember what the Catholic sexuality educator Brian McNaught said in his video *Growing Up Gay*. He described the suicidal feelings that led him to drink a near-deadly substance, out of fear he wouldn't be loved anymore—especially by those who were most important to him. My fears are somewhat the same. I have, in fact, experienced painful losses as a result of who I loved.

Nonetheless, I have decided to take the risk and share some of my story. I am grateful for the early pioneers of GALA and later the Welcoming Community Network, without which we might not recognize the need for publishing an updated, second book of stories. I applaud every person who ever attended a GALA retreat and found a life-changing community there! It has been in loving circles like these, where, for many years, I have experienced joy, a sense of belonging, healing laughter, and profound inclusive worship. And without the persistent work of WCN, many congregations wouldn't hear the call to celebrate diversity in deeper, more dynamic ways.

From 2002 until 2004, while I served as executive director for GALA, I was richly blessed. Part of my job was to work closely with a network of Welcoming Church Program leaders. It was from these faithful people, representatives at least ten other denominations, that I learned much about perseverance. While never denying their own painful denominational practices that excluded LGBT people, these leaders taught me about the miracles of "practicing presence" within my own faith community. Sharing our stories with each other has always been a significant element of bringing about healthy change. To some extent, I've become more willing to share my own story now, as a way to "pay it forward."

In our training to help people work more effectively in their own churches, I was grateful for the panels where I was asked to speak about bisexuality. I still believe that of the letters L, G, B, and T—B is the least discussed, though I'd understand if those who are transgender think differently. In all the years I've been a spirituality and sexuality educator, I've found common misconceptions about bisexuality. In the early 1980s, when I first fell in love with a woman, some in the gay community assumed that bisexual people were confused about their sexual orientation or hadn't yet fully accepted a lesbian or gay identity. At that time, I was told that bisexual persons just wanted to "cling to a remnant of heterosexual privilege."

Another belief was that bisexuality implied that one wanted intimate relationships with partners of both genders, often at the same time. This presumed that bisexuals wouldn't want or be capable of monogamy. This has not been my personal experience, although I do not deny these descriptions do reflect the experience of some people, regardless of their sexual orientation.

Eventually, there came a time in my life when I wanted to talk more openly to my own family. During a Community of Christ World Conference, I decided to share with my mother some of what I'd been going through. I explained to her that I was bisexual and in a significant relationship with a woman for whom I cared deeply. I will never forget that moment. After my explanation, which required a lot of courage, my mother looked at me and said, "You make me want to vomit!" My response was stunned silence, and for the next almost ten years I never talked about being bisexual again. I did not feel safe.

That first relationship, while in my thirties, grew rather naturally out of a deepening friendship, much like it might have in an opposite-gender friendship. Before that time, I knew very little about bisexuality and had no language to describe my feelings. I wasn't so much confused about what I felt, as I was hesitant to discuss it openly, because I didn't know other people like me. When the words bisexual and transgender came into more general use, especially within the Welcoming Church movement, I felt a huge relief.

Though I understand the need for using these labels to describe various aspects of human sexual experience, I also look forward to the time when their use is not so important. Also, I find the word "lifestyle," when talking about homosexuality, to be unhelpful. If asked about my lifestyle, I might say that I'm active in my local congregation, I was recently married, I pay taxes, I eat popcorn, and I like to hike. But often when people talk about the lifestyle of a LGBT person, they are referring to some imagined behavior of what they do in the bedroom. Most of us wouldn't want our parents or close friends to be described by their intimate sexual behavior.

Therefore, I am extremely grateful for the efforts of those who write about the value of a well-thought-out sexual ethic. When Marie Fortune, author of the book *Love Does No Harm*, was given the 1998 Peace Award by Community of Christ, I had not yet read her book. I highly recommend her writing, because she writes so well about the principles that make behaviors and relationships abusive, and presents ethical discernment as being very different from rule-based ethics. The "love ethic" she describes has been a valuable tool to help me think about how we bring our best selves to intimate relationships. I admire churches that have comprehensive sexuality education in both their adult and children's church school curriculum. It inspires individuals and families to choose actions based on the values they want to embody, not just on the community norms. In Ms. Fortune's work as an ethicist, she describes well the foundational attitudes about relationships that exhibit healthy sexuality, intimacy, and wholeness.

Within Community of Christ, I think the value of holding up principles, rather than sexual behavior guidelines, would best be done in creating a sexual ethic. This was started over ten years ago by a committee that worked tirelessly to write one. I believe a revised version of it from 2001 was introduced for discussion within the recently Expanded World Church Leadership Committee. I can only surmise that the fertile ground from which that document grew needs to be cultivated more fully so such a statement could come into wider use.

To its great credit, I think Community of Christ made a giant step forward in publishing what are called the *Enduring Principles*. They were published in 2010 as the second edition of *Sharing in Community of Christ: Exploring Identity, Mission, Message, and Beliefs* and are now available in tract form. I believe deepening our understanding of how to live out these core principles lessens the need for everyone to subscribe to identical beliefs. It is the underlying principles of the worth of persons and respecting the dignity of each human soul that allows us to celebrate our differences.

Within the underlying principles of Christlike love and dignity for all, there is no need for the dualistic practices of labeling which sexual orientations or gender identities merit full inclusion. Being "one in Christ" is a reconciling umbrella under which we are all welcome to gather.

To that end, I find inspiration in section 164:6a and b of the Doctrine and Covenants:

> As revealed in Christ, God, the Creator of all, ultimately is concerned about behaviors and relationships that uphold the worth and giftedness of all people and that protect the most vulnerable. Such relationships are to be rooted in the principles of Christ-like love, mutual respect, responsibility, justice, covenant, and faithfulness, against which there is no law.
>
> If the church more fully will understand and consistently apply these principles, questions arising about responsible human sexuality; gender identities, roles, and relationships; marriage; and other issues may be resolved according to God's divine purposes. Be assured, nothing within these principles condones selfish, irresponsible, promiscuous, degrading, or abusive relationships.

I look with hope to Community of Christ as it takes its unique place in the circle of the churches and faith communities that offer full inclusion to all who seek fellowship with us. This is possible when we move beyond labels and an all-or-nothing thinking. In so doing, we will more fully celebrate the incredible diversity represented in God's creation!

14

The Story of Walnut Creek, California

Kay Fletcher

THE STORY OF WALNUT CREEK, California, Community of Christ is a shared story of people yearning to be followers of God's plan for their congregation. It is a story of listening to God and to one another, recognizing needs in a community of believers, and following the gentle—and sometimes not so gentle—direction of the Spirit.

During my six-year tenure as pastor, our congregation began to vision our future. We decided we wanted to maintain a presence in the city, grow and thrive spiritually in our congregation, and reach out to our community. We began to pray. We prayed for God to awaken people to come into our midst and hear the story of Jesus and his mission the way we could best tell it. We prayed we would be open and accepting. We committed ourselves to identifying and overcoming our shortfalls. We became more scripturally sound by taking

Temple School classes together, and we invited world church leaders to teach us.

One Sunday, as I was preaching, a guest entered the back of the sanctuary. I felt God's Spirit shape my words. I spoke more clearly, in a different way than I had prepared. Prayers were raised that the heart of this visitor would be touched by God's message contained in my words. There were those who witnessed tears rolling down the face of our guest, and, soon thereafter, we learned his story.

His name was Keith, and we later found out he was gay. He had grown up in Community of Christ but, due to the prejudice he experienced, left the fellowship for seventeen years. He witnessed of the Spirit of God moving in his life as he responded to a call to return to church and share his story. Unsure of the reception he might receive, he still walked through the doorway into our sanctuary and was welcomed. Gently, our congregation was taught to really listen to each person's story.

Over the next several months and years, we were guided into a greater understanding of how we, as a congregation, could respond to those who were marginalized by our society and members of the Christian faith due to their sexual orientation. We talked about how to create a mission statement that was inclusive. Our intentions were good. We wanted to invite everyone to worship, learn, and fellowship as participating members of our congregation.

During the process, we invited the Welcoming Community Network organization to lead us in a weekend workshop. Together—as brothers, sisters, disciples, and ministers of Jesus Christ—we expressed our desire to understand and welcome those who were lesbian, gay, bisexual, and transgender. In our discussions, however, when we were asked why we hadn't invited LGBT members and why we might be afraid, there was a deep silence in the room. Someone, anyone, needed to speak up to identify what some may have seen as "the elephant in the room." Desperate that a response be provided and a safe space be created to share, the pastor gave voice to the question. Perhaps we were afraid we might discover we were hypocrites. If people who were very different from us came to visit, would we be confronted by our own nonacceptance?

The break in the ice could not have been more thunderous—workshop participants began to openly share their concerns and fears in a loving atmosphere. The next day, we shared the communion bread and wine, and felt the Holy Spirit's comforting presence move in, around, and through us. This began our journey in a focused and inclusive manner, as we continued to expand our worship to be more expressive of the many ways people approach their relationship with God.

More recently, we have sponsored a booth at the San Francisco Pride Festival and handed out the *Enduring Principles* brochures from Community of Christ that answered questions posed by visitors to our booth. The message that our congregation now sends is that all are loved and invited to God's table to share in community and fellowship. We have been blessed with the presence of new individuals in our congregation who are warm and loving, some of whom just happen to be LGBT, as well. Our congregation members have become interactive participants sharing in one another's journey through the challenges of life.

In time, it became clear that Keith had a call to the priesthood office of elder, but I had grown to love and respect him, and I struggled with processing his call. What if he fell in love and, due to church policy, would not be allowed to continue his ministry? Perhaps, even worse, what if he fell in love and chose to turn his back on life's love so that he might function in the priesthood office to which he was called? I agonized for months, yet God's persistent lead, coupled with the reassurance of God's love for Keith, encouraged me to move ahead. I knew that God would prepare the way for the ministry to be incarnated. Keith was ordained to the office of elder in 2010, and the blessing to our community and congregation has been great.

Our congregation continues to be transformed as the power of God's Spirit pours out blessings in ways that invite members to reach out to bring justice with ESL (English as a Second Language) classes, discernment groups, and ministry to recovering addicts. We invite everyone to come to God's table of forgiveness, love, celebration, acceptance, and service. God's love is for everyone, at all times, and in all places.

It is our congregation's story, and my individual witness, that God's love and mercy pour out in measure beyond understanding for all who would seek the Divine. We have met many who courageously live their lives with integrity. Our congregation has become a safe space where LGBT children of God may claim their rightful place as God's beloved.

15

Left Twice but Still Here

Saundra Merth

Music has played an important role in my life, ever since I was a child. One of my first memories of singing in front of a group was when I was singing in a church Christmas play dressed as an angel. After our regular Skylark meetings, I would stay after all the other girls had gone home and sing out of the gray hymnal with our leader playing the piano. Summer reunions at Lake Doniphan in Missouri also hold a special place in my musical memory, because there were always people in attendance who could sing well, and I was able to sing the alto and tenor parts, harmonizing just to delight in the sound.

Having been raised in the Midwest, surrounded by people who all looked like me, in a town where everyone seemed to follow the same set of rules, I knew at an early age I was different. As I grew up, I moved out of my parents' house and got married. Attending church just seemed like the thing to do on a Sunday morning and getting married to a man, also, seemed like the thing to do. Many years later, I was still singing in church choirs and Christmas plays. I was creating banners to hang and celebrating all the special and not-so-special seasons during the church year. But I still didn't feel like I belonged.

Then, while married to my husband, I met a woman and fell in love. And everything changed. My husband and I had a good marriage by all standards. We bought some land, built a house, and enjoyed our families, who were close by. After two weeks anguishing over how I was to tell him, I simply said to him one night that I was in love with a woman. As we gazed at the night sky, he stopped looking heavenward, turned to me, and said, "I guess if she were a man, I would have to punch her or something."

I distinctly remember that it was a Saturday night, because we went to church the very next morning. We weren't looking for guidance or answers, but we went because it had become a habit. I don't remember exactly how the sermon began, but I knew the man speaking had confidence in his premise that specific actions would land you in hell for an eternity. Of course, being gay was one of these choices, and when we left church that morning, I only returned once, a few years later, to sing at a funeral service. No one came up to me and asked me where I had been. No one approached me at all, and I left a second time.

My husband and I remained friends through this coming-out process. The closeness we shared was a blessing to me. When we lived near each other, we shared the holidays and milestones in our families. But, one night stands out in my memory even now, twenty years later. He had chosen to start attending a different denomination closer to home. We still occasionally shared our homes with each other, especially when I would have late night rehearsals making my commute too long. One evening, he said to me that he feared I would be going to hell, because his preacher had specifically said all gays would end up there. I explained that I believed God made me just the way I was—a lesbian. I also told him that he had come into my life for a reason. How could I ever choose someone else over him—man or woman? He loved me with all my shortcomings, and treated me with dignity and respect—before, and after, my coming out. We both cried that night, and, to this day, we remain close friends.

I was lucky enough to find an outlet for my musical passion by joining a large chorus in Seattle that performed classical music with an orchestra. We went on two musical tours: one to the Soviet Union, before the fall of communism, and the other to Australia to sing at the 1988 World Expo. During one of our performances, I had the opportunity (because the primary soloist got sick) to sing a solo with the entire group backing me up. In a word, it was magical. As a group, we performed three or four times a year—including New Year's Eve—where I had the most amazing musical experiences of my life. I got to experience my passion everywhere around the world—except in my church, where the passion was born.

It was several years after leaving the church the second time, that I heard about GALA and its annual Labor Day retreat. That particular year, it was to be held in the beautiful Pacific Northwest at the Samish Island Campground. I loved that area and decided to go, even though I really didn't know anything about GALA, and only knew the person who invited me. I longed to somehow get back in touch with my church roots but wasn't sure that was possible after so many years. I wasn't sure I wanted to go back to a church that still didn't accept me right where I was. A church that was willing to throw away anyone—gifted or not, just because they were gay—wasn't something I was interested in embracing.

It wasn't long before I realized how angry I was at everyone at the retreat who was straight and a church member. How could they impose themselves—here of all places? This was *our* safe space, if only for just one weekend. It took me a while to understand that they were our allies and were supportive of all of us in our journey within the church. But my anger wasn't that easily conquered. I realized I was still hiding from my church family, and I had some work of my own to do.

I experienced harassment at work, because I was a lesbian, but a change in jobs and a move to California settled me into a new place where I was determined not to hide who I was from anyone. It was after moving, that my partner, my teenage son, and I visited another Community of Christ congregation for the first time. This congregation had a tradition of newcomers standing and introducing themselves. We knew only a couple of people there, but I spotted an older couple sitting in front of us who looked a little familiar. As they stood up and spoke, I realized they were from my hometown in the Midwest. Now, I really didn't want to get up and announce to everyone that I was gay. What if they went home and told? I stood up anyway, and introduced my partner and our son, and quickly sat down. No one said anything derogatory to us afterward, and, later, I felt like this experience somehow brought my journey full circle and released me from my anger.

Over the years, I worked my way back to the church, and, it would appear, the church worked its way toward me. Although it still has a way to go before it joyously and openly embraces everyone, regardless of their sexual orientation, I am willing to stick around and see it through. It breaks my heart to hear the stories of all those who have left the church, looking for the open-arm embrace of another denomination, because I feel their longing for unfettered acceptance. Each and every one of us is on our own spiritual path of learning and understanding, no matter where we end up on a Sunday morning.

Now, I attend church with a purpose and not just out of habit. I am blessed to belong to a congregation that went through the process of becoming a Welcoming Community Network congregation that has adopted specific language welcoming the lesbian, gay, bisexual, and transgender community. Singing is still a passion with me and a gift I willingly share with my congregation, or with others, when called upon. I feel welcomed and accepted in my church community and, most importantly, comfortable in my own skin without the anger. I long for the day when all those who are a part of the LGBT community know they can enter any Community of Christ congregation and feel the same welcoming spirit that I now enjoy.

16

God's Love: Enough and to Share

Kay Fletcher

When I was seven years old, we lived in England. At that time, my baby sister, Saundra, was born, and I marveled at her mystery and beauty. As she grew up, I became aware that she was bright, articulate, and a joy to be with. We lived in Kansas when I was baptized into the RLDS church, then we moved to Independence, Missouri, the next summer.

One day, when she was about four years old, Saundra stopped me in the living room. I can remember where I was standing, with the sun shining through our living room window. She looked up and asked me, "Was I adopted?" I was stunned. I dropped to my knees to hold her and look in her eyes. I told her, "Of course not." She was my little sister—she looked like all of us with her beautiful brown eyes, and, besides, I remembered Mom bringing her home from the hospital. She later asked me several more times, and I continued to reassure her. I didn't know where those questions were coming from, even though life was turning upside down for us right then. Our father had left the family home, and there were lots of changes in our lives.

Saundra and I shared a room together—our beds were on either side and our windows were open, with the ceiling fan pulling in the hot summer air. In the cold winter, we snuggled together under the blankets. Holidays were spent with cousins and aunts and uncles, and Saundra's haunting questions of being adopted soon stopped. Our mom remarried, and our stepdad adored my sister; he was good to me and was great for our family. Saundra was baptized in Community of Christ at Lake Doniphan the same day as our stepdad. What a celebration of family and loved ones it was!

Just five short years later, I was married and moved to Texas. Saundra soon finished high school. Our stepdad died a year later. I moved to Washington State, and she married and moved to Florida. Though our paths didn't cross much, our love for each other never wavered.

Some years later, Saundra divorced and moved to Washington to join me. There, we had an opportunity to renew the close bond we had as children. She was gifted with an eye for beauty and balance. She had a wisdom that I marveled at, and she was blessed with a voice that sang our beloved hymns like an angel. She even went on a peace tour to Russia with the Seattle Choral Company.

My daughters were a part of the church school, and she was their teacher and beloved aunt. She took them on vacations, helped them bake surprise birthday cakes, and read to them. Saundra and I were as close as two sisters could be—sharing our aches, dreams, hopes, and sorrows.

One day, we were driving in the Seattle area, and she said to me, "I want to tell you something, but I don't know if I can." As she started to pour out her heart's concern, I could only reassure her that there was nothing she could tell me that would stop or hinder my love for her. Then, she told me she was lesbian. "Really," I said. "How do you know? What does that mean?" I must have had a thousand questions. She told me how she had been to church a few weeks before, and the minister had spoken from the pulpit that anyone who was homosexual would go to hell. I was so angry. The God of love, I knew, would not send anyone to hell for the way they were born.

I didn't know anything about homosexuality—I just knew we needed to learn more about it. We both remembered her asking me about being adopted and nervously laughed. Somehow, she knew she was different and didn't have the words to describe it, and I didn't know how to guide her. But we were going to find out.

Over the years, we both moved to California, and I became the pastor of the Walnut Creek Community of Christ congregation. One Sunday, as I was preaching, a man entered the back of the sanctuary, and I began to feel God's Spirit shape the words I was speaking a bit differently than the way I had prepared. Part of me prayed that the heart of this visitor would be touched by God's message. I watched as tears rolled down his face, and I soon learned his story. He was homosexual and grew up in Community of Christ, but left the fellowship for seventeen years due to the prejudice he experienced. He felt God's Spirit call him to return to church and tell his story.

Over the next several months and years, we were guided into a greater understanding of how we, as a congregation, could respond to those who were marginalized by society and Christianity because of their sexual orientation. We invited the Welcoming Community Network organization to come and share with us in a weekend workshop, so that we, as ministers and disciples of Christ, could better understand and welcome into our congregation, those who were lesbian, gay, bisexual, and transgender. Our outreach ministry led us to sponsor a booth at the San Francisco Pride Festival where we handed out the *Enduring Principles* brochures from Community of Christ. Our message was that all are loved and invited to God's table to share in community and fellowship. Our congregation has been blessed with the presence of new individuals who are LGBT, especially as they journey through the challenges of life and share their ministry with us.

It is my story and my witness that God's love and mercy pours out in measure, beyond understanding, for all who seek the divine, so every person may claim their rightful place as one of God's beloved children.

17

God's Call to Return to Community

Keith Carter

I am consumed in perfect love and overwhelmed with the best feeling I've ever known. Yes, I know what this is. I've experienced this before. The Spirit of the Lord is upon me. But why is this happening to me now? My thoughts go to past experiences of knowing God's Spirit upon me.

> Suddenly, I'm back in the year 1983, sitting around a campfire with members of the RLDS church at a senior high camp. We meet every year at Big Spruce Camp to share in a week of fellowship. We've come together for a campfire with singing and worship. Eager for the experience, we yearn for and seek God's touch. We start out by singing campfire songs that quickly turn to the more serious side of worship. Then, we start sharing in testimony of our past experiences of God and how it changed us. As we seek and affirm God within our lives, sharing and yearning for that experience, we are not denied. God envelops us with

his loving grace. We experience the best expression of a Loving Creator. We all sit around the campfire, sharing and embracing the love God has to offer. This is what we yearn for. We revel in God's presence. We never want this to end. We could stay there forever in this perfect community, sharing in God's love. This is what we've come to know: Seek God and he will not deny.

How does one explain the experience of God? Words cannot fully explain this experience, as it is too large to be expressed. The only way I can think of explaining it is to tell you to think of someone you love. Think of someone close to you who makes you feel warm inside. It's kind of like that feeling—that innermost, warm feeling you get when you think about someone you love. Now, take that feeling and expand it a million times so that the feeling of love is so strong that it overwhelms and consumes you. It is the most consuming love you have ever experienced. It completes you. When I experienced this, the feeling of love was so strong I knew I could not have produced such a feeling myself. I do not have the capacity to create love this strong. But there it was—put upon me, put upon us. All I know is that I would love to have this experience forever.

Every year, God extended his grace upon the youth gathered specifically for that purpose. They were gathered, because once you've experienced God's grace, once you know where to get it, you keep going back. If only the rest of the world could know this kind of love.

Well, that was a long time ago. I've left that life behind. I'm gay. The world, for the most part, excludes me. I am chastised and told I am sin. I prayed for way too many years to be normal, and it didn't work. I'm still gay. I'm told I'm not part of God's plan and that I must change. I would if I could. I don't want to be gay.

Here it is, 2006—twenty-four years later—and I sit here on my couch overwhelmed with God's love. But why? What is God trying to tell me? I'm not with a group of like-minded individuals seeking God at a church campfire. So, I turn to the only place I know I've experienced this presence before—the RLDS church. However, they are now known as Community of Christ.

Since I left the church in 1983, a lot has changed. Descendents of Joseph Smith Jr. are no longer the leaders of the church. Women are now called into priesthood. And they've built the Independence Temple, dedicated to the pursuit of peace.

I wonder if God is still speaking to the church I once knew. I pull up the website for Community of Christ on my computer and find a link to Doctrine and Covenants, section 162—words of council to the church from President W. Grant McMurray in 2004. With God's nudge, I begin to read, and the words jump off the page at me:

> 1b. Listen to the Voice that echoes across the eons of time and yet speaks anew in this moment. Listen to the Voice, for it cannot be stilled, and it calls you once again to the great and marvelous work of building the peaceable kingdom, even Zion, on behalf of the One whose name you claim.

I've often thought what Zion would be like. If it has anything to do with that all-consuming love of God I've experienced in the past, then count me in—I'm there. I want nothing more than to be constantly in communion with that love. If the world could just experience what I experienced as a youth, then everyone would be working to bring forth Zion. We would all want to share in the experiences of God and never leave.

Okay, if you're trying to tell me something, God, what is it? I read further with a yearning to see what God is trying to tell me:

> 3b. That Spirit is even now touching alive the souls of those who feel the passion of discipleship burning deeply within. Many others will respond if you are persistent in your witness and diligent in your mission to the world.

Wow! Is this really talking about me? Somehow I feel it is:

> 6a. From the earliest days you have been given a sacred principle that declares the inestimable worth of all persons. Do not forget.
>
> b. The One who created all humankind grieves at the shameful divisions within the human family. A prophetic people must work tirelessly to tear down walls of separation and to build bridges of understanding.
>
> c. You hold precious lives in your hands. Be gentle and gracious with one another. A community is no stronger than the weakest within

> it. Even as the One you follow reached out to those who were rejected and marginalized, so must the community that bears his name.

I am overwhelmed. God is speaking my language. Yes, I sense that these are the words of God. But why am I here reading them? I'm not ready yet.

I'm thankful for this experience. I've missed you, God. Yes, I know better. I know you don't condemn me for the way you've created me. But the world has it wrong, and there is nothing I can do about it. I know that you love me unconditionally. I've experienced the love you have for me, and I'm gay. The one being I can't lie to or hide from is you, God. You know me.

***

It's now been several months. It's 2007, and I'm back at my computer responding to the gentle, yet persistent, nudges of God's call. A few months ago, Community of Christ held its world conference. Section 163 was given by President Stephen M. Veazey. As I read the introductory statement, I can understand the president's explanation of "the limitations of the human vessel entrusted with responsibility for articulating divine encounter." The experiences I have had with God are not easy to articulate into language. God is so much more than we are able to express into words. As I read section 163, many parts of the counsel to the church jump out at me:

> 2a. Jesus Christ, the embodiment of God's shalom, invites all people to come and receive divine peace in the midst of the difficult questions and struggles of life. Follow Christ in the way that leads to God's peace and discover the blessings of all of the dimensions of salvation.
>
> 3a. You are called to create pathways in the world for peace in Christ to be relationally and culturally incarnate. The hope of Zion is realized when the vision of Christ is embodied in communities of generosity, justice, and peacefulness.
>
> b. Above all else, strive to be faithful to Christ's vision of the peaceable Kingdom of God on earth. Courageously challenge cultural, political, and religious trends that are contrary to the reconciling and restoring purposes of God. Pursue peace.

> c. There are subtle, yet powerful, influences in the world, some even claiming to represent Christ, that seek to divide people and nations to accomplish their destructive aims. That which seeks to harden one human heart against another by constructing walls of fear and prejudice is not of God. Be especially alert to these influences, lest they divide you or divert you from the mission to which you are called.

I am once again overwhelmed with God's grace and call to return to relationship. I am being called to be a witness to the grace and love God is extending to me—a gay man. It seems God doesn't have a problem with me like the world does. As I read the following verse, I am shaken to the core:

> 7c. It is not pleasing to God when any passage of scripture is used to diminish or oppress races, genders, or classes of human beings. Much physical and emotional violence has been done to some of God's beloved children through the misuse of scripture. The church is called to confess and repent of such attitudes and practices.

I weep with the overwhelming love of God within me. I know of the emotional and physical violence done to the gay community in the name of God. I've lived it for the past forty-two years. I see the fractured lives and brokenness of the gay community. I see the results from people being told they are not included or wanted. They are told that the desire, attraction, and love they feel is wrong, because it's for people of the same sex. Gay is not right. It's not normal. It's not in God's plan. If you're gay, you're unworthy of God, because you're not part of the plan.

The world doesn't want gay people. In some countries, being gay is against the law. A person can be imprisoned and even sentenced to death by stoning or hanging—just for being gay. In other places, they actually burn homosexuals in the streets. Who wants to be gay? Many gay people commit suicide—the shame of being gay is just too tough to endure.

These are the enduring principles of homosexuality—shame and unworthiness. Such enduring principles create a brokenness that only a loving people can fix.

My tears subside enough to read section 163 a bit further. My final call is loudly announced:

> 10a. Collectively and individually, you are loved with an everlasting love that delights in each faithful step taken. God yearns to draw you close so that wounds may be healed, emptiness filled, and hope strengthened.
>
> b. Do not turn away in pride, fear, or guilt from the One who seeks only the best for you and your loved ones. Come before your Eternal Creator with open minds and hearts and discover the blessings of the gospel anew. Be vulnerable to divine grace.

God is calling me back into relationship. I'm being called forth to embrace divine grace, without pride, fear, or guilt. But can I really have a relationship with God in the community I once knew?

Weeks later, I stand in front of the Walnut Creek Community of Christ, looking at the front doors. They are waiting for me to open them. I yearn for God's touch once again. I'm about to enter this church as a gay man, without shame, and know that I am loved with an everlasting love that delights me to the fullest. I'm here to proclaim the good news—God's love for all of creation—and we're leaving no one behind. I feel confident, as the words of counsel have assured me that God has gone before me. He has prepared the way.

I step into the church and am consumed in perfect love. My journey begins.

18

By Love's Chance

Della Mowrey

I have a hard time conceptualizing people living in this world without knowing God. My life couldn't function without a relationship with a supreme being who has a purpose or a plan for me. I would feel deadened, hopeless, and forever lost if this loving Creator didn't comfort me when I am sad, lonely, and defeated. In turn, he is also the one who rejoices with me in celebration during the times that I've reflectively recalled my many blessings.

My first experience with the GALA organization was the precise time that I recalled discovering that *God loves and accepts me just as I am!* Every GALA encounter has been a life-changing experience for me. A minister from Community of Christ led me to this organization, and I shall be forever thankful for this light in my life.

My story begins the moment I was born. Unloved, abandoned, and left by my biological parents to die in my infancy, my life was immediately thrown into survivor mode. My adoptive parents shared a deep love and an abiding faith in God that led them to entrust me to the elders of their church. I was placed in their hands for administration, the sacrament of healing grace. This is where I received my first miracle—life. I was no longer a delayed infant who was malnourished, crippled, and whose diagnosis was fatal. The love of God restored my damaged, broken body; my spirit was loved and accepted. As third-generation members of the Reorganized Church of Jesus Christ of Latter Day Saints, my family has instilled in me a belief system of values that has continuously permeated my soul. This church became my family, foundation, support system, and village, as it had for generations of others before me. I grew up with a framework to form my life around which created a sense of balance in my world.

It all seemed like a perfect plan until one day in my early adulthood—things were not as they appeared. No one told me I would have these types of feelings toward other women. There was no one I trusted enough to share my secret with. In my desperation, I approached the church ministers, and they were sympathetic. But they had no idea of what to do, beyond a few supportive words. It added to my confusion and the feeling of being lost without a clear path ahead of me. I felt like the topic of sexual identity was being moved off a back burner to be set aside to become a cold and ignored topic. I felt abandoned by my church family.

As I grew, I was continually reminded of God's unconditional love for me. I was also told that certain acts were sinful and against Christ's way—following those ways would take a person to eternal hell. The conflict within my soul was unceasing, and I chastised myself daily for what I understood was a natural part of me. I hated myself!

Following the expected norms of my family, church, and society, I married a man who was a minister and who had also grown up in the RLDS church. Within the first few months of our marriage, I realized I had compromised myself, and I was devastated. My falseness was not only injurious to him but was also harmful to me. I was living a heterosexual life, but my body, mind, and spirit knew my natural state of being. Living a double life caused me great pain and anguish—it tormented me for over twenty years. I was the mother of three, fulfilling my duties as wife and mother with every ounce of love and dedication I could muster. An accumulation of many things led to divorce, which resolved, for me, the battle to be honest that raged within me.

My children were raised with the same concepts and values as I had been—with one notable exception. They were taught to love all people without judgment. I left the church for several years, because I could no longer find solace. Despite the perceived damage done to my heart by the lack of acceptance and understanding by the only church I had ever known, I faithfully drove my children to church camps every summer. I wanted them to have the same opportunity of experiencing those personal moments with God that I had been given. It was my way of sharing my heritage with my children.

During summer vacation in 2001, my youngest son, Daniel, wanted me to take him to Sacramento Mountain Retreat in New Mexico. Eager to fulfill his wish, I gladly complied. Upon our arrival that warm Saturday in July, everyone was seated in the dining hall having a midday meal. We joined them and conversed with a few people I recognized. Lunch was soon over, and I watched as everyone scattered with their trays in hand, leaving the site.

There was an awkward silence as I found myself sitting with just one other person—a woman across the table. Peering at her, I saw her eyes were filled with love and compassion, and I was transcended into a place I had never known. Out of her mouth spilled the word GALA, and she told me of a place where I would be supported, loved, and accepted just as I am. She indicated that it was a place where God was the core, and I did not need to hide anymore. My heart skipped a beat as she spoke. She somehow knew my story without words being exchanged.

She told me her name was Karen. I instantly felt unconditional love as we embraced. Like a shadow, I followed her around the campground into the late evening, soaking in every word she shared. Before I left, Karen and her husband, Aubrey, administered to me, and I felt another healing begin to take place in my life.

I rushed down the mountain with tears streaming down my face as I made my way home. Rapidly racing into my house, I immediately booted up my computer, wrote the GALA organization an e-mail, and bought a plane ticket to Missouri for the GALA Labor Day retreat. Arriving at the Kansas City airport, I was warmly greeted by two men, Chuck and Mike Hewitt. They graciously took me to Camp Doniphan where my life was forever changed. I spent the weekend being smothered with love and affection, shedding tears, and sharing laughter among a group of people who immediately became my family.

During the final worship service, I became aware of God's unconditional love for me. As the closing service approached, I bounced down the stairs, running a few minutes late. I walked into the room and noticed a circle of people with one empty seat on the opposite side. In the center of the circle was a long table that contained different-sized glasses set for communion. As I stepped into the circle, I became drenched with my own tears. The Holy Spirit flooded over me like a wave of new beginnings, and I could hardly make my way to the empty seat across the room.

God, the heavenly parent I had always known, touched my heart, opened my eyes, and showed me I was home. This was where I belonged. My loving Lord broke through the chains of guilt, with which I had allowed myself to be bound, and wiped away the shame and self-hate I had allowed to grow around me. I realized I was loved unconditionally, just as God created me, and I didn't need to be any different. This was my family—my family of God. My spirit was reignited. It was because of God's love and my GALA experiences that I decided to attend church again.

Over the years, there have been many ongoing changes in what is now Community of Christ. I had the honor of attending the 2010 World Conference, and I had the heartwarming experience of being a delegate for my region. I witnessed a different church than the one I had experienced in the past. I saw a church that was accepting of all people, by ethnicity, and now by sexual orientation, too. My church welcomed me and many others like me. They showed us that we are unconditionally loved just as we are. During the GALA banquet, I approached one of the ministers I had shared my dilemma with many years earlier. He and I embraced, and thanked the Holy Creator for this greater understanding and love that we now equally shared.

For the past several years, I have lived my life as a lesbian in two long-term relationships. I've experienced some difficult times due to the prejudices that still encompass our society, but, internally, I am free. "By love's chance" I have survived the neglect and abandonment that life bestowed upon me. I have become a warrior in the army of God—exercising love for all, not just for some. I am a living miracle. I am loved unconditionally!

19

My Small Town Story

Todd Davison

It was a clear, crisp, beautiful June morning in Macon, Missouri. It was Father's Day. As I got dressed, I could look out my bedroom window at the Reorganized Church of Jesus Christ of Latter Day Saints where I was about to be ordained to the office of priest. At the age of seventeen, I was the youngest priesthood candidate I knew. I'd always been a good kid. I had grown up in the church and was quite secure in the knowledge that the church and I, together, had something unique to offer the world. I had read, studied, and prayed in preparation for ordination, and, on this special morning, I knelt beside my bed and bowed my head.

As a good Zion's Leaguer, I knew how to pray—first, give praise and thanksgiving; second, offer specific petitions for my friends, family, church leaders, and the upcoming service; and then, I prayed for myself. I asked God to bless my ministry as it would expand as a member of the priesthood. I asked that I would be humble, helpful, and discerning. Then, I asked for the biggest blessing of all. I really didn't understand or have the right words to describe it, but I had this secret—a part of myself I was pretty sure no other person knew about, but I knew God did. I asked that when the elders placed their hands on my head to ordain me, God would remove the unnatural, un-Godly urges that I'd felt, and I'd be made clean and whole.

You see, about two years before, our district had held a youth preaching series in a central congregation about an hour from my home. This wasn't a series of services planned by youth or featuring youth speakers, as one might assume, but it was a series of sermons preached by adults with a specific focus on "things today's youth need to know to be equipped for the very real battle between good and evil." During one of the sermons, the speaker told the story of his brother who had been "possessed by an evil spirit that made him desire men instead of women." After the brother had been administered to, "the evil spirit left him, and he had a normal desire for women." This story hit me like a ton of bricks. Even though I didn't understand my feelings, I knew that I must be possessed by that same evil spirit.

As luck would have it, the speaker who had the gay brother was a close family friend and was assisting my father with my ordination. I was a little troubled that I had not confessed my feelings to this man, so that he'd know about his important extra role in my ordination. But I figured, if I asked God, sincerely, the whole thing could be taken care of in one fell swoop, and no one needed to be troubled with the details.

During the next ten years I experienced periods of denial, exasperation, and cluelessness, but never thought of myself as gay. In fact, I wasn't even sure that *real* homosexual people existed.

I had plenty of dates in high school, but was always too busy to "go steady" with anyone. Because I was a musician and theater person, instead of being athletic, I was sometimes teased and even called a "fairy." But I hardly ever let such insults get me down. My involvement in the church was very important in my life. I knew lots of scriptures and rules. I even developed a sense of righteous indignation when my peers talked about girls. I certainly was not going to cross any forbidden line with a girl before I was married!

At Graceland, I soon developed a reputation as a fun (and safe) date. I enjoyed dramatic dates and parties and was invited to lots of formals. Once a male friend suggested we could be "more than friends," but I was shocked and flustered, and I left his car right away. I had three relatively serious relationships with women in college, but they all ended with my ambivalence. I eventually just didn't care if I saw them again or not. I always chalked this up to the idea that I just hadn't found "the right woman."

My relationship to scripture, God, and the RLDS church changed and deepened while I was attending Graceland. I was challenged and inspired to examine the ideas of my youth and was sometimes surprised at what I found myself thinking. I had never been to world conference for more than a day or two, but, in 1984, I was a delegate and really felt like I was a part of something worthwhile. During my senior year, I was an assistant to the campus chaplain, and believed I was really helping people and preparing myself for greater service. Before leaving Graceland, I was ordained an elder.

After college, I worked at various jobs, became pastor of my local congregation, and stayed "too busy for dating." Finally, a woman whose schedule appropriately matched mine began to spend a lot of time with me. I certainly enjoyed her company, but one fateful night, she finally came right out and asked me why I wasn't physically demonstrative to her at all. I had no answer, other than the fact that I wasn't physically attracted to her.

In the spring of 1992, I was once again a delegate to world conference. During an informal conversation in the hall one day, a friend of mine from Graceland was described in a completely nonjudgmental way as being "as gay as they come." I was shocked—and intrigued. During the conference floor discussion on the resolution on Human Diversity (WCR 1226), I turned to the fellow sitting next to me and asked, "Do you think there really are homosexual people? How do they get that way?"

During the next three months, I suddenly discovered that some people really *are* homosexual—and I knew a number of them. Suddenly, my own life experience made sense to me. I was one of them, too! It wasn't that God forgot to remove my gayness when I had asked so fervently at age seventeen. I believed that God didn't care if I was gay any more than if I was right handed, Caucasian, or able to whistle through my teeth. I found supportive gay folks right in my own town, and among high school and college friends. Within a few weeks, I had told most of the people I was closest to, including my parents and sister, about my self-realization. There were some tears and lots of misunderstanding, but no one was ugly or rejecting—until it came to some members of my congregation.

Soon after my personal coming out, I made an appointment to talk with my district president. I was a pastor, and I thought she ought to know I was gay, and advise me about what I might need to do. I surprised her in the midst of her family's own struggle to understand her gay son. She was very supportive, and we decided I would continue on as pastor.

I had discovered some very helpful books about gay folks serving in other denominations. The idea that Christian people were integrating their gayness into their church lives was heartening to me. When I was invited to my first GALA retreat, I really felt like I had come home. Here was a bunch of men and women who shared more in common with me than I had ever imagined. I thought I was alone, but, suddenly, I was part of a community. Eventually, I was able to mesh my GALA community with my biological family. Both of my parents and my sister have their own GALA stories to tell.

While many people around me were able to assimilate this new information about my makeup, some have not been supportive. Instead of sewing sequins on my dress shirts, filling my yard with rainbow flags, or organizing a gay pride march in Macon, I chose to simply live my life a little more personally grounded and not deny the places where my gayness leaked out a little. I didn't try to cover or hide, and if anyone wanted to ask or talk about it, I was game. However, most people in my local congregation didn't want to talk about it.

After getting a frosty reception at church, two weeks running, from a certain couple, I asked if I might come over to their house and talk to them. These folks had been in our congregation since I was in elementary school and were my Zion's League leaders throughout high school. When I got to their house that night, I didn't beat around the bush. I just said I felt like they had been avoiding me, and I wondered if it had anything to do with the fact that I was a homosexual person. It did. They said it was "all over town" that I was gay, and it was embarrassing to them. They told me they were disappointed and appalled that I would continue to act in a leadership position in the church. The man who had been pastor and processed my first priesthood call thought he may have got it wrong—or I had changed. They said the fact I could walk into the Auditorium and not be "detected" was evidence that the world church leadership was not "as strong as it used to be." I don't remember what I said to them that night. I just remember feeling lonely and sad.

In fact, it *was* all over town. I ran my own business and was very well known, so a number of curious folks whispered, and a few bold ones talked to me. In one infamous scene in Walmart, a toothless young woman of my acquaintance hollered down the aisle, "Todd Davison, I heard you married a man!" In time, another family from our congregation decided they could no longer worship with me if I was going to be speaking from the pulpit. It was okay for me to play the piano, but they didn't think I had authority as a leader. After they left, a minister friend from another denomination sought me out to offer his personal support, even though his own congregation was not supportive of "the gay lifestyle."

My experiences of being gay in Community of Christ have been a decidedly mixed bag. I have witnessed people saying, and doing, terrible and ignorant things to one another. However, for every cousin who writes to tell me that I am a cancer in our family, there is a mother who seeks my advice for welcoming her gay high school son's boyfriend, a lady at the bank who asks if I'm dating anyone because a very nice man just moved to town that she thinks I should meet, and a six-year-old who throws his arms around me with unconditional abandon. I pray that I may live to see a time when we wonder what all the fuss was over.

20

Invitations

Douglas Graves

I am a minster. I am an active member of Community of Christ. I am a homosexual. I am not an ordained priesthood member. The first two statements are direct responses to invitations I have received. The second two do not matter. Unless someone asks, I volunteer the information, or (as I have allowed them to in the past) they become limitations in how I serve. It took the love and patience of several people, and my own time of healing and discernment, to arrive where I am currently in my journey of faith. The journey is just beginning in many ways, but it began with a simple invitation.

In June 2006, I received an e-mail from a former youth minister, who was a huge influence in my life during my high school and college years. He had discovered, through a member of GALA that I was working on a musical production, and got my e-mail address. In the e-mail, he asked if I would consider helping out at SPECTACULAR (SPEC). When I was growing up, this camp was called SPORTS SPECTACULAR, so I didn't really see how I would fit in there.

Through e-mail exchanges, he told me about changes in the camp programming to include leadership classes, and visual and performing arts opportunities to the high school-aged youth who attended the camp. He asked me to help with the technical features of the performance aspects of camp (I am a professional audio engineer). I responded that I would think about it. I was going to be moving to another city in a few months, to set up a production of a musical there, and would have to find the time off. However, I informed him that I was going to be in the city where he lived and would gladly meet up with him and discuss it.

In October 2006, I met with him at his family's home. This was our first meeting in fifteen years, though he had been in my thoughts many times during that period. I met his children and reconnected with his wife, whom I knew from college. The kids went off to bed, while he and his wife and I began to talk about the camp. I came there willing to listen, but I also came with a series of self-made roadblocks that I was convinced would keep me from being able to participate in this camp. Each one that I placed in front of him was gently pushed aside, so I threw down my biggest one.

"I can't go back in the closet."

"I don't want you to."

***

A little personal history: I left the church—okay, I received a letter in 1995 saying that I was placed on the inactive membership list. Before that time, I was becoming more comfortable in my sexuality, and I was struggling with reconciling being a gay man and being a member of the denomination I had been born into. I was in graduate school and had transferred my membership to a small congregation near the university, but I became inactive in congregational life. No one from the congregation had contacted me in several months, and I was struggling with the idea of leaving the denomination. So that letter became my answer to my struggle—I didn't belong in this denomination.

I grew up in Community of Christ. My father was the pastor of two different congregations. I was active in Boy Scouts (I received the rank of Eagle Scout). I was active in church youth groups. I ended up at the denomination's sponsored college, and I became a summer camp counselor, lifeguard, and campfire leader. However, I knew that I couldn't be gay and be in this denomination. Nothing was ever said, but I knew that being gay wasn't acceptable because of the content of church documents. So to protect myself from the pain that I was sure would come, I distanced myself. Still, God was inviting me to be a part of this community.

I discovered GALA through an online contact in 1999 and was encouraged to attend a retreat. My first retreat was in 2000, but I had not told my parents about my sexuality. How painful and silly is it that you can't tell your parents that you are going to a church retreat, because you aren't "out" to them? After the first retreat, I attended another GALA retreat in 2002, where then-president Grant McMurray shared his ministry with us. The challenges and difficulties that he spoke about gave me the perspective and encouragement to come out to my parents.

Two years later, I attended the 2004 World Conference—not as a delegate, but just as a person to stand in the GALA booth. This was my way of reacting to legislation being introduced that would limit the ability of lesbian, gay, bisexual, and transgender members to serve in the denomination. This piece of legislation was sponsored by a regional delegation where I had served for two summers as lifeguard at their campground. The thought of this legislation coming from that area was very painful for me.

These few events, from 2000 to 2004, were my only physical contact with members of the denomination for over ten years. So, I didn't understand why I would even be asked to be a part of one of the largest gatherings of denominational youth.

During our meeting in 2006, my former youth minister said, "I feel a calling for you here." If you grew up in this denomination, you might understand the impact that those words had on me. I always felt close to God and never understood why I hadn't been called to the priesthood. This may also give you some insight into how startling those words were to me in that moment. I was no longer faced with just deciding if I was going to lend a helping hand at a camp; I was being challenged to respond to a calling. We ended the evening, and I said I would still have to think about it. I had a lot of fear to work through.

***

Flash forward to the spring of 2007, and I have agreed to help out at the camp. Jump ahead to July 2007, and I am at the camp. There is not enough space here to express what I experienced at SPEC my first year on staff. I made some peace with God and with myself. I found other people who would take the time to listen to my stories, fears, frustrations, and still walk beside me on those first steps of this journey back into activity in Community of Christ. I hoped to come back and serve again the following year at SPEC, but when was a good time to ask if it was okay to come back? Someone then asked me on the final night if I was going to return—another invitation.

Several months after SPEC, I took some time away from my professional life and made the decision to begin attending a local congregation. The first Sunday I showed up, I was asked to do a reading—so much for my idea of just showing up there and sitting in the congregation. Then, I received other requests to serve in the congregation. I was asked to do readings, give prayers, and share in the ministry of music during the services. I had become a part of that congregation.

One of the invitations I received my first year at SPEC was to help with the audio of the International Youth Forum (IYF) in 2009. I was timid at the time, but I said if I could work it out with my professional work, I would be willing to help. IYF took place right before SPEC, which allowed me to do both events. Once again, I could write an essay on the powerful experience of serving and the experiences of God's Spirit at IYF. This led me to extend my own invitation. Bill Russell was teaching a class at SPEC that summer on the book *Homosexual Saints: The Community of Christ Experience*. I offered to share my story with his class, if he needed someone to do that. My invitation was accepted, and another powerful experience of God's Spirit was added to my life.

I returned home and received an invitation to be part of a church-planting team. This meant I would be a part of a leadership team to help create and serve a new Community of Christ congregation. Once again I had my reservations, but the pastor gently helped me to agree to be part of this endeavor. A few months later, I was asked to attend the SPEC committee meeting, where I was asked to become a member of the committee. That invitation was much easier to say yes to, after three years of being loved into that community.

I was suddenly involved in—not just a local congregation—but as a church-planting team member; and I also became a member of the SPEC committee. I felt as if I had become a part of the denomination in a way I had never imagined in my youth, when I was longing to be an ordained priesthood member. I was being a minister (which several friends had to point out to me), and it didn't require a priesthood card.

I was looking forward to taking part as a delegate, my first time, in the 2010 World Conference. Before conference, I was invited to a meeting with my pastor and the regional apostle to discuss my feelings on the document that would later become section 164 of the Doctrine and Covenants. I was humbled by this—and a little more than shocked, when the pastor excused herself and left the regional apostle with me in the coffee shop to speak privately.

We talked about the language of the document and the implications it would have on the LGBT community. I was then informed about a non-legislative session that would be held where a member of the denomination would be asked to share their story with the delegations. I offered my support in whatever way was needed. A few weeks later, I was invited to share my story in that session. I accepted and compressed the past 1,700 words you have read, into 350 words and a one-and-a-half-minute presentation (which took longer, to allow for simultaneous translations for the international delegations).

My journey had taken me to a place that I never thought I would be when I removed myself from the denomination fifteen years earlier. All of these events started with an invitation. While I can say that I was invited, there is a more important aspect to this. I *accepted* the invitations. No one begged me. No one put pressure on me to accept. I had to be willing to accept what was being asked of me. I now continue to accept invitations to serve in Community of Christ. I also exercise my agency to say no when I have to say no. There is not a blanket yes to every request.

I have been blessed to learn of discernment and to listen to where the Spirit is leading me. This has led me to other places where I had been fearful to attend and be a part of, because I thought it was only meant for certain people in this denomination. I attend the local LEADS (Leadership Education And Discipleship Studies) classes, which are courses to help develop the ministers in our local mission center, and I am currently pursuing a master of arts in religion through the seminary program at Graceland University. All of these things have helped me in my role as part of the ministerial team for my home congregation, the church plant that was started in 2010.

I have even begun to invite people to denominational functions. I have invited people to come worship with us on Sundays. I have invited people to attend retreats. I have even invited people to attend SPEC as campers and as staff. Not everyone has accepted those invitations but I have put them out there. I do this because someone did this for me, and I will always be grateful for that simple gift of invitation. We are all continually being invited, every person, to be in closer communion with God and with one another. All are called. How you choose to respond is between you and God.

21

A Competent Elder Lost: The Story of Dave Russell

Bill Russell

My brother Dave was four years older than I—the third of four children born to Eleanor and R. Melvin Russell. From the time the four of us were young children, Dad was a full-time, paid "church appointee" minister, as they were called. Reta, the oldest child, was not eligible for the priesthood, being of the wrong gender; but she married a young man, Richard B. Lancaster, a year before he went under appointment.

Of the three Russell boys, Dave was the one we thought would most likely be the son who would follow in Dad's footsteps and become a church appointee. He was the most religious of the three sons. But Dave had one serious problem with regard to a career in the church. He was gay. He was in the closet until he was fifty-two, so he spent most of his life denying who he really was.

Our oldest brother was Robert, and he and I were much more interested in sports than in religion. We both loved mathematics and had a lot in common. Dave was not into sports at all. He later told me the only time he really enjoyed athletic competition was when he took a touch football class at Graceland College, where he attended from 1952–54. They played a seven-man game. Dave, having little or no athletic ability, was assigned to be the one lineman whose only assignment was to block the defensive linemen as they came through to tag the quarterback. He enjoyed pushing the defensive guys around. But the other more skill-demanding positions were not his cup of tea.

Dave was the most outgoing of the three brothers and, probably, because of his greater spirituality, was called to the priesthood at a younger age than Robert or I.

Dave was drafted into the US Army in 1956 and served most of his two-year hitch in France. He once told me that if you are discovered as a homosexual in the military, you will be discharged—I presumed dishonorably. He hid his sexual orientation by doing such things as visiting a French brothel with some of his army buddies.

After his discharge from the army, Dave returned to our hometown of Flint, Michigan. He began teaching at Longfellow Junior High, just three short blocks from where our family lived when I was in junior high, and Dave and Robert were at Flint Northern High. Dave met a local church woman who was the soloist at my wedding, and they married eighteen months later. Again, this was a good cover for his sexual orientation.

I assume the Saints at the Hamilton Avenue congregation in Flint were very happy to have Dave back home. He had been a popular teenager in the congregation when Dad was the appointee pastor, and he had many good friends there. Two of the longtime families had Dave live with them for a period of time before his marriage.

Soon Dave was the church school director for the congregation. He was an educator and worked hard to develop the program, which included an extensive church library of materials. But when my wife and I visited Dave and his wife in Flint, they seemed frustrated, feeling that they were not well-accepted in the congregation.

Eventually, Dave began a master's program at the University of Michigan, first in English and then in library science, so he resigned as the church school director. He felt that his successor ignored the work he had done with the curriculum and with the library. Possibly it had become known, or suspected, in the congregation that Dave was gay. At any rate, for some reason, Dave and his wife did not feel accepted.

I was an editor at Herald Publishing House in Independence, Missouri, when, to my surprise, I learned that Dave had quit going to church and, for all intents and purposes, was *quitting* the church. I don't know if he ever resigned his priesthood or membership, but he quit attending. He had been an active elder for only about six years. This was in 1966, approximately.

Dave was a religious person, though, so he began attending other denominations. He had no interest in fundamentalist Christianity, regarding as indefensible their biblical literalism and refusal to accept science when it conflicted with the Bible. Over the next fifteen or twenty years, he tried virtually every other nonfundamentalist Protestant denomination, but did not find them satisfactory, either.

Occasionally, Dave would feel guilty about abandoning the church that meant so much to his parents, so he would return to the Reorganized Church of Jesus Christ of Latter Day Saints and give it another try. Most of these visits happened after he and his family moved to Iowa City, Iowa, and then to Cheyenne, Wyoming. He was very close to our mother, and he would typically write her a letter and tell her they had attended the local RLDS church the previous Sunday. It seemed like this would occur around Mother's Day.

But the RLDS church in Iowa City and Cheyenne were no more satisfactory than the Hamilton Avenue congregation in Flint. Although Dave remained in the closet, he no doubt sensed a lack of acceptance of gays in the other denominations, as well. He was a married man for twenty-four years (1962–86), and very few Protestant denominations had become sensitive and accepting of LGBT people in that period. It wasn't until the mid-1970s that various professional organizations began to change their view of homosexuality as a mental disease.

Finally, Dave found a home in the Unitarian Universalist Association, the only church of any size in America at the time that wholly accepted LGBT people. His family history was a westward movement: from Flint to Iowa City to Cheyenne and finally to Ashland, Oregon. His wife had remained with him despite a longtime suspicion, if not a clear knowledge, that Dave was gay.

Finally, when I was divorced in 1986 and wrote to Dave in Oregon, he replied with a letter that said his marriage had been going downhill for fourteen years. I wrote back that he should make some major adjustments and, if that didn't work, end it. You can't have a marriage that is continually getting worse. He wrote back, saying that the problem was that he was gay. But, reflecting his natural desire to remain in the closet, he wrote back in the next day or two and said to ignore his previous letter, because he was *not* gay. Finally, just a few days later, he wrote again and said to restore the original letter, and—yes, he *was* gay.

Dave came out of the closet, and, soon, he and his wife decided to divorce. I recognized that it was good for Dave's mental health to come out and no longer have to deny who he was. But I hoped he would not tell our mother, a loyal church appointee widow, as Dad had died four years earlier. Dave was in Oregon, not involved in the RLDS church. Mom was at Resthaven in Independence, Missouri. There was no reason to believe that Mom would hear about Dave unless he told her. But, I should have known that Dave would tell Mother. They had been very close over the years. As a young child, Dave would walk around the house in Mother's shoes or put on one of her dresses, long after it was an embarrassment for the rest of us.

Dave probably didn't know for sure how Mom would react. She was a loyal church member and proud of her appointee husband, now deceased. And Dave no doubt knew that gays who come out of the closet cannot be sure how their parents may react, no matter how loving they appear to be. When Dave told our mother he was gay, she was completely accepting. "I always suspected it," she said. And while she was normally a fairly quiet person, whenever someone at Resthaven would say something negative about gays or lesbians, she would rebut them vigorously. I'm sure Mother's acceptance meant more to Dave than we can imagine.

On the other hand, Dave had one longtime friend from Flint who corresponded with him for many years—his best continuing friend from Flint, it seemed. But when Dave wrote to her and told her he was gay, he never heard from her again. This hurt him deeply.

When Mom died at age ninety-three, we were very proud of the fact that she had been so supportive of Dave when he came out of the closet to her. I'm glad Dave told her, as Dave's siblings were able to be proud of her for her stand in support of her gay son. After all, no matter what the church taught, she knew he was a good man. And he was her son and she loved him.

At the time of Mother's death in 1999, Dave suffered a stroke and declined over a period of eight years until he died on April 30, 2007. If Dave had been born a generation later, he might very well have found a supportive community of LGBT people and their supporters within Community of Christ or in one of the many other Protestant churches he attended in his quest to find a spiritual home.

22

AIDS AND THE GAY EXPERIENCE*

David Russell

IN NOVEMBER 1988, two years ago, Ballot Measure 8 was passed by Oregon voters. This measure not only rescinded Governor Neil Goldschmidt's executive order that prohibited discrimination of state employees on the basis of sexual orientation, but it now permits discriminatory practices by state employees based on sexual orientation. It specifies that no personnel action may be taken against a state employee who practices such discrimination.

I am able to stand before you today in this public place as a self-identified gay man because of the passage of the 1988 Ballot Measure 8—for with its passage, I became radicalized. Certainly, that was not the first time that discrimination against a people became public policy, but this time it was about me—a new experience for one who had formerly enjoyed the privileges that come with being a white, Anglo-Saxon, Protestant male. It was time to stand up and speak out.

*This essay was originally presented in observance of World AIDS Day at the Unitarian Universalist Fellowship on December 2, 1990, Ashland, Oregon.

When Brad and I were planning this service, we agreed that I would present the response of the gay community to the AIDS epidemic. What I present today are the perceptions of a particular gay man, filtered and influenced by my own life history.

Perhaps the greatest limitation of my ability to speak on this subject is that I did not come out of the closet and join the gay community until four years ago, when I was already past the age of fifty. I am a gay man who was in a heterosexual marriage for twenty-four years. I am the father of three grown children who are central to my life. I was raised in a Mormon denomination, and I was active in that church for several years as an adult.

The Mormon denomination I was a part of is known as the Reorganized Church of Jesus Christ of Latter Day Saints and is headquartered—not in Salt Lake City—but in Independence, Missouri. This is relevant to my story, only because that branch of Mormonism does have full-time salaried ministers, and my father was such a minister for forty years. So, I had the onus of being a "PK," or a preacher's kid. Church was the family business. Church is in my blood.

I might add, parenthetically, that one of the statements that I frequently heard at church while growing up was Joseph Smith's admonition to the Saints: "You are called to be a peculiar people." Because I knew at least by the age of ten that I was different from the majority of my agemates, I had no trouble identifying with Joseph Smith's dictum. As a gay child, I felt peculiar, all right—but not in the way Joseph Smith had in mind!

At one of my father's pastorates, the boys in my Sunday school class named me "Angel Face" and, more than once, tried to force me to have sex with them. I was just entering adolescence and was sexually innocent, so what they proposed frightened me. I pulled rank. I told them vehemently that I would tell my father, their pastor. Could it be that they recognized in me something that I did not acknowledge by name and, because of our society, they knew that I was vulnerable—as are virtually all gay people sometime in their lives, especially those in the closet?

I did try to deal with my sexuality by going to see a psychiatrist when I was twenty-six, about two years before I was married. I felt so desperate, so out of control of my emotions that I was open and frank from the first session on. I don't remember the psychiatrist's words, but he glossed over the issue. He did say, in response to my concern about confidentiality, that he was professionally bound to keep our sessions confidential. Unless, he added gratuitously, I were to molest the boys at the school where I taught, a comment as irrelevant to my situation as any that can be imagined—that old, unearned stereotype. In fact, I sometimes wonder if gay men have been made scapegoats for the sexual behavior of nongay men, particularly in light of what we have recently come to know about the shockingly high statistics of sexual abuse and incest. (The scapegoat image is that of the ancient Hebrew custom of symbolically placing the sins of the people upon the head of a goat and banishing the goat to the wilderness.) At any rate, my psychiatrist could not deal with my gayness, so he put me on large doses of valium, a drug dependence I was able to break only four years ago.

Thus, began a succession of therapists from Michigan to Iowa to Wyoming to Oregon—five in all. It was not until I was on the brink of a nervous breakdown here (the drugs quit working) and my physician insisted that I get counseling that, with the support of a local clinical psychologist, I was able to accept myself for who I am. This was the first therapist among the five who was willing to center on the major issue of my life and, also, to assure me that I was still okay. Is homosexuality a choice? Anyone would have a hard time convincing me that gayness is not a condition of birth. The real choice that I finally exercised was to act upon my gayness. By so doing, I not only gained the whole world, but I came into possession of my soul.

Self-styled agnostic though I have come to be, my religious past sometimes reaches forward and claims me. Those of you with a Jewish or Christian background may remember the experience of Isaiah in the temple (Isaiah, chapter 6) where he beheld the Lord, high and lifted up, and was filled with a sense of the mystery and beauty of the world. "The whole world is full of ... glory." Then came the voice of the Lord, "Who shall I send? Who will go for us?" And Isaiah responded, "Here am I. Send me." I had been so nurtured by the organized gay community here that Isaiah's response to a vision of a better world became my response to my vision of a better world.

I have gone into my own story at some length for two reasons. First, my experience is not unique. The individual stories of gay people—women and men—are almost universally stories of struggle and pain in coming to terms with their sexuality and in dealing with the world around them. I believe that it is difficult to understand the spread of AIDS through the gay male community without a sense of what it has meant to grow up gay in this country and why we have formed the communities that have made us so receptive to an epidemic such as this. My second reason is that I am not an outside guest speaker who will leave and go away following this service. I am not an exotic freak imported for the occasion. I am a member of this fellowship, but I am a *recent* member. Although, I have been a Unitarian Universalist in other places, you don't know me very well. I have to live among you, a member of this religious community. In fact, it seems to me that the building of community is the most important task facing this congregation, which has grown so phenomenally in so short a time. I want to be a part of that process.

In describing the response of the gay community to AIDS, let me first deal with the question: What was gay life in the United States like prior to the AIDS epidemic?

Stonewall 1969 refers to an event as important to American gays as the *Declaration of Independence*. Stonewall Inn is a gay bar on Christopher Street in Greenwich Village, New York City. On June 29, 1969, at three o'clock in the morning, police raided the bar for operating without a license. The customers were allowed to leave and it seemed at first to be just another police raid. Then three drag queens (it was illegal to cross dress) and a lesbian were roughly shoved into the paddy wagon. Catcalls began, and then the crowd threw coins, followed by bottles. Cries of "pigs" changed to "Overturn the wagon." The crowd closed in and a riot ensued. Rioting erupted again three of the four days that followed, drawing thousands of people into its wake. Although the *New York Times* ran only small news items in its inside pages, news of the Stonewall riots traveled through the gay grapevine and electrified gays throughout the country.

Stonewall, of course, did not happen in a vacuum—gays did not come marching into American history out of nowhere. The disruption of social patterns caused by World War II and the dislocations that followed the war resulted in gay migrations to such cities as New York and San Francisco where a colorful gay life was centered in bars, the only institutions gays had at that time—and even they were illegal.

We had experienced the civil rights movement of the 1960s, which had taught us that laws could be changed and people could successfully demand basic human rights. Women and other disenfranchised groups were also pressing for their rights. It was a time of profound social change.

As for the mood in New York the day the riots erupted—feelings were running high. Police had decided that summer to crack down on unlicensed bars, reputed to be Mafia-owned—for who else could afford the payoffs? Earlier that month, police had raided other gay bars, and among those arrested was an exchange student from Columbia University. Afraid of being deported, he jumped from a third-story window and impaled himself on an iron fence. It took the fire department several hours to free both him and the iron bar to take them to the hospital. The young man lived, but he was maimed for life.

Stonewall did not begin the gay rights movement, but it marks the beginning of a new era for American gays. A momentum had been building. Gay organizations had been forming, such as the Mattachine Society, founded in Los Angeles in 1951. By 1953, Mattachine had chapters in New York and other cities. Its purposes were to unify the isolated, to educate toward an ethical homosexual culture, to provide leadership as socially conscious homosexuals, and to assist the victimized.

At first Mattachine leaders pressed for assimilation, believing that conformity would bring toleration. The name itself stood for masked societies in the Middle Ages and Renaissance. In time, tension developed between the assimilationists and newer members—activists who pressed for gay identity and minority rights. This tension exists to this day throughout gay communities, including the Rogue Valley.

By the time of Stonewall, most major cities had small homophile organizations where the assimilationists were gradually losing ground to the activists. Thus, Stonewall marks a new era for gay liberation, the 1970s, which seemed an enchanted time for gay men—many of whom acted out their long-repressed feelings.

It is a common experience for gay men to enter a kind of second adolescence when we come out of the closet—for, during our teenage years, many of us have been denied our feelings. The culturally sanctioned rites of passage as sexual beings experienced by nongay adolescents do not exist for us. Think of how irrelevant to our existence a senior prom must be.

It is with a sense of absolute joy, of exhilaration, that many enter the gay community, no matter what age one is at the time. At last I can be myself. I may not know very much about what that gay part of me will turn out to be, but there is joy in the journey.

Those who achieve a gay identity may have a bit of the outlaw about them. After all, to be gay puts one in violation of the sodomy laws in twenty-five states and the District of Columbia, and sodomy is broadly defined. Gay identity puts one beyond the protection of the law in most states, if not all, and puts one firmly in the category of "sinner," according to most of the prevailing moral codes of this country. To be gay subjects us to: ridicule, trivializing or even denying our existence; various forms of harassment, including gay bashing; possible loss of jobs, promotions, housing, and, at times, the love of our families. Under conditions such as these, there may be few limits to our behavior.

Coming out is an acknowledgement that one is a sexual being. In a sex-negative society such as ours, that alone may take courage, and brings with it a release from former constraints. The affirmation of sex may have taken too extreme a form in the 1970s—I don't know. Nevertheless, in a sex-negative society, affirming sexuality remains one of my cherished affirmations.

And, finally, there is the reaction on the part of many gays who say, "Why should we imitate the social norms of the nongay world?" Fifty-one percent of marriages end in divorce. How many of you were virgins when you were married or expect your daughters, not to mention your sons, to be virgins? How many of you have been faithful to your partners? Your institutions and moral codes cannot be respected, because they have not included us, have not served our needs. How can you wall us out, excluding us from your institutions, and then accuse us of being immoral?

We have come to see ourselves as a people, very much like an ethnic group. Our friendship networks are similar to kinship systems. Two men in their early twenties look to me as a father, for example, and have put it in so many words—a compliment to me, for I will not be coy about my age. Both have made their archetypal journeys: one to Seattle and the other to Miami. One of them called me last evening and announced that he had just been released from jail. He had joined the "die-in" staged by ACT-UP (AIDS Coalition to Unleash Power) on Interstate 5 in the middle of Seattle, and they had all been arrested. As he put it, "I'm not asking them to understand me. I'm not asking them to respect me. I'm only asking them to let me be."

We can, however, join with others of goodwill in common cause. Let us join together for play—the healing release of laughter—and to nourish each other, as well as to work for a time in which all people, even those among the most despised and reviled of this earth, can go about the business of living and can experience the joy of loving with equal freedom. In the words of our closing song:

That's what friends are for.
In good times and bad times,
That's what friends are for.

23

Why I Am a Member of Community of Christ

John Hamer

In my own lifetime, the transformation in North America from a culture of widespread, hardened bigotry against homosexuality to one of broad acceptance has been both radical and remarkable. This transformation has meant that most recent generations of gay men, lesbians, bisexuals, transgenders, and others have grown up in very different environments. Although every experience is individual, people growing up in earlier decades found an environment much harsher than those of us who have come of age more recently. Indeed, it was the often heart-wrenching experiences of the pioneering generations—the people who risked everything to come out of the closet and found the LGBT movement—which caused the societal transformation that has made life so much better for all of us who have come after. It is with awareness of my own debt to those pioneers that I am able to tell my own story as one of the first gay men fortunate enough to have grown up without any negative experiences.

I was born in 1970 in Aurora, Illinois, the eldest of five children, and I grew up primarily in the suburbs of Minneapolis, Minnesota. The members of our family were baptized in The Church of Jesus Christ of Latter-day Saints—the LDS church—and were active members. My mother came from an old-line Mormon family, and my father was a convert. Ours was always one of the core families in our congregations (or "wards"). From my earliest years, I was very interested in church, and I was very mature and articulate for a child and later a teenager. As a result, I was always the one called upon when adult leaders wanted a kid to say a prayer. And I also regularly held all of the youth leadership positions: deacon quorum president, Boy Scout patrol leader, president of the seminary (the youth education program), leader of the priest's quorum, and the like.[1]

In my childhood, being gay never arose as an issue. Looking back, I always knew I was attracted to other boys and not to girls, but this was still an era when you could know this information and yet not know that it meant you were gay. There were no gay people on television, in any movies I saw, or in the media that I was aware of. I never once met an openly gay person while I was growing up. In such an environment, I fell back on classical and scriptural examples to explain my feelings. My attraction to my good friend was like the great friendship between the biblical Jonathan and David. It was the Roman ideal of *amicitia*, as espoused by Cicero. As the classics articulated, such friendships between men transcended the marital relationships between men and women.

Given how intensely the LDS church has fought in the 1990s and 2000s to deny basic civil rights to gay people, one might expect antigay bigotry was even worse among LDS leaders in the 1970s and 1980s.

[1] In the LDS tradition, all boys are routinely ordained to the office of deacon at the age of twelve, teacher at fourteen, and priest at sixteen. In the LDS church the term "seminary" does not refer to an actual seminary; it is the name of the church youth education system, the equivalent of CCD in the Catholic Church. Boy Scouting is an official and required part of the LDS youth program for young men. I earned my Eagle Scout award at age thirteen.

And it was. However, the backwardness of the church on other social issues meant that homosexuality was hardly the most visible concern on the radar screen in the past. The average Mormon growing up in the sixties and early seventies would likely understand that they were supposed to oppose civil rights for black people. In the seventies and early eighties—when the LDS church successfully dealt a death blow to the ratification of the proposed Equal Rights Amendment to the US Constitution—the average member (like me) was aware that they were supposed to oppose equal rights for women. During my childhood, worrying about denying civil rights to gay people was still far off in the future.

These factors—the fact that I was not out to myself about being gay and the fact that the church was more worried about denying rights to blacks and women—combined to keep my orientation from ever troubling me. If I didn't date girls much as a teenager, that was fine, because good Mormon kids weren't supposed to date much.

At the same time, the visible civil rights issues actually were troubling to me. Although the LDS church finally reversed its racist priesthood ordination and temple marriage policies in 1979 (when I was nine years old), church leaders did not apologize for the former policy, nor did they renounce past doctrines.

I was even more unsettled by discrimination against women in the church. Living in a mostly white community in a mostly white state in an all-white congregation made racism a more esoteric question. Sexism, by contrast, was apparent everywhere. All important leadership positions in the church were priesthood positions, and women were denied priesthood. Although, as a devoted son, I believed my mother was the smartest person in the congregation, she was not qualified to be bishop.[2] She could be (and sometimes was) president of the women's department[3] or president of the young

[2] Unlike in the early church and in Community of Christ, bishops are not financial officers in the LDS church. LDS bishops are the same as pastors in the early church and in Community of Christ.

[3] The women's department in the LDS church is named the Relief Society in similitude of the Nauvoo Women's Relief Society.

women's group, but she was denied priesthood that was systematically doled out to all twelve-year-old boys.

I believed that it was wrong to discriminate against women, and it had been wrong to discriminate against black people, and I saw that the LDS church did both. The church was therefore wrong. As a teenager, this led me to question what else the church might be wrong about. Of course, this was long before the existence of the Internet and, living in Minnesota rather than Utah, I simply had no access to any printed information about Mormonism, other than what the church itself produced. My own research, therefore, focused on the scriptures.

By sixteen, I had become a closet doubter; however, I still enjoyed the church as a social organization. I determined that I would not throw away two years of my life on an LDS mission, but I imagined that I would otherwise remain active in the church going forward.

When I graduated from high school, I made the decision to attend Brigham Young University. In part, this was because I was easily accepted, and I was offered both academic and art scholarships. In greater part, this was because I knew my best friend's parents were making him go to BYU. Although I didn't identify it as such at the time, I had a terrible crush on him, and he was the first person I ever fell in love with.

However, I was one school year ahead of him, so I went out to BYU first. Moving to Provo in Utah County, Utah, was an eye-opening experience for me. The Mormon population in Minnesota is small; there were just three members in my high school graduating class of six hundred. Being a member of a tiny minority, I was able to maintain my impression that Mormons were something unique and special. Living in the heart of Mormondom quickly shattered that vision. Mormons weren't any more special or righteous than the broader society I grew up in. Indeed, I judged Mormon society, to which I was now exposed for the first time, to be superficially righteous, inherently dishonest, and completely hypocritical. One week after I moved to Utah, I decided that the church was false, and I had no interest in being a part of it.

In my second year, as I had anticipated, I was joined by the friend I had a crush on and also by my sister—both had been one grade behind me. We three joined the staff of the unofficial university newspaper, the *Student Review,* and consequently began to connect with the liberal and/or disaffected Mormon community in Provo.

At the end of my second year, when my friend left to go to the Missionary Training Center, I was devastated. It was the kind of crushing blow that frequently attends the end of your first love—in this case, the unrequited love I'd had for a straight boy.

As I traveled around Europe that summer on a Eurorail pass, staying in youth hostels, I made the conscious decision to finally leave my Mormonism behind. I would tell no one of my background, and I would excise that entire portion of my identity. The first night I was on my own, I was at a youth hostel in Strasbourg. I met a fellow student traveler and went out with him to a tavern. There, I had my first taste of alcohol—a beer. I'd never had anything so vile! It tasted like hairspray to my virgin palette, but I drank it down and pretended that I was an old hand at drinking. At one point, my companion said he thought I was really cool. Cool! That's one thing I'd never been, growing up Mormon! The month I spent in Europe was the best time I'd had in my life—and I experienced the whole thing as a non-Mormon, without even acknowledging to anyone that Mormonism had been a part of my past.

Returning to Provo was a letdown, but I still had good friends on the newspaper. In December 1990, I went with one of them to Salt Lake City, and she introduced me to a friend of hers who was gay. This was the first time I'd ever met an openly gay guy. He was a couple of years older than me—smart, artistic, and good looking. We talked all evening and again on the phone during the next week. Within a week, it was all crystal clear to me. I was gay. There was no doubt about it. This was welcome information to me! It all made sense now. I immediately came out to my sister, and my other friends on the paper, and in the liberal community. Everyone was very supportive; some were positively excited. Within a month, I told my parents, and, although I'd steeled myself for the worst, their reactions were also extremely good. My father spent the weekend reading half-a-dozen books, and when I talked to him next, he said that what's important is that you're our son, and we love and support you.

During the new year, I began seeking out the local gay community. As one might expect, Utah County, Utah, in 1991, was not exactly the ideal time and place to be gay. The only gay institution was a support group that met weekly. Although I was only freshly out, I quickly learned I was in relatively good shape. In contrast to my experience, many others in the group had received terribly negative reactions to their news from family and friends. Worse, almost all of them were dealing with crises of faith. Thus, not only did they have to process their gay identities, they were also being confronted for the first time with the idea the LDS church was false. In short, their entire worldviews were being shattered. In the year-and-a-half of remaining time I spent at BYU before graduating, two gay friends attempted suicide. It's no wonder to me that the suicide rate for young, gay Mormons remains so horrifically high.

When I went to graduate school at the University of Michigan in Ann Arbor, I stepped through a social time warp. If Provo had been socially twenty years or more behind the times, Ann Arbor in 1992 was already one of those islands that anticipated a future where the LGBT community achieved full acceptance. It was absolutely no big deal to my professors or any fellow graduate students that I was gay. Nor was it a big deal to the students I taught as a teaching assistant. In fact, when I went looking for a weekly support group—like the one I'd experienced in Provo—I found out that such groups didn't really exist anymore in Ann Arbor. In some ways I missed what I'd had, but it seemed that gay people in the utopia of Ann Arbor didn't need that kind of support. If you wanted to socialize, the queer alliance threw parties in the student union each month; otherwise, the main dance club in town had gay night every Tuesday and Friday.

I was attracted away from graduate school to work in publishing—drawing maps, illustrating, and typesetting books for academic presses—but I continued to live in Ann Arbor. I'd dated a lot and had one serious relationship, but it was becoming clear to me that the pool of gay people on my little island was too small, and I wasn't likely to find the perfect partner to marry. I decided to move to California, but I traveled there by way of my parents' home in Minnesota. I had two freelance jobs to do in Minnesota, drawing maps for museum exhibits.

Thus, I had a month to kill in Minnesota. Although I'd grown up in the state, I'd never gone out to a gay bar there. I said to the state, "You have one month—find me the perfect guy or I'm moving to California!" That night, I went out to a large (and somewhat seedy) bar complex called "The Gay 90s," and it was there that I met Mike Karpowicz. We hit it off immediately, and after only a few days, I realized I wasn't going to have to move to California after all. I was going to move to Minnesota.

I decided to read about Mormon history, and I picked up a copy of Fawn Brodie's legendary biography of Joseph Smith, *No Man Knows My History*. Fawn Brodie showed me how wrong I'd been. Mormon history wasn't dull at all. It was just the way Mormons wrote their own history—sanitizing it—that made it seem dull. Mormon history was, in fact, extremely interesting.

From Brodie I moved on to the rest of the historians of the "new Mormon history," and became relatively well read in the field. For Mike and me, this evolved into a shared hobby, and as we began to take road trips around the country, we included Mormon history sites on our itineraries.

Finally, a few days after my thirtieth birthday, Mike and I went to Kirtland, Ohio, to see the temple there. We knew it belonged to the RLDS church, but we'd had no prior contact with the Reorganization. Having been to several LDS visitor centers, we expected to find missionaries there strong on propaganda (trying to sell us on their church) but light (frankly, misinformed) on any facts about the historical site itself. However, we found something completely different.

We arrived at Kirtland Temple on April 6, 2000, when many of the regulars were attending the world conference of the Reorganized Church of Jesus Christ of Latter Day Saints in Independence, Missouri. Two older volunteers, Al Bachman and Ray Cain, were staffing the visitor center, and Mike and I were able to visit with them at length. These RLDS volunteers made quite a different impression than LDS volunteers we had been used to. An older LDS volunteer at the St. George Temple Visitor Center told us stories about how the temple was built on the site of an ancient Nephite temple and about Brigham Young's miraculous stubbornness in insisting it be build at such-and-such a precise spot rather than somewhere else his architects or engineers thought was better. Al and Ray, by contrast, told us about the world conference and where they thought their church was headed. We heard about the name change—the conference voted to adopt the name "Community of Christ"—and we also heard how upset Al and Ray were that the church was moving so slowly on the issues of gay ordination and marriage.

This was a surprise. As much as Al and Ray thought the church was being delinquent, to outsiders like us it seemed that action on these issues in 2000 would put the newly renamed Community of Christ in the vanguard of progressive churches. I'd read a little about the disruption in the RLDS church over the issue of women's ordination, and I actually cautioned patience—it seemed better to me that the church navigate a bit slower to build consensus than risk a second catastrophe.[4]

Accustomed as we were to LDS historical sanitizing, Mike and I were also pleasantly surprised by the honest way the church's history was presented on the tour of the temple itself. The collapse of Joseph Smith's bank was not papered over; indeed, we purchased facsimiles of the bank notes in the visitor center. We were also astounded by the quality of the history books for sale.

In contrast to the regressive Mormon church we knew that was actively fighting to suppress fundamental civil rights for gay people,[5] we found a progressive church working toward total equality for gay people. And instead of a church that actively sanitized, suppressed, and lied about its own history, we found a church that embraced hon-

[4] This was, of course, a general institution prescription. Obviously, inasmuch as this might have been good advice for the institution, it would still necessarily cause suffering for the individual members facing discrimination.

[5] The LDS church had already taken part in the campaign to prevent marriage equality in Hawaii.

est, professional scholarship. Mike and I came away from Kirtland thinking, "These aren't the kind of Mormons we're used to."

Mike and I next encountered the newly renamed Community of Christ again the following summer in Nauvoo, Illinois. Nauvoo occupies a pivotal place in Mormon history. The last and most substantial of the early church's gathering places, it was here that the church split apart after Joseph Smith's assassination. Nauvoo also held a pivotal place in my own history. I had been there once before in the summer of 1983 at a mass gathering of Mormon Boy Scouts. Touring the restored town made a huge impression on me as a thirteen-year-old boy. Nauvoo became a theme for my artwork and a subject of my junior high school history reports. I even built a replica town out of Legos, complete with a restored temple. Nauvoo was my last attempt as a child to connect with my religion. If I could connect my innate interest in history with Nauvoo and church history, perhaps I could find value for myself in the church experience. As I mentioned previously, the attempt failed because the official, sanitized accounts of Nauvoo history that I was exposed to as a child failed to hold my interest. Nevertheless, for a time, as I did my paper route in the early morning, I would think of plans to build a replica of the Nauvoo Temple, the original of which had been destroyed by arsonists in 1848.

Now, all these years later, the LDS church had actually built a replica. Although the original temple had been open to the public for tours, LDS temples are closed except for a brief window prior to their dedication. Mike and I timed our trip to coincide with that window and were on one of the first public tours. We also visited the Nauvoo LDS Visitors' Center and most of the restored sites owned and operated by the LDS church before making our way down to the sites and visitor center owned and operated by Community of Christ. It suffices to say that we had the same experience in contrasts as we moved from a church that was actively distorting and misrepresenting history, to one that was being honest and open about history. However, one additional experience stood out. While shopping in the Community of Christ bookstore—stocked, like Kirtland, with real history books rather than faith-promoting, apologetic stories—Mike pointed over to a man in shorts and a T-shirt. "That's Grant McMurray," he said. Indeed, it was! We went over and introduced ourselves to the president and prophet of Community of Christ, who was very cordial and seemed happy to meet us. (Like us, he was in town to tour the new temple—although, unlike us, he had been invited to a personal tour by leaders of the LDS church as a courtesy given his position.)

It's scarcely possible to overstate the reverence Mormons hold for their own prophet and apostles. In Salt Lake City, we had witnessed a crowded public room in the Joseph Smith Building go absolutely silent when an elderly Mormon apostle entered in his wheelchair. No conversation resumed until the man was wheeled across and out of the room. It's not unfair to criticize this degree of reverence as outright leader worship, with all of the negative implications this charge carries. By contrast, here was the Community of Christ's prophet himself—in a T-shirt and shorts, no less. He was just a regular human being like the rest of us. Our experience in Nauvoo gave me the determination to visit the headquarters of Community of Christ in Independence, Missouri.

While we were having our first encounters with Community of Christ, I was simultaneously encountering, online, a community of other ex-Mormons like myself. When I'd left the LDS church as a teenager, I had no access to outside information on Mormonism. The World Wide Web did not yet exist, and I had to feel my way out on my own. The advent of the Internet rapidly made my childhood experience researching Mormonism as dated and archaic as my coming-out experience in the world before general gay visibility. Now there were hundreds of websites debunking Mormon truth claims and whole online communities of Mormons discovering this information for the first time.

Mike and I took our first trip to Independence, Missouri, on April 6, 2003. I'd become fascinated with the Community of Christ Temple there, but at the time its Internet footprint was meager. Visiting was the only way to get a real sense of it. Mike and I had visited a dozen LDS temples by this time, but the Community of Christ Temple in Independence was something altogether different. Larger and taller than any LDS temple, the Independence Temple is uniquely possessed of actual architectural significance.[6] In its exterior form, the Temple is a magnificent spiral reaching to the heavens. This pattern is matched inside, as a "worshippers path" leads upward, around the center, and finally into the heart of the sanctuary. I couldn't help but be impressed by this wholly modern and original expression of my personal religious heritage.

Our guide was a dear, elderly lady who echoed what Al Bachman and Ray Cain had told us back in Kirtland. She believed the church was dragging its feet on the issue of full equality for gay members, and she didn't want to wait for change.

Waiting to get married and uncomfortable with the sham wedding option, Mike and I decided to look outside the box. Unlike the United States, it turned out that Canada, in addition to embracing full marriage equality, was possessed of a rational immigration policy. Whereas US immigration policy is primarily racist (or at least anti-Hispanic), Canada understands that immigration in the twenty-first century is about the global marketplace. If Canada can attract highly educated, highly skilled immigrants, fluent in English (and/or French)—still in the prime years of their work lives—Canada will reap the harvest without having had to pay all the costs that went into their education and development. Because of our fluency, university degrees, and skill sets, we easily qualified for Canadian residency. Meanwhile, we had frequently visited the city of Toronto—Canada's principal cultural Mecca, and the most diverse and vibrant city on the planet—and discovered we liked it better than any city in North America.

Although I didn't find the community I sought among ex-Mormons online, by 2005, when Mike and I became executive directors of the John Whitmer Historical Association, I had begun to find a real home in the church history community. Although JWHA is explicitly open to all regardless of religious affiliation, its core continues to consist of Community of Christ members or secular people who grew up in the RLDS church. I thus began to develop close friendships with

[6] The Independence Temple was designed by Gyo Obata, the architect who designed the Smithsonian Air and Space Museum and the international airport in Riyadh, Saudi Arabia.

many members of JWHA, who were also members of Community of Christ—Ron and Anne Romig, Bill and Lois Russell, David Howlett, Barb Walden, Steve Shields, Billie Young, Ken Mulliken and Wendy Bachman, Lachlan and Christin Mackay, Mark and Rita Scherer, Dick and Barbara Howard, Alma and Kay Blair—to name just a few.

In August 2007, I drove with Ron Romig and Bill Russell from Independence to Salt Lake City to participate in the annual Sunstone Symposium. Sunstone is a venerable, independent institution within Mormonism. Founded in 1974, Sunstone has provided a rare, open forum for open discussion of Mormon issues. Unfortunately, LDS leaders do not value open discussion of Mormon issues. When the church decided to crack down on intellectuals, beginning with the excommunication of the "September Six" in 1993, it similarly declared war on Sunstone. Church employees, including faculty of church-owned universities, were forbidden to participate in the symposium, and both Sunstone and freethinking became increasingly marginal in the LDS church. Bill and Ron were both longtime supporters of the symposium, but this was the first time I attended. It proved to be very worthwhile, although the overall effect could not help but be a bit depressing.

The many presentations and enlightened discussions inevitably highlighted the fact that while productive thought continued to exist in Utah Mormonism, liberals and intellectuals were utterly marginalized in the LDS church itself. And no signs remained that there would be any improvement in the foreseeable future. Indeed, by standing still while society progressed, the LDS church had clearly regressed, in a relative sense, since my childhood. And if the position of intellectuals was utterly hopeless, the outlook for the large contingent of gay Mormons I met at Sunstone was worse than hopeless.

Although I felt that I had made peace with the LDS church and embraced an essentially secular Mormon or cultural Mormon community at JWHA and the Mormon History Association (MHA), I found out in 2008 that the LDS church had not made peace with me. On May 15 of that year, the California Supreme Court correctly ruled that the state's ban on gay marriage was simple, unjustifiable discrimination—and the court threw the ban out as unconstitutional.

Marriage equality was instituted and thousands of gay couples and lesbian couples married legally in California for the first time. Conservatives reacted immediately by having a proposition added to the ballot (known as "Prop 8"), which, if enacted, would strip gay people of their rights and enshrine discrimination into the state's constitution.

Although many religious groups, including notably the Catholic Church, supported Prop 8, it was the participation of the LDS church that proved decisive. LDS leaders called for total mobilization in the state. Members were routinely exhorted from the pulpit. Tithing lists were employed so that local leaders could press members to donate to political front groups. Mormons in good standing were expected to go door to door, to campaign, and to staff phone banks. Donations flooded into California from Utah. In the end, the LDS church provided the organizational backbone for the Prop 8 movement, and Mormons ended up swaying the election completely out of proportion to their numbers.

Because of Prop 8, my policy toward the LDS church changed. In taking so fierce a political stand, LDS leaders showed that they could not be ignored. The LDS church has long been a consistent and effective enemy of civil and human rights—unsuccessfully opposing civil rights for African Americans in the 1960s and successfully opposing equal rights for American women in the 1970s. Although Mormon leaders had changed their targets, they had clearly not repented of their reactionary political policy or of their general bigotry.

The one slender reed, the sole ray of hope in this bleak wasteland, provided the only conceivable answer to all these questions—Community of Christ. Yes, compared with the LDS church, Community of Christ was miniscule. But compared to all other independent institutions within Mormonism (MHA, Sunstone, Signature Books, *Dialogue*), Community of Christ was massive. For Mormons leaving, Community of Christ offered an alternative destination to simply being gone from the equation. For Mormons of good conscience, fervently praying to see their church reformed—honesty in history, eradication of sexism in ordination, an end to leader worship—Community of Christ had already blazed that path and achieved those reforms.

Inside the LDS church, intellectuals, liberals, and all other members of good conscience were effectively doomed to be permanently marginalized—their voices utterly ignored by totally unaccountable leaders. Outside the LDS church ex-Mormons were destined to be forgotten—themselves freed in their own lives but dead to the movement. Inside Community of Christ, however, both groups would be noticed. I believe that a significant movement into Community of Christ is the sole potential avenue that liberal Mormons have at their disposal to reform the LDS church.

That vision—the revelation of this potential—provided a calling for me in the movement. I feel called to build that bridge. I began to serve on a committee advising Steve Veazey, the new prophet and president of Community of Christ, about how Community of Christ could become a spiritual home for disaffected Mormons. This eventually became known as the "Latter-day Seekers" program. At my next Sunstone symposium, I functioned as an unofficial part of the Community of Christ delegation led by Apostle Susan Skoor. I spent the conference sharing my vision with disaffected Mormons.

One evening of the symposium, Susan Skoor declared that she ought to ordain me a seventy, then and there, for my missionary zeal. And at a dinner at Lavina Fielding Anderson's, after I'd made my pitch to Lavina, she asked me, "Are you going to join Community of Christ, John?" I answered, "Yes, but the time isn't right yet," which caught Susan by surprise. She said, "When the time is right, I hope you'll tell me, because I'd like to be a part of it."

When Al Bachman and Ray Cain were complaining about foot dragging regarding ending discrimination against gay people in the church in 2001, I believed (as an outsider) that their concerns were premature. I felt about the same when our tour guide in Independence confided the same feelings in 2003. But I will concede that if Community of Christ had had its house in order by 2008, it's possible that some of the Mormons who simply resigned their memberships due to Prop 8 would have been willing to cross the street. By 2010, the time was clearly ripe for the church to act.

In advance of the world conference to be held on the 150th anniversary of the Reorganization (and the 180th anniversary of the Restoration), Steve Veazey published his inspired counsel to Community of Christ, destined to become Doctrine and Covenants, section 164. The revelation affirmed that "God, the Creator of all, ultimately is concerned about behaviors and relationships that uphold the worth and giftedness of all people and that protect the most vulnerable. Such relationships are to be rooted in the principles of Christ-like love, mutual respect, responsibility, justice, covenant, and faithfulness, against which there is no law" (Doctrine and Covenants 164:6a). A Godly relationship such as marriage, therefore, was not identified by being between "one man and one woman." Rather, Godly relationships were characterized by their Christlike love, mutual respect, responsibility, and the rest—qualities utterly consonant with my own relationships. The document provided a path for a functional compromise within the international church—national conferences would be established to deal with the subjects of gay ordination and marriage equality within different jurisdictions. For example, the church in Canada would cease to be held back by the church in Haiti.

The document also proposed changes to the conditions of baptism. Following a year-long, church-wide discernment process, the revelation proposed that Community of Christ begin to recognize other Christian baptisms as valid.

All of these counsels and other personal signs inspired me that the time was now ripe to join the church myself. I chose not to wait for section 164 of the Doctrine and Covenants to be canonized, potentially recognizing my prior baptism as valid. I wanted to join the church openly. I chose the key date of April 6, 2010, for my baptism. April 6 is a special date in the Restoration. The church was organized on April 6, 1830, and the church was reorganized on April 6, 1860. It is also a special date for my connection with the church. I encountered the church in Kirtland on April 6, 2000. I visited the temple in Independence, met Ron Romig, and entered the church historian community on April 6, 2003. And I asked Ron to baptize me on April 6, 2010—four days after my fortieth birthday.

The baptism service was held at the Walnut Gardens congregation in Independence. Walnut Gardens was historically the most liberal congregation in the church, leading the movement to reform in the 1970s and 1980s. My friends in the church all participated in the ceremony: Bill Russell presided, Barb Walden gave the charge, David Howlett played the music, Steve Shields and Mark Scherer provided prayers, and Susan Skoor performed the confirmation, accompanied by Apostle Dale Luffman. When the service ended, Steve Veazey, Susan Skoor, Dale Luffman, and Andrew Bolton vied to be the first to shake my hand, welcoming me into fellowship. Steve joked, "It's not every new member that has the prophet and three apostles on hand at his baptism"—especially not given the importance of the date and the otherwise intensely busy schedule of church leaders in the lead-up to world conference. Susan Kisslinger—a friend from JWHA and a member of the Walnut Gardens congregation—said to me, "I don't know why you'd want to join our church. But the fact that you did gives me hope!"

I attended the full world conference as a member, participating in the prayerful consideration of the inspired counsel in small groups and watching the debate among all the delegates in the Auditorium. Although it went unspoken, everyone understood what the document's subtext meant. And, yet, as each verse was read, it was approved by the delegates almost unanimously. Finally, when the whole document was approved, all the spectators like me were invited to rise and vote in support of adding the counsel to the Doctrine and Covenants as section 164. Susan Kisslinger (who was serving as a delegate) later told me that when she saw me stand and raise my hand in the galleries, it made her weep with joy.[7] For the whole church assembled, it was an intensely moving moment.

I want to bear my testimony that this church is good and that its path is true. I know that I am called to be a part of it, and I affirm my commitment to honoring and fulfilling that calling.

---

[7] Susan passed away earlier this year (2011). I am happy to have known her and to have called her a friend. She will be missed and remembered.

24

Transforming Grace: So Let Your Light Shine

Gayle Humphrey

I was born into the church. My family's heritage goes back at least four generations. My father and mother were very dedicated members and involved themselves deeply in the life of the church. My father was the pastor of just about every congregation where we lived at one time or another. I have to think really hard to remember if there were any times while I was growing up that we weren't in church twice on Sunday, once on Wednesday, and at other times during the week. At one point, my father was the pastor of two congregations concurrently—eighty miles apart. I developed a deep faith in God early in my life.

As I grew older, I became immersed in the life of the church. I was called to the priesthood office of deacon at the age of fourteen and was ordained at fifteen. Immediately, I became active in the local visiting program, and started preaching and teaching. The church, in one way or another, was almost my complete personal identity for a number of years. I was eventually called and ordained to the priesthood office of priest.

In 1986, the ordination of women into the priesthood caused a rift within the Reorganized Church of Jesus Christ of Latter Day Saints. My entire family—father, mother, brothers, sisters, and their families, as well as my own—left the RLDS church and began worshipping with others who left. We became a part of the Restoration movement and attended one of the independent Restoration branches. In the Restoration movement, I was called and ordained to the priesthood office of elder.

After almost twenty years, my partner, my family, and I left the Restoration movement and returned to the RLDS church, now known as Community of Christ. One of the main reasons we did this was because of the intolerance we would have faced if we had stayed within this movement.

My parents had taught me that God is omniscient. Knowing this, I had no trouble accepting calls to different priesthood offices, because surely God knew what was in my heart and everything about me. If God accepted me and chose to call me, why shouldn't others accept me as well? However, it hasn't worked out that way for me.

My relationship with God has been somewhat confusing, especially to me. On one hand, I know that God loves me—or at least I hope so. On the other hand, I was taught and learned very early that sharing my thoughts and feelings wasn't the best thing to do. Over time, I was taught that my thoughts and feelings were evil and wicked, and, somehow, I was an abomination in the eyes of God. My parents made it very clear to me that I couldn't hide my thoughts and feelings from God, so I knew I was damned for sure. It was better just to keep my mouth shut, lie if I had to, and stuff my feelings deep inside. No one was to ever know what really was hidden deep within my heart. On the outside, which was the most important thing, everything seemed to be all right. It has taken me a number of years to overcome some of those early teachings and really see God as loving and kind. My parents did the best that they could. I am not attempting to speak badly of them; however, I do feel they overemphasized certain aspects of the scriptures that have been harmful to me.

My father had three great loves: the US Air Force, the church, and my mother. I can remember waking up many mornings to military march music blasting throughout the house. I had a flattop haircut with gobs of hair grease in it until I was old enough to decide for myself how I wanted my hair to be fixed. (It immediately became long.) I remember Dad's starched uniforms, polished, black shoes, ribbons on his uniform, and several stripes on each sleeve. I drew a picture of him once where he was "Sarge" from the Beetle Bailey comic strip. He was so proud of that drawing that he hung it over his desk at work.

Just as much as my father is remembered as a military man, my mother was the person that I remember as always being there for me. We talked, spent time together, and had fun as well. My father, who it seemed was almost always gone doing church work several nights a week or at a new duty station, wasn't around for teaching me at home. His presence was mainly at the public worship experiences on Sundays and Wednesdays. It was my mother who taught me how to pray, read stories and the scriptures to me, and encouraged me to walk closely with God. She was my spiritual giant. Other people looked up to my father; he was a great teacher and gifted at working with people. But I looked up to my mother, because she was there for me.

I was blessed as a child to have the opportunity to live overseas. I lived in Germany for three years and in the Philippine Islands twice for a total of three years. In our travels, we had opportunity to visit with the missionaries as they came through our area. I still remember their names— Zonker, Deville, Compier, Neff, Butterworth, and Black, to name a few. They often stayed in our home and shared meals with us. While they were in our home, I would sit by the hour and listen to their exciting stories. I dreamed of becoming a missionary one day. It's a dream that I still carry with me today. The church and my family were my mainstays as I grew up. I thought that I would always be able to count on them no matter what happened.

My first inkling that something was different with me was when I was about five years old. There were the times that I got caught with my mom's makeup on or wearing my sister's clothes. But more deeply were the feelings and thoughts that I had going on inside of me. Because my parents were very religious and had definite, concrete, and immovable ideas about right and wrong—and because of my father's comments about "queers" and the subsequent repercussions for being caught with makeup on or wearing my sister's clothes—I did what I was supposed to, and that seemed to make my parents happy.

When I was in the seventh grade, I couldn't stand it any longer and told my mother about my feelings. My mother immediately told my father who promptly sent me to see a psychiatrist who tried to make me well. That was the first of five different psychologists I saw over the next several years. In my parents' eyes, as well as in the eyes of many others, being LGBT is a choice—a choice that you must turn away from and overcome if you are "righteous."

Growing up in the 60s and 70s, I had no idea what transsexual meant. The only reason I knew about homosexuality was because my father used terms like "queer, fairy, and fag" a lot of the time. From a very early age, or about the time that I noticed that things were different with me, I remember him calling me those names daily. And because he was always right, I knew that I must be those things—even though I was never attracted to men in the way that gay people are drawn to each other. I knew that I was attracted to men, but no differently than any other straight female would be. The idea of being drawn to men as a man was not something that interested me. I didn't find out what a transsexual was until I was about twenty-two years old. By then I was married.

I tried very hard to be a normal male all through school and through the early years of my marriage. I went into the military, rock climbed, and played football. I really tried hard to be what I thought a good man ought to be. I cried to God to be delivered from my inner hell and torment. I asked for administration several times. I prayed, I read my scriptures for hours at a time, and I fasted regularly. I threw myself into church work, as my father had done, in the hope that total immersion would take my "evil thoughts and desires" away.

None of these things relieved the growing hatred that I had for myself. Nothing fixed my desire to be rid of the lie that I was living, so I might be accepted by my family and the church. I knew in my heart that I wasn't a man and had never been one—no matter what I had done or would ever do.

I was in a real bind. I could either live a lie and be accepted, or I could stand up and tell everyone my true, inner identity. The need to be loved and accepted was so strong that I chose to continue to live the lie until I was almost fifty years old and extremely suicidal.

It was at that point, when I couldn't go on any longer, that I came clean. Almost immediately, the dark, black cloud which had constantly covered my mind, lifted. After about three weeks of telling others, I was off all my depression medication. The people I went to church with in the Restoration movement no longer spoke to me. They avoided me in the stores in town and continue to do so to this day. When I am at a function where they are involved, I do not exist to them. My parents passed away several years ago, before I began my transition from male to female. My brothers and sisters haven't spoken to me in about four years. They believe that they must avoid evil and cling to that which is good. In their eyes, what I did to become whole was evil.

Transsexuality is a biological condition where the biological sex (body) and the gender (sexuality identity) do not match each other. The latest scientific research indicates that in biological males the testosterone bath, which takes place in the sixth to seventh week of gestation and covers the male brain, does not take place in approximately one out of 150 thousand births. If the testosterone bath doesn't occur at that point, it never will, and the brain will be different from the body. Transsexuality and homosexuality are entirely two different things. Transsexuals are not necessarily gay. One has to do with sexual identity and the other has to do with sexual orientation.

My experience in Community of Christ has been much different than my experience in the Restoration movement. The first Sunday I attended the Walnut Gardens congregation, I felt loved and accepted. When I told them about my situation, their love for me didn't change negatively but, instead, positively grew. Their expression of love for me expanded, especially when they learned how transsexuality happens. The thing that impressed me the most was that they were willing to listen. Their minds were not closed to different ideas. However, at times, I know that my experience in the church has been very limited. If I were to go to another congregation or overseas in some areas, I might not be accepted and might even be killed. People like me are killed every year for simply being different than others.

My transsexuality has made me a much better person. Although I have sustained loss, I have gained so much more. I have come from hating my situation and asking God the question, repeatedly, "Why me?" to being in a situation now where I wouldn't want my life to be any different. I am more compassionate, less judgmental, and more loving than I believe I would ever have been otherwise. I am happy for the first time in my life—I feel whole, complete, and good in my own skin. Everything finally fits, and my mind and body are finally one. My immediate family—my spouse and my children—have remained by my side and are my mainstay. We left the Restoration movement after twenty years and now have a new church family who loves me for me. I currently wait to hear if my priesthood will be reinstated. I am hopeful that my authority to act as a priesthood member will be given back to me someday soon, so I might eventually realize my dream of traveling to faraway lands and teaching others about Jesus.

25

SEEING THROUGH A GLASS DARKLY

Joyce Humphrey

I HAVE KNOWN GAYLE since I was in the sixth grade. At that time she was known as Guy—she was a female in a male body. Our families lived and attended church in Anderson, California. My family had a long heritage in the church; I am a direct descendent of E. C. Briggs. When I first met Gayle, she was seen and treated as a male. I thought of her as a boy. Little did I know, at that time, of her struggles and inner turmoil. She was friendly and kind to me, and I remember her family coming up to the mountains where we lived to socialize together.

One time in the winter, Gayle and I were at a church youth group function in the mountains close to my home. We were having a snowball fight, and Gayle hit me in the face with a snowball, winding me. She immediately ran up to me to see if I was all right. At that moment, I knew that she was special.

Gayle's family moved away from the area, as they often did, and I did not see her again for four years. Later, out of the blue, my family received a letter from Gayle in Fresno, California, where we had moved. The last line of the letter read, "If Joyce would like to write me, I'd like to hear from her." I wrote her and was able to see her from time to time, whenever the ship that she was on was in port in San Diego. Still, at this point, I had no idea that she was a woman. From the time that she was very young, Gayle had been conditioned to stuff all of her feelings deep down inside, so not even those who were very close to her were aware of the struggles that were taking place inside of her.

I had never seen myself as being gay. I had never been drawn to other women and thought that I was in love with a man. Like most other women of our time and upbringing, I dreamed of being married to a man, having children, and settling down to a very long life filled with love and laughter. It has turned out pretty much the way I expected it—except, I fell in love with someone who later turned out to be a very beautiful and happy woman.

Gayle told me about her situation either right before or soon after we were married. I don't remember the exact timing. In any event, when she told me, I began to sob. I saw all of my dreams crashing down around me. I was extremely confused and wondered what to do. My first reaction was denial. I told Gayle that I would never accept her as a woman and expected that she was going to be my husband. I told her what she was thinking was evil and wrong, and that God could, and would, take those things away from her if she just tried hard enough. For a number of years, she tried very hard to do what I and others expected of her. We did not talk of her transsexualism often, and when we did, it was only in terms of how to overcome it.

If it were possible for someone to overcome being gay or transsexual, it would have been Gayle. She often studied the scriptures for hours a day. She prayed. She was administered to countless times, and she fasted often. None of it removed the feelings that she had inside and with which she was struggling. I wasn't much help at the time, because I was scared about what others would think of us. Over time, I reluctantly allowed little changes to take place as long as she remained where no one would see her or could ever know what she was doing. In fact, I asked her to remain closeted and never allow herself to live openly and honestly. That is one of my regrets. At the time, I didn't realize how my actions affected her.

Over time, Gayle became very depressed and suicidal. It was then that I understood just how serious the situation had become and that we needed professional help. We turned to someone Gayle had found, after three years of searching, who worked with transgender people. She was a counselor named Caroline. As we sat in her office one day, I asked Caroline if Gayle really had to go through a sex change in order to heal. She told us, "Yes." It was actually the only way to find healing and wholeness. It wasn't the answer I wanted to hear, but I wanted so much for Gayle to find connection with herself. I was finally willing to consider a sex change as a possibility. Caroline was correct—the only way that a transgender person could find peace, happiness, and wholeness was by connecting the inside person with the outside person.

I was sorry I didn't come to that realization sooner. For too long, I listened to people who were very judgmental of those who did not follow the social norm. For too long, I did not see the answer that was right in front of me. If we had it to do all over, Gayle would have transitioned earlier in life.

Our church, the Reorganized Church of Jesus Christ of Latter Day Saints, played a role in this process. In 1984, when the policy of women in the priesthood was accepted by the church, our family left and followed the Restoration movement. Gayle was silenced as a priest, and for twenty years we attended different Restoration groups. At first, I accepted all that was taught in this movement, but in the back of my mind, I began to formulate questions. I sat on the sidelines watching as people fought over doctrine and followed priesthood members around like groupies. I watched as people were shut out of the fellowship when they did not conform. Over time, I began to ask myself, "Would Jesus act this way? Would he treat people this way? Can I find Jesus if I continue worshipping with these people?" Through much prayer, the answer I discerned was, "No!"

A couple of years before Gayle began to come out and transition, I began begging her to find another church movement to attend. When Sunday came around each week, I dreaded going to church. By the time she had her sex change, we both knew that the Restoration movement would not accept us—years of dealing with them told us so. After determining that we could no longer attend any of the Restoration churches, the next question was, "So, where do we go?"

Our lives and heritage in the church had remained intact. We did not want to leave the church where we had grown up. Knowing this, our counselor suggested that we attend a congregation of Community of Christ which she had heard was accepting of lesbian, gay, bisexual, and transgender people. Gayle was the first to check out the Walnut Gardens Community of Christ congregation. She came out as a woman only a few weeks after we began attending. In fact, the first sermon that we heard included statements from the pulpit about how glad the speaker was that Community of Christ and Walnut Gardens congregation, in particular, were so open and accepting. As we began to become more acquainted with the people there, Gayle began to talk to different members about our situation. It was finally presented to the whole congregation in a meeting. Almost unanimously, we were embraced by everyone. We had come home.

It is now four years later, and I still feel that way about Walnut Gardens—they are my family, my children's family, and Gayle's family. Looking back, I realize God had answered our prayers. Transitioning was the answer. From this experience, I learned to look at people differently—not by what I saw on the outside, but by what I recognized came from the inside. This is what I believe Jesus wants all of us to do.

26

Coming Out: A Search for Self

Gabe Horner

I don't know if I really have enough life experience at age eighteen to have a story, but I'm certainly going to try. I grew up in a liberal, accepting family. Being gay had always been okay. I was taken to my first pride parade at around three years of age, so it came as a surprise to me when I struggled with my own sexuality.

When I was growing up, I didn't believe in God—despite having a pastor for a father and my family being active in church. I didn't see how there could be a God who would make me so screwed up. I always joked with friends that telling my parents I was atheist was going to be like coming out to conservative parents, but I spoke too soon.

During the time I was growing up, my family and I should've realized I was a "transman" (born in a female body but having a male gender identity). I hated dresses, long hair, and just about anything considered girly. I was asked, over and over again, if I was a lesbian—to which I very adamantly replied I was not, because I wasn't. I didn't identify that way. The reason it took me so long to come out to my very liberal family was because I had never heard of a gay transman—a trans person who was attracted to the sex they identified with. Inconceivable! Information was widely available. I just hadn't thought to look up such a thing on the Internet.

I went to my first GALA retreat in September 2009. It was an amazing experience of love and community, and the first time I had heard of a gay trans person. I was rooming with my uncle who told me about a lesbian transwoman in his congregation. I was shocked to discover that I wasn't an unheard of "freak of nature," after all. I was going to come out to my mom *right then*—I had an in! I walked down the hall to her room at the retreat and told her about this lesbian transwoman—and right before I could tell her that this was kind of like what I was, she said, "Well that's weird!" In her comment, she had unknowingly called *me* weird. My reply? "Yep, weird!" and I turned around and walked away. How could I come out after that? It wasn't an option. Back into the closet I went.

Thanksgiving, that same year, was my breaking point. My mom was on the phone with an unidentified family member and, while looking directly at me, she said, "I've asked her if she wants to be a man, and she says no!" I swear this conversation never occurred. If it had, then the answer would have been yes! My very first memory is of sitting on my brother's lap telling him I wished I was a boy. That whole weekend I was haunted by my mother's statement. She thought I didn't want to be a man. How could this be? Being a man had been the only thing on my mind for quite some time!

Sunday night while I was talking and crying to a friend online, I decided I would come out the next day. Being a wimp in the technology age, I decided to come out by e-mail. I do not recommend this avenue—it involves a lot of waiting, as you don't know when your e-mail is going to be read. Halfway through the school day, I received a text from my mom that simply said, "I love you." However, this was not the reaction I felt when I arrived home.

When I got home, I was told a therapist would be calling the house to set up an appointment—not a gender therapist, a regular one. Also, after coming out, my mom sat me down to have a frank discussion about my transness. She didn't seem to understand how I could be gay and trans. I remember her saying she thought I was mixing up their (my parents') political battle with my life. They thought maybe because they'd been so pro-gay my whole life, I thought I needed to be trans. Neither of these actions felt very loving to me.

Once the idea had set in and I had come out to more people, I felt an overwhelming sense of calm in my life. Everything was balanced. I started to experience God in the relationships around me. What had been keeping me from a real spiritual awakening all those years wasn't a lack of God—it was a lack of inner peace. I needed to find out who I was and be calm with that, before taking on bigger things. God had always been there, I just needed to find me first.

As of June 2011, I have been on testosterone injections for three-and-a-half months, I have been living as a male for a year, and I am in a "hopeful relationship" of nine months. I am now trying to balance my spiritual, social, and college lives into something remotely cohesive.

27

Parenting: A Challenging Reflection

Jana Horner

If I knew where to start this story, it might be easier to tell. I know that telling this story can't be done in a few short paragraphs, but what I hope is that this will be the start of a conversation between you and me. I grew up in a household where the wonders of human diversity were something to be celebrated. For that, I am grateful. I am a daughter, sister, wife, and mother. I would also say there is nothing in life that prepares you for the vulnerability of being a mother. Like most mothers, I want my children to have a fulfilling life, blessed with loving companionship.

There is so much that goes into what makes a person who they are. There will probably always be the debate about nature and nurture—which is the more powerful shaper of the human essence? As a mother, I have always hoped that the environment in which I raised my family would nurture them to be the best that they could be. And at the same time, they could overcome any deficiencies that nature gave them. So, it is through the eyes of a mother that I tell this story.

I have three children. I could write volumes about the joys, sorrows, and surprises that children bring to life. We did all the things parents do with children who live in the United States—we participated in church, school, athletics, lessons, movies, and family time. Even though all my children have made it to age eighteen, I still worry, and wonder when the worry will stop. I'm experiencing a bit more worry now than I thought I would at this point.

I still remember the day I opened the e-mail from my youngest child. I hated getting the news this way, but there I was, sitting at work reading an e-mail that informed me that this child, who I had always thought of as female, was male. It would be a lie to say that I felt joy in the moment. It was more of a feeling that drops deep in your gut and then, the worry started. I wasn't sure where to begin or what to say to whom. So, even though there have probably been things I could have done better, the first thing I did was tell Gabe I loved him.

My mind then ran through everything that might have given me a clue as to my child's identity. To say that things started making sense immediately would not be truthful; but, since that day, I have learned a lot about what it means to have a transgender family member. I guess there were a few signs along the way, if I had been a bit more perceptive. Maybe I would have picked up on them, if only there had been someone along the way to tell me their story.

Here are just a few things I really never thought much about at the time, but now I know to be clues: I had a child who didn't like to use public restrooms, wasn't really interested in picking out a swimsuit and going swimming, and never wanted to wear a dress. There must have been other signs that I did not see. We do not have everything worked out. As a family, we are just at the start of this journey, being taken to places we don't know much about.

Transgender people face many challenges that many of us don't think about— widespread discrimination, hate, fear, and violence. I am proud that my son simply had the courage to be different. Because of his courage to live openly and authentically, by simply embracing who he is, I am given hope for a better world. Our journey is ongoing. We often see new things and even have a few new surprises. It has unfolded at a pace that is sometimes faster than I am ready for, but it gets easier with time.

I wasn't sure what would happen in our home congregation when we shared the news. Our family's journey has been one of transformation, even if we were scared at first. When we invited our church family to join us on our journey, we found the church to be a place of welcome and warmth. Although our home congregation is a place of safety and support, I still hunger for a larger community that accepts all of God's children. I yearn for a place where the larger body of believers is inclusive and welcoming in all aspects of church life, including ordination, marriage, and programs that consider the special needs of our LGBT sisters and brothers. I pray that day will be soon.

28

My Name Is Rebecca

Rebecca Chesnutt

My name is Rebecca. I am a male to female transsexual. The terms gender and sex mean very separate things, though they are often considered interchangeable by the less aware. To clarify, *sex* refers to physical form and function, while *gender* is a component of identity. Because the brain is structured in many sex-differentiated ways, there can be some legitimate overlap between the two, but the brain is the seat of one's identity. However, with regard to the dilemma of the transsexual, the difference between sex and gender are at the core of the issue.

In a transsexual's brain, the sex-related structures that define gender identity are exactly opposite from the physical sex organs of their body. Put even more simply—this individual has a mind that is literally and physically trapped in a body of the opposite sex. This hurts them so much that they are driven to fix that problem or die trying.

Transsexuality begins in the womb and occurs in many animals besides humans. Transsexuality and homosexuality seem to share a common prenatal causality, but they are *not* the same thing. Transsexuality is sometimes associated with things it is not really related to, such as cross-dressing for social or political reasons. A transsexual person, born to all appearance within a given physical sex, is aware of being of a gender opposite to that of their physical sex. This conflict between gender identity and physical sex is almost always manifested early and is the cause of enormous suffering. It is common for transsexuals to be aware of their condition at preschool ages. I realized this when I first went to kindergarten—I noticed that I preferred being with girls rather than boys. Since I was physically a boy, the girls wouldn't associate with me. There were times when boys would beat me up while I was walking home from school, just because I was not normal in their eyes.

The agony felt by transsexuals can and does lead to self-destruction unless properly treated. The incredible difficulties that surround achieving treatment are often agonizing. In reality, some 50 percent of transsexuals die by age thirty, usually by their own hand.

Transsexuals have always existed. In the ancient world, they were both accepted and respected. Throughout the ages, transsexuals have attempted to correct the error of their bodies with varying results. The modern, technological world at last provides a real chance for the transsexual to finally, truly correct the errors of nature.[1]

I remember how kindergarten gave me my first taste of shame—I experienced ridicule by adults and peers that will be with me the rest of my life. Later on in my early childhood, I knew something was wrong, and I continued feeling shame and embarrassment, but I always felt it would work out okay. I thought that if I just hoped and prayed hard enough, I would wake up a girl, and my family and friends would then accept me. On many occasions, while I was walking home from junior high school, I would be the target of boys who wanted to beat me up. Many times I was captured and very badly beaten. I often changed my path home just to avoid being beaten up again.

---

[1] Some of the information above has been adapted from the website *Transsexuality*, http://www.transsexual.org/.

I became a member of the Reorganized Church of Jesus Christ of Latter Day Saints when I was nine years old. Before that time, I had read the scriptures of the denomination—the Inspired Version of the Bible, the Book of Mormon, and the Doctrine and Covenants—completely through. I had taken it upon myself to learn as much as I could about Jesus in order to be a good Christian. I made it my goal to read the three scriptures through every year. Every time a book was published about Jesus Christ, I would read it through and derive from it those things that I could then incorporate into my life. As years went by, I read the scriptures along with their commentaries, so I could understand what scholars understood about the scriptures. Most of the time, I would meet God in the temple of the outdoors, praying about my life issues and the scriptures I didn't understand. I believed, like Joseph Smith Jr., that I would be taught, through love, what I needed to know in order to live a Christlike life.

Throughout my life, in an effort to serve others at home and around the world, I was active in programs to help other people. As a youth, I served in Older Youth Service Corps (now called the World Service Corps) and was assigned to La Quinta Restamex in Saltillo, Mexico. I worked in Central America, as well as the United States, to help others to the best of my ability. I felt then, even as I do now, that I was answering the call to maintain "an eye single to the glory of God" in the service that was offered through my life.

Coming out to my family was difficult for everyone. It was as if they had suddenly been blindsided. It must have seemed to my children and my wife that there was a strange woman breaking into their lives that was killing their father and husband. The pain and suffering was felt deeply by everyone, and I sincerely apologize for this. I continue to carry a profound love for my two sons who have supported me through my transition. I still love and care about my ex-wife.

In raising my boys, I attempted to teach them to be accepting toward other people, regardless of who they were and what they thought. My desire was, and still remains, that my children would be interested in studying about Christ, Community of Christ, and our church's scriptures.

Many members of my family, including my grandparents, have been members of Community of Christ for years; several have served in the priesthood. A member since 1955, I was ordained a deacon at the age of sixteen. In subsequent years, I was called and ordained a priest and then an elder. I served for a couple of years as pastor of the Buffalo-Clarence, New York Branch. I have remained an active priesthood member. In my home congregation in Davenport, Iowa, I am active in various roles.

My contact and experience in Community of Christ has been and continues to be one of a positive nature. All of my life, I have agreed with the overall religious position of the church. Many times when I have had concerns about the direction of the church, I have noticed that these same concerns were already being addressed in a way I would have taken, but with greater thought. Community of Christ will be my church, and I have dedicated the rest of my life to work as a servant within it.

During my life, I have attempted to live in service to those with whom I come in contact. I believe that the journey of peace starts with one person helping another. Because of this belief, I have volunteered, through personal service, to serve others in many ways—I've given aid to the homeless, helped battered women find safe shelter, and assisted drug addicts with their rehabilitation. I've tried to help them receive the community service they most desperately needed. God has recognized the actions that have been given in service to others and has provided a blessing in each life that has been touched.

Matthew 25:34–40 (King James Version) has inspired my life, even when I was a little child. It goes as follows:

> Then shall the King say unto them on his right hand, Come, ye blessed of my Father, inherit the kingdom prepared for you from the foundation of the world: For I was an hungred, and ye gave me meat: I was thirsty, and ye gave me drink: I was a stranger, and ye took me in: Naked, and ye clothed me: I was sick , and ye visited me: I was in prison, and ye came unto me. Then shall the righteous answer him, saying, Lord, when saw we thee an hungred, and fed thee? or thirsty, and gave thee drink? When saw we thee a stranger, and took thee in? or naked, and clothed thee? Or when saw we thee sick, or in prison, and came unto thee? And

> the King shall answer and say unto them, Verily I say unto you, Inasmuch as ye have done it unto one of the least of these my brethren, ye have done it unto me.

I have dedicated my entire life to God by helping others, and this scripture has helped me know where to start and has guided me every step of the way.

I would like to conclude by saying that all this has been done regardless of my gender. However, I believe that being a woman has helped me in my ministry for God. I know that whoever I am, God loves me all of the time and is always reaching a hand out to lift me up in times when I need guidance.

29

Lazarus, Come Out!

Skip Frizzell

"He cried with a loud voice, 'Lazarus, come out.' The dead man came out."

—John 11:43–44

I was dead.
Good Heavens, man, I was dead!
In the grave, rotting, corrupt,
a lump of cold, dead dust and clay.

And now I can laugh and sing,
smell wet dew on the morning grass,
feel the warmth of yearling sheep,
taste the bitter tang of grapes,
bursting in my mouth.
I, who was dead, *am now* alive!

You ask me, was this man come from God?
Perhaps you did not hear me well:

As I say, I was quite dead. Dead!

Touch me—quite a lively corpse I make, eh?
What spirit ever had warts and moles,
and feet that needed washing?
I am alive, as you can see.

It is a long story, and I shall not go into it,
because, knowing what I now know, I know that I
was dead long before I died.
Dead—dead of soul, dead of spirit,
dead to the love of God
and his life.

And then came God, walking in the
guise of a workman of Galilee.
Oh, it was *God all right—*
that was my tomb just there,
behind that garden plot.

My spirit was dead and then, incidentally,
my body died.

And then God came, garbed as a carpenter,
as my friend,
and said:
Lazarus, come out!

And now I know why.
For now my soul *is alive,*
and I no more fear my body's second death,
for now I know that I shall die
unto life![1]

Like Lazarus, I'd like you to try to grasp my seventy years of self-imposed secrecy, lies, deception, and feelings of shame. A part of

[1] David C. Hill, *These Met the Master: 40 Portraits of Persons Who Met the Christ* (Minneapolis, MN: Augsburg Publishing House, 1967).

me hated myself, because I was taught that I was bad. Growing up in the years preceding and including the 1960s, in a society where homosexuality was unspeakable, forced me to find ways to mask, hide, disguise, and bury my true self for fear of exposure that could ruin what was becoming a brilliant, satisfying, and all-consuming career, marriage, and family life. I was living with the possibility of exposure and utter failure. This is my story:

As far back as I can remember, I felt different than other boys. I was not good at catching or batting a ball. In elementary school, when choosing teams for recess games or sports, I was one of the last chosen. Being chosen last hurt my feelings, and made me feel worse. I wanted to be invisible. I felt inadequate and distanced from the other boys. I don't remember being bullied or made fun of—I just wasn't chosen.

I can clearly recall having a crush on another boy in fourth grade. I wanted to be around him and walk with my arm around his shoulders. I learned quickly, I wasn't supposed to do that. It's amazing how quickly we learned the code of acceptable and unacceptable behavior. We learned what society allowed and did not allow us to do.

Later, in junior high school, if someone criticized my walk, I tried not to swish or swing my shoulders. If someone criticized my talking voice, I tried to sound more like how I thought a man should sound. When my dad wanted to take me fishing, I didn't much like that, but I worked hard to be what I was not.

On the other hand, I started taking piano lessons at the age of eight, and I liked it. In seventh grade, I started clarinet and, because of my earlier piano lessons, I was able to proceed faster than the other kids. Music class and band quickly became my favorite activities. I hated gym class, because we mostly played team sports by choosing teams. I tried not to be the worst player, but with little success.

While I was noticing and admiring certain boys, I was also noticing the girls. In seventh and eighth grade there were school dances, and I wanted to be included. I had a growing awareness that I wanted, and probably was expected, to grow up, get married, and have a family. Indeed, in the 1950s, there were no known options or expectations to marriage and family. In my case, my teen years in our family life were not happy ones.

In the 1940s and 1950s, there was no talk of gender difference. There was no talk of sexuality. We sort of grew into our sexual roles through ignorance and whatever we learned observing the examples around us. I remember, in fifth or sixth grade, the girls were excused from the regular classroom one day, while the boys were left behind. It was always a puzzle what the girls learned that day, while the boys were excluded. There was no sex education of any kind unless we got "the sex talk" from our parents. I received none in our family I. I literally learned my male capabilities from classmates in the restroom when I was in junior high school.

In the years leading up to the 1960s, words for gender differences didn't exist. The only words I was aware of, for males who didn't comply with common expectations, were "sissy" and "queer." I was ignorant of the 1969 Stonewall event in New York City until I was well into adulthood and seeking out historical information. The Stonewall event was an actual incident that ignited a turn in history that grew into what we now know as "gay people." The revolutionary Kinsey report on sexuality in 1948 provided us with the words "heterosexuality" and "homosexuality." The words "faggot" and "gay" have completely taken on different meanings other than those originally given. My old Webster's dictionary defines gay as "excited with merriment, merry" and faggot as "a bundle of sticks." If you look on a French music conductor's score, faggot is the word for the bassoon, which, in fact, resembles "a bundle of sticks." Unfortunately, these words are currently and commonly used slanderously, as negative terms often by youngsters completely ignorant of their distorted value.

During my teenage years, I had both life-shaping and life-changing experiences that provided a platform for the rest of my life. There was an opening in our high school band for a drum major. I thought I would like to try out for that and was accepted. Along with the new position came the opportunity to go to a week-long summer camp to learn how to fill that position of leadership. It was a profound event. I not only learned the techniques of how to lead a marching band, but, also, how to be an effective leader, and skillfully and objectively lead others to plan and fulfill a group's goals. The training was extremely competitive and intense. I took to it so well that I went back the next summer as a squad leader and became one of fourteen to earn the camp's highest award. I returned as an instructor for many years. During those young and impressionable years, I found these experiences created a boost in my confidence level. I had previously felt less able to compare my skills, abilities, and expectations with those of other boys.

Throughout junior and senior high school, I was dealing with dueling struggles and desires. On one hand, I was becoming more aware of my attraction to boys and men and, equally, my desire for a successful family life in the future. I rationalized that I would outgrow my attraction to men as I grew into my increased desire for marriage and family.

In college, the voices in my head and the desires in my heart grew louder. Dad's alcoholism and our parents arguing also moved to the forefront of our lives. Dad lost his good job, and our parents divorced. The unhappiness in our household was seemingly balanced by my increased desire to find the ideal marriage companion with whom I could spend a lifetime.

At about age fourteen, I started a prayer life to find, with God's help, the right partner with whom I could build a happy family. Without any doubt, whatsoever, God led me to that ideal partner. When I was seventeen, my grandfather, Evangelist John Grice, asked me to go with him to Eastland congregation in Detroit and play the piano at a service where he was the guest preacher. I did, and there she was—Ann Gault. Our romance and courtship began and, once married, was followed by forty-eight years of a blessed marriage. We had our problems and trials along the way, but God undoubtedly brought us together.

During our marriage, I had an amazing career as a high school music teacher and choir director. I did not do it on my own. I was blessed with people who offered support, and events that let our creative lights shine. God's intervention made it all possible. I was fortunate to have had students who performed in Carnegie Hall, and a show choir that placed seventh in the nation at the Young Americans competition in California. We also experienced concert tours of Europe where we visited twenty-one countries on an every-three-year rotation, and countless other achievements.

Eventually, a man moved into the school district where I was teaching choir and suggested that our schools' choirs could establish a tradition of singing together. We could perform together as a live "Singing Christmas Tree." He took me to California so I could see his idea in person, and he convinced the parent organizations of our choirs that they should buy a giant contraption to hold three hundred kids in the shape of a tree. The choir parents did so, and the next six years, right before my retirement, we established the tradition of performing the Singing Christmas Tree.

During those first six years of performances, we sold fourteen hundred tickets five times each Christmas season. In 1986, the Singing Christmas Tree opened the ABC television network's morning show, *Good Morning America*. In 2010, I attended the twenty-fifth anniversary of the Singing Christmas Tree. The parent support organization for this choir worked tirelessly raising huge amounts of money in support of their children's activities.

Simultaneously, while I was fully involved with school activities, my wife—the love of my life—was feeling distanced and separated from me. I had allowed my professional life to consume all my time. Feeling left out, Ann detected an opportunity where she could blend our companionship with my zeal at school. I was producing a stage production at school, and the librarian-media director was ill-equipped for designing and operating the show sound. Ann stepped in and learned how to be an expert sound technician. She developed expertise in the area and operated complicated stage shows with as many as twenty-six microphones, and she was in demand to do the same in the community for theater and symphony concerts. Ann found a way to blend our family life with the demanding activities I was creating at school. Sadly, the love of my life passed away many months ago.

During those years of family and professional life, I had dark and foreboding times which I became expert at never revealing. I was hiding a secret. This secret built inside of me to where I thought I would explode. It was a secret that, if revealed, could result in a sudden end to everything good in my life.

One day, a parent volunteer was in my office. I had a free hour during the second class period and was trying to tie up some loose ends at my desk and around the classroom. The volunteer pulled me into the office and shut the door. She told me she recognized, in my face, the same expression that she had seen in her face when she was on the brink of a nervous breakdown. She knew something was wrong and didn't want me to go through what she had experienced.

Well, that was a wake-up call for me. I had long ago seen the handwriting on the wall and admitted to myself that I was a homosexual. That had been a long and painful struggle. The self-imposed pressure building up inside of me wasn't as well-hidden as I thought, as I tried desperately to bury it. I came out to Ann in 1986. It was tough. I decided beforehand, that whatever the consequences—whether to stay or leave the marriage—I would accept them. We were both very emotional, and it was not as simple as I had expected. Although it was not an immediate decision, she decided to stay.

Over the next couple of years, Ann and I both struggled with continuing emotional issues and mental adjustments. She revealed she had sensed there was something wrong or missing in our marriage along the way. Although she could never put her finger on what it was, now she could name it. Our marriage healed after a long time. She never wanted me to come all the way out, and I have respected her wishes. I, also, had a strong will to fulfill our marriage vow. I continue to miss her each and every day, but I now feel I can lift the veil of hiding over a long, hidden life.

My coming out has been a long and slow process. Five years ago, my wonderful sister, my brother-in-law, my mother, and Ann were sitting around the dinner table when my sister—with tears in her eyes and wavering voice—recalled a time when I was in high school leading the band. My dad and his drunk buddies were in the bleachers ridiculing me. The time frame for this was about 1956, when there were very few boys who led high school bands. Their remarks had been filled with innuendo and verbal abuse. It was at that moment that I decided it was time to come clean and admit that I was gay. My brother-in-law immediately came to my defense. There were tears all around, and my mother said, "That comes from your father's side of the family." I think I responded with something like, "Well, I guess that makes me a flawed person." Mom said, "You are my son and I will always love you." That was good enough for me for that day. Mom struggled with the issue, but we have had lots of talks since then. I found it humorous that, since then, Mom has recalled some folks on her side of the family who were possibly homosexual. Mom continues to struggle, but she has come a long way.

Four years ago, my siblings and Mom had an adult gathering during the summer, and I came out to my two brothers. My older brother has done a wonderful flip-flop regarding his views. I felt that, a few years ago, he was mostly homophobic. He has made it a journey to seek a larger view, and I think he has changed remarkably—especially, since he is a professional counselor. My younger brother is open and accepting, but I think he has conservative views.

I came out to my daughter, Amy, two years ago. She is remarkable. She said to me, "Dad, God is allowing you a time to live your life to fulfillment that you haven't had until now." Whew!

I was afraid to come out to my son, Aaron. In the past, he had done a little act mocking effeminate men. It had really annoyed me, but I held my tongue. In recent phone conversations, he had been pressing me on some personal issues. So, about three months ago, I got up the courage to tell him. All is well, and after I told him how offended I was with his cute little act, I asked him to never do it again. I'm sure he never will.

I realize now, that in 1962 when I started teaching school, or for that matter when I retired in 1990, I would have been unable to have gotten a teaching job if I had come out. I am also positive when I was hired as a worship service coordinator at world church headquarters, from 1994 to 1998, that I would never have been hired if I had been out. However, I am quite sure it is a different and better situation today.

I wish there were words enough to express how freeing, enabling, and emancipating it is, that God has allowed a series of people to come into my life, shaping the events that allowed me to be a whole person. Every time I have outed myself to someone, I have felt another layer of guilt and shame lifted. I have felt richly blessed. It is part of our human nature that we tend to forget the bad and remember the good. When our prophet told us to go to the "bruised and brokenhearted," I felt my eyes fill with tears, as in my heart, I heard the response, "They are us."

I feel it is important and necessary to openly share my highly personal story at this time. I think it is especially relevant with the scheduling of Community of Christ's USA National Conference in April 2013, where we shall deal with issues regarding homosexuality, ordination, same-gender marriage, and the church policies developed from the 1982 Standing High Council Statement on homosexuality. I think every time we see a human face relating to the issues, we gain further insight.

Cornerstone congregation, Community of Christ, has overwhelmingly voted in favor of being a welcoming congregation and published weekly its mission statement and welcoming statement. I am hopeful that those people who knew me, loved me, and supported me before my coming out, will continue to do the same knowing me as a gay man. I am the same person now, but I am known better. God created me in his own image. He loves me just as I am. I was born this way, and I give thanks for his blessings in my life.

30

Nudge Us into Paths of Righteousness

Bud Perrin

Thinking back to when change happened in your life helps you realize how great God is, and how fortunate we are to be blessed by a Spirit that is patient and willing to nudge us into paths of righteousness. There have been many spiritual nudges in my life that have led to changes I thought would never happen. I remember feeling called to be a delegate at the world conference of Community of Christ and going through the process of being elected for this opportunity in our mission center. Feeling fortunate to have been chosen and wanting to be responsible with my obligation, I read the legislation printed in the *Herald* (the monthly denominational magazine of Community of Christ) that would be discussed by the conference delegates. One piece of legislation that was scheduled to come before the conference for the first time, had to deal with the issue of homosexuality and the church. My immediate reaction to this was, "Not in my church." I was outspoken on the issue and sure this would be something that would be easily dismissed, and we would move on to more proper work.

Feeling it was my responsibility to follow the obligation I made when world conference began, I attended the discovery sessions where the legislation was presented to and then discussed by the delegates. Stone Church congregation was packed, and I was surprised at the amount of stir this proposal caused. I was still convinced that this issue would be quickly handled and wouldn't happen in my church. What I experienced in that meeting started me on a journey that has been life changing on many levels.

As I listened to homosexual children standing beside their parents, telling their painful stories of rejection, I was filled with a loving spirit for those families. I cannot say I was changed in an instant, but something stirred within me to cause me to look deeper into my response—I had prejudged without first seeking knowledge or fact. I was so touched by their testimonies that on my walk back to the Auditorium I was overcome by a spirit of repentance, and had to sit on the hill by the Church of Christ building and recompose myself. I remember hoping no one would come along who knew me, because I was not sure I could explain my experience.

Since then, I've taken many opportunities to grow in my knowledge of homosexuality and the church. I have to say that what I've learned has led me into a deeper understanding of God and his love for all people. My experience has been enhanced while serving as a co-missioned pastor for the Cornerstone congregation, Community of Christ. Coming to Cornerstone from another congregation has been a fulfilling and challenging opportunity for me and my family. One of the first couples we met was Chuck and Mike Hewitt. Although other same-sex couples had attended other congregations where I had previously been the pastor, they had never been as invested in mission as Chuck and Mike. We quickly became friends, and I began another journey of understanding and education of God's love for all.

I feel more blessed than I deserve when I look back, not many years ago, to a time when I easily said, "Not in my church." I now have knowledge of God's love for all. As I think about my own journey and growth, I can only begin to imagine how hard the journey has been for homosexual Saints—our brothers and sisters who have felt left behind, ignored, and pushed away by many in the church. My prayer and support is for those who are today's pioneers, who are bridging the gap and helping those of us who lack understanding. The challenges that have been faced and the progress that has been made will be a blessing for many who will follow, as we grow together as a community and a church, sharing God's love as we are nudged into paths of righteousness.

31

Michigan to Missouri: My Passionate Journey

Michael J. Albers-Hewitt

Born in a small Michigan town, I grew up in a large family with seven boys and three girls. As the middle boy, I was surrounded by brothers who excelled in sports and popularity. Unfortunately, I was neither athletic nor popular. I knew at an early age that I was different from my brothers and other boys. Everyone in my family knew I was different. Some welcomed my difference—this included my mother and sisters. Others were embarrassed by and ashamed of my difference—this included my father and brothers. I was regularly made fun of at home and school. My father physically abused me, thinking he could beat me into being like my brothers. I became a boy who shied away from men and most boys, and preferred the company of girls and women. Yet, I was very attracted to men. This was confusing to me and was cause for my development of self shame.

Church was the one place where I found solace from the abuse. In church, I received love and care. I enjoyed Sunday school and sitting in church with my family. It was in church that I met the first boy to ever be friends with me. We enjoyed a special connection and were close until, at the age of fourteen, he got into drugs. He was taken to a state home for boys some miles away, and we never saw each other until we were adults. He lives as a heterosexual man.

Church was a large part of my life, until my mother died when I was sixteen. She had been a strong support for me and protected me from my father. I was not sure I could live without her. After her death, my church attendance severely lapsed. My father threw me out when I was seventeen, and I went to live with my oldest sister.

The summer after my mother's death, my oldest brother took my youngest sister and me to a church reunion. While attending that reunion, I met my first openly gay person. I finally knew what I was and had an identifiable name for it, but shame drove me from a relationship with him.

Between my junior and senior year, and again for a year after I graduated high school, I was a summer exchange student to Sweden. There I lived with two different families and pretended to be heterosexual, so I would fit in. Later, when we finally reconnected, I discovered that my best friend in Sweden was gay. I still call him frequently.

During my first year of college in Michigan, I entered a program to change into a heterosexual. The program was emotionally painful and, of course, it failed me, and I felt that I had failed the program. I tried to commit suicide during this time by taking a number of pills. They made me very sick and I threw them up. I prayed to God to change me and later, after moving to Minnesota, the change came. I met a lesbian who took me to a gay club in Minneapolis. I was amazed by all the people and felt a sense of belonging I had never felt before.

I longed for an intimate relationship that would provide me with a sense of togetherness. Shortly after coming out, I met my first partner of several years. I wanted to reconnect with the church to share my love of God with him. We started to attend a local Reorganized

Church of Jesus Christ of Latter Day Saints congregation, but we did not feel welcome. My partner did not understand my church, so regular attendance became an issue. My partner had a drinking problem and became very jealous of relationships I developed with friends and co-workers. Our journey together ended painfully. I loved him very much. The following two years I had a short relationship, but it ended because of physical abuse.

I attended church occasionally during this time. I would cry during the services, but I still did not feel comfortable being open and sharing my sexuality. I was never questioned about my tears or about who I was.

Then, I met the man of my dreams—or so I thought. He was a very handsome man and was studying to become a doctor. We were together a couple of years when he came home one day and told me he had acquired HIV from another person. It was a few weeks later that I found out I also tested positive for HIV. I was devastated, because I thought I had been in a monogamous relationship. Health officials told me I would be dead in the near future. I needed support.

Unfortunately, there seemed to be no place where I could receive support—especially not from my church. I felt completely alone and ashamed. I started to prepare myself for dying. I ended up telling my closest sister but swore her to secrecy. People with HIV were being treated like lepers. Those with HIV were dying all around me. I felt I must keep this AIDS disease a secret from everyone—no one must find out. My partner and I split and went our separate ways. He died a couple of years after that. Fortunately, I did not die. Neither did I get sick until years later.

In 1989, I moved back to Michigan with a new partner who was aware of and comfortable with my HIV status. He was HIV negative. We bought an old farm house with a cottage next to it and proceeded to remodel them. We opened a bed-and-breakfast, and I planted huge flower and vegetable gardens around the property. I started attending a small mission group in Holland, Michigan, with my sister. It was in this setting that I came out with my sexuality and my HIV status. The pastor was accepting, as were some in the congregation, but others were not supportive, except to say, "Love the sinner, not the sin."

I attended reunion with my sister and felt moved by the Spirit to share my situation about my sexuality and health. It was not received well by other reunion campers, especially parents. They would run screaming for their children to get out of the men's bathroom every time I entered. I have not attended a church reunion since. I learned that it was not okay to share my HIV status with people with whom I went to church. My partner at this time was Catholic and refused to attend church with me.

In 1993, I became very ill, and my HIV developed into AIDS. Although I was prepared to die sometime soon, new medicines became available that allowed me to combat AIDS and achieve some level of recovery. It was a long and painful experience, as, again, my friends were dying around me. During this period of illness, I became acquainted with two people from GALA. They visited me frequently and suggested I attend a GALA retreat that was being held outside of Chicago. I went, even though I was in fragile health. It was my first of many retreats. My partner became unable to cope with my illness, so we sold the house and parted ways after moving to San Francisco, California.

I sought out the San Francisco congregation and found a friend from GALA attending there. Church again became a major part of my life. The San Francisco congregation, for the most part, was very supportive. The pastor was a kind, gentle man who drew me into congregational life. I enjoyed the warm, loving fellowship that I found there. Yet, I didn't have someone special with whom I could share my church life. One night, I remember praying to God for "one last person to love." I prayed for someone who would love me and love my church.

In the fall of 1999, a church friend and GALA member encouraged me to attend the annual GALA retreat at Camp Doniphan, located outside of Kansas City, Missouri. It was there that I met Chuck, and we found that we had similar interests and goals for our lives. I, a wounded and lonely soul, found that God had not forgotten me and had answered my prayer with Chuck. I returned to San Francisco and made plans to move to Kansas City where Chuck lived.

Chuck is HIV negative and had a previous partner who was positive like me. I had never been happier, because I found someone who loved me and understood my spiritual connection with my church—now *our* church. We had a commitment ceremony in September 2000 at Peace Chapel in downtown Kansas City. The ceremony was presided over by Curt Filer. Chuck's parents, aunt, and uncle attended, as did my youngest sister and eldest brother. Many friends and church members also came to share in our special day. We attended Peace Chapel until 2002 and, during that time, headed up the worship and pastoral care committee for the congregation.

In December 2000, we bought a house and moved to Independence, Missouri. In the fall of 2002, we decided to find a Community of Christ congregation closer to where we lived. After visiting several, we finally found Cornerstone congregation, where we were truly welcomed. By the spring of 2003, we had transferred our membership to Cornerstone. We quickly became involved in worship planning for two years and then headed community outreach until May 2011. We were allowed to teach Sunday school, vacation Bible school, and preparation-for-baptism classes. We cooked a neighborhood Thanksgiving dinner, as well as helped with other fundraising events. We began singing in the choir. We have become an important part of the Cornerstone congregation and feel loved and accepted there.

In May 2009, Chuck and I were legally married at Roy A. Cheville Chapel, Graceland University, in Lamoni, Iowa. Curt Filer presided over the ceremony once again. This became quite an unintentional scandal with the university president and Community of Christ. World church leaders launched an investigation into the ceremony.

We attempted to announce our wedding in two of the local Kansas City newspapers. Both refused to print the announcement. We called a local Kansas City television station, and they came right away and interviewed us. Soon, we had most of the local television stations and the national news covering our story. On July 5, 2009, the *Kansas City Star* decided to print our announcement, but the *Independence Examiner* has continued to refuse to print same-sex announcements.

As of 2011, we have been together twelve years, and we continue to attend the Cornerstone congregation. We have found that even though Cornerstone is welcoming, we need to always be vigilant to remind them of what it really means when we say, "*all* are welcome!" Our journey and our work together are not yet finished. We shall continue to help guide our congregation and our mission center by always being active participants in our church family!

32

THE LONG, WINDING ROAD

Chuck Hewitt

I WAS BORN GAY! No doubt, no questions—I knew I was different at an early age.

Growing up in Montana, I was raised in the Reorganized Church of Jesus Christ of Latter Day Saints where Dad was an elder and Mom played the organ. Over the years, Dad would share being pastor with two other men in the priesthood, each taking a year or two, then passing it back and forth. Mom always played the piano, and my three brothers and I sat in the front row whenever Dad was giving the sermon. At times, Dad would reprimand us from the pulpit if we were misbehaving—but that only took a few times. Early on, I became involved in the church through youth groups and activities, Zion's League, mowing the lawn, and attending reunions. I was taught the foundational values and beliefs of the church, and developed a strong connection with God and the Holy Spirit from the beginning. I can't express how much I appreciate my parents planting the seed that would save me later in life.

As I look back, growing up in Montana actually wasn't that bad. In sixth grade, during the seventies, kids were calling me gay, so I knew I had to work on showing them that I was okay. I wouldn't allow them the pleasure of upsetting me. I found a group in high school who would accept me. They called themselves the Hoods. And you can guess what that meant—fun, drugs, drinking, and rock and roll.

As I started figuring out who I was, I learned an old word with a new meaning for me. When I was a junior in high school, I admitted to myself, *"I am gay."* Oh, what a relief it was to say it and truly understand that I now had purpose and direction. I had several boyfriends from grade school through high school and beyond, so saying I was gay just fit and seemed natural to me. I knew that when I grew up, I could leave Montana and go find my Prince Charming. But don't forget, I also found that wonderful world of drugs, alcohol, parties, and later—sex.

I dropped out of high school and entered a drug and alcohol rehabilitation program. My parents helped out by sending a couple of us to counseling where my drug and alcohol problem first came out of the closet, so to speak. After treatment, instead of getting a GED certificate, I went back to high school to graduate. The feeling was weird. I was nineteen years of age, living on my own, and, yet, I was a senior in high school. I knew I was gay, and my friends and classmates knew it, but I couldn't tell Mom and Dad. See, there was the church thing that now stood in my way, and my being gay just wouldn't work for them. So I moved out and, for the most part, stopped going to church. I would always ask to be scheduled for work on Sundays as a convenient excuse to be unavailable to attend church.

After high school, I eventually left Montana and, in the early eighties, picked Kansas City, Missouri—of all places—to call my home. Within the first couple of months there, a friend asked me if I would like to go to a function of gay and lesbian members of the church. I went to my first GALA meeting in 1985, in Arthur Butler's home in midtown Kansas City. I remember meeting Curt Filer and several other people at that first gathering. It was fun, but I never attended again until years later.

I lived there for a few months. I had determined that I no longer needed my parents' help financially, and it was time to come out to them. Mom was visiting one week—it might have been for the church's world conference—so I decided that would be a good time. After I told her, I couldn't believe it. Her response was, "Your father and I have known for years. We figured you would say something when you were ready." The funny part is, I figured *they* would ask *me* about it when *they* were ready.

Around that time, I realized I no longer had a drinking and drug problem, so it seemed only logical to me that I could start using again. Guess what else I discovered. There are gay bars and clubs where I could find my Prince Charming, and I could get married and live happily ever after! Yeah, right! Back to reality! I went to church a couple of times, never quite feeling comfortable. I discovered that staying up late on Saturday nights made getting up early Sunday morning a problem.

I found someone, and we were together for ten years. During this time, I continued drinking and drugging. While I was being faithful, I found that my partner wasn't. When I found out, my reaction was, "If you can't beat them, join them." In my heart, I knew that this was the beginning of the end in our relationship. When it finally came to an end, there was a quick and hard downward spiral. During this time, I was mostly drunk, and my world opened up to crystal meth, a seemingly wonderful drug. I was clubbing and having a great deal of anonymous sex with multiple partners. My drug-fueled lifestyle went on for several years.

I was unable to recognize the downward spiral from the inside. I didn't realize I was in my own personal hell, even when I found myself getting up in the mornings still drunk from the night before, using crystal meth to get myself going, and closing one eye to drive to work because of the double lines. Shaking so badly during work, at noon I started drinking vodka from a water bottle to maintain myself through the workday.

Then, on April 23, 1999, three days after my birthday, I was fired! Everything finally caught up with me. My work, which kept me somewhat sane, was now gone. I lived alone. My drug and alcohol friends were gone. I had finally reached the bottom. I was unable to type a resume, because I was shaking so badly. I drank to stop shaking and then passed out by noon—just to start the cycle all over again. I was in pain physically and emotionally. I was lost and so very alone. There was no one to whom I could turn. My world came crashing down all around me.

Now, at age thirty-five, I needed help or I wasn't going to make it. There was someone I had worked with at the bank who got sober through Alcoholics Anonymous, and I knew I could go to that acquaintance for help. I knocked on his door on May 4, 1999. He was now my *only* friend, and I stayed with him while he helped me get off the drugs. He helped me while the drugs worked out of my system, and he took me back to AA, after all of those years. In AA they talked of a higher power—believing in something greater than one's self. It didn't matter if the higher power was a rock or a force. I knew mine was God. Not only did I have to believe, but I had to allow this power to work in and through me. Once again, I knew where to go. Thank you, Mom and Dad, for planting the seed. It saved me!

I called the local mission center office of Community of Christ to find a church in my neighborhood. They put me in contact with Peace Chapel in downtown Kansas City. I called them and found out their service times. The person on the other end of the phone was excited that I would be visiting and assured me that I would fit in just fine. Now, keep in mind, it had been more than ten years since I had stepped into an RLDS church. I had been gone for a long time. I was sick, lost, and just trying to survive. I was scared and afraid that they might not accept me. I was still learning how to function without alcohol and drugs, and I was gay. In my mind, it sounded like I should not be going to church. After all, I'm gay, and you just can't fix that.

I built up my courage and went one Sunday morning, even with all my harbored misgivings. I walked in nervously and was greeted warmly, ever so warmly. Then, I noticed others were already there, and they, also, warmly greeted, welcomed, and comforted me. I was no longer alone. The biggest thing I noticed was that most of the people gathered there for church were gay. I thought, "My goodness,

I have been away from church for a long time, but, *wow*, we are accepted!"

What I soon learned was that Peace Chapel was a congregation that helped the broken, and took in anyone, regardless of who they were, helping them to heal and grow. Many of the people who passed through those doors entered broken and lost, and were helped to gain strength and grow to become disciples for Christ. Many later left the comfort and safety of Peace Chapel, able to share the love of the Christ on their journey.

It was June and I was still attending my AA meetings. At church one Sunday, someone mentioned a GALA retreat at Camp Doniphan. Well, I knew what GALA was, and I found out that Camp Doniphan was the reunion grounds for Central Mission, Community of Christ, so I decided to go.

The retreat was Labor Day weekend, and I packed up my things and went. I had the weight of the world on my shoulders—I had been in recovery four months and had finally started working again. I was healing, but I was still feeling low and thought I was the only one with problems.

During the retreat, there were classes for learning and social mixers for getting to know one another better. The first day, we broke up into small groups of about twelve to fifteen people. We were asked to tell our stories and were encouraged to speak of our struggles, hopes, joys, and pain. After listening to the stories of others, I began to have an understanding that I was not alone. I realized that others had painful experiences just like me. I discovered that, in a number of cases, the pain and agony of others was so great it made me feel that my problems weren't that bad.

I shared my story that morning and also listened to the stories of others. I know that their stories helped me in my journey, and I was truly filled with the Spirit that weekend. It was as if I was a kid again, after a week of camp and my battery was recharged. God filled my soul and showed me new life. I realized that the love of God is great, and no one can take that away. I now know that I am God's servant, placed here to help others, and that means everyone without reservation.

During that wonderful GALA retreat, something else amazing happened, but that is another story. I will give you a hint, though. Do you remember when I said earlier in my life I wanted to meet my Prince Charming?

33

It Began with a Prayer: The Buffalo-Clarence, New York, Congregation Story

Nancy Cervi

It began with a prayer—a prayer for children to fill our congregations.

Those of us who worship in Buffalo, New York, have experienced a couple of difficult years. In 1976, our congregation decided to move our physical facilities from inside the city limits to a location in the somewhat rural surroundings of suburban Clarence, New York. There, we continued to grow and share in faith. We were blessed with an attractive, modern church building, but suddenly the rooms were empty. Our numbers were cut drastically when three key families moved out of the area, taking with them half of our youth. In addition, there were some deaths of prominent leaders in our congregation. We were going through a transition period where our grief and mourning was taking a toll on those of us left behind.

And so we prayed. We began with a prayer for children to fill our congregation. We prayed for children's voices and the pattering of small feet to once again echo through our church building. We prayed that there might be people led to our doorway, so we could open our arms wide and welcome them into our family.

We had expectations that God would send us families with lots of kids. And, lo and behold, our prayers were answered—but instead of sending children, God sent us two remarkable women. These women were a couple and turned out to be the true answer to our prayers as we began to recognize and understand the challenge of exactly *who* were God's *children*.

Buffalo was already blessed to have an active and loving priest in our congregation who was a gay man. His quiet ministry was never a threat, and we loved both him and his partner (who joined the church during this time). I believe that some of our members only saw them as roommates but, none the less, their ministry was truly appreciated. With the addition of these two lovely ladies, we now had to confront those issues we hadn't spoken of. For the first time, we had to confront the message of acceptance that we had been practicing but had never spoken about.

In 2002, some of us traveled to Camp Bountiful in Ohio for the GALA retreat where President Grant McMurray was invited to be a guest. It was here that I met the forgotten children of Community of Christ. Here, stories were shared of those who had come out to their families and congregations, and some who had come out while at Graceland College. I heard, firsthand, of the pain and ignorance of prejudice. When the sharing service was over, I was numb. As a convert to the church, my rose-colored glasses had been shattered. Up until this time, I was not aware that we, as a church, could preach one message and, yet, harbor such un-Christlike thoughts.

During this time, I was asked to perform a union ceremony for these two ladies, who had now been baptized and were active members of our congregation. Actually, because of their background in social work, they became the spiritual conscience of who we were as a congregation. They not only raised our awareness of homosexuality, but of other social issues, as well. I think all three of us were very surprised when they did not get the 100 percent support we anticipated. While everyone in the congregation truly loved them (you couldn't help it)— there suddenly was a public statement to be made.

The details of the struggles we went through at that time remain a spiritual blur. There were discussions, meetings, phone calls, and many, many prayers. As part of the pastoral team, I heard the objections and the confirmations. There were families who just couldn't support the ceremony but could attend a service of blessing. A lot of words were used to describe what was going to be perceived as a marriage ceremony.

Having been asked to perform other wedding services, it was strongly impressed on me that no other couple had ever approached me with this simple, heartfelt request: "We would like God's blessing on our relationship. Would you perform this ceremony?" As a new elder in the church, I knew that I would never deny a request of any blessing that was asked of me. It was when I was on my knees, asking for relief from my personal turmoil and that of my congregation, that I received my call to the priesthood office of evangelist. It was made known to me that a spiritual calling isn't a reward for being diligent, but God was strengthening me for even more difficult challenges.

I am pleased to say that the union ceremony was held on a beautiful, autumn evening with many friends there, to not only support Sharon and Nance, but to publicly announce that our congregation was ready to move ahead. We were well equipped to welcome other gays and lesbians into our church home. We had been through the difficult days and seemingly learned, without hesitation, to offer love and acceptance to others, especially those of the LGBT community. Our arms had always been open to anyone who walked through our doors; we thought of ourselves already as a "welcoming church."

It was not long before two more gay men found their way through our doors and into our hearts. Around that time, we began periods of study and discussions about what it meant to be a welcoming church. During the discussions, it was pointed out that welcoming churches (although emphasizing ministry to persons from the LGBT community) must be open to offering ministry to everyone without exception. It was indicated that if we truly believed and acted as a welcoming church, then we should verbalize our sentiments. Perhaps printing and posting such sentiments would continually keep them in front of us, as well as on our minds. We heard from our LGBT members that the exclusion from churches and worship settings had been so negative and severe over time, that there was a need to hear and know that they would truly be welcomed, accepted, and fully included in all aspects of church life.

The process of study, prayerful consideration, group interaction, discernment, and guidance lasted over a period of a couple of years. Members of the congregation were invited and encouraged to take ownership in the process of becoming a people who were truly welcoming in all of our gatherings. Our mission statement was developed and approved by every member in attendance and first appeared on the title page of our local church directory. It stated: "We are called to be a welcoming church, open and affirming … sharing the peace of Jesus Christ with all, especially the disenfranchised including, but not limited to, the LGBT (lesbian, gay, bisexual, and transgender) community … a continually discerning and prophetic people." This publicized statement indicated that in addition to "talking the talk" that we "walk the walk" in our congregation. We have chosen this path and have offered love and compassion to everyone who has walked through our doors.

Today, we are blessed with the talents and ministry of two more remarkable men who have found a home in the Buffalo branch. They are leaders who continue to challenge us to meet the needs of the LGBT community. We have been blessed each time they offer ministry in our worship services. Participation in our church reunion has changed for them, and for us, because of the light that they have provided. We have become founding members of a new, local organization that seeks to bring together people of diverse faiths that offer open and affirming ministries within their sacred walls. This organization helps people, whether LGBT or straight, find full inclusion and participation in worship settings of their faith choices.

We have chosen to discern the will of God for us in this part of the garden. We shall continue to cultivate the garden and look for ways to increase the bounty. We shall continue to reach out to those who are disenfranchised and provide them with uplifting ministry. We shall be about the tasks of bringing hope to those who sense hopelessness, love to those who feel unloved, compassion to those who are hurt, and peace to those who feel alone.

We are all God's children designed by our Heavenly Parent. We are flawed, fickle, and fearful. We are afraid of the dark, and we long to be held by a loving parent when life is unfair. While we have life and breath in Buffalo, New York, we are ready to comfort anyone who enters our door. We have learned that God answers prayers, but not always with the answer that we expect. May we all rise to the challenge of ministering to *all* of God's precious children.

34

Desperately Seeking a Community to Call Our Own

Nance Gerbracht

I have started and stopped writing this story so many times. It's difficult to sit down and put into words all the ups and downs that my partner and I and our congregation have gone through in the process of its writing.

Let me begin by sharing the story of my church. I belong to the Buffalo, New York, congregation of Community of Christ. My partner and I have tried so many different churches and congregations, desperately trying to find a place that was welcoming to us and fit us. We had basically given up on ever finding a church to call our home, when we talked to a friend of ours who could not stop telling us about his church. He said that he and his partner attended the Buffalo congregation, had Bible study in their home, and felt welcomed and accepted.

We finally got up the courage to try attending church just one more time. I know that might sound crazy to some people—needing to get the courage to try church just one more time—but, after so many rejections, so many words of hatred and bigotry from the pulpits of so many churches, one can become jaded and protective, and we certainly did. So, that said, we decided to attend this church that our friend told us so much about. The first time we walked into that church, I felt an overwhelming sense of peace and rightness. I think I knew—this was what we had been searching for. It was not that the people in the congregation were just like us. In fact, they could not have seemed more different. It was the love, kindness, and genuine welcome that the people offered to us when we walked in and again as we were leaving. We tell everyone that we were loved into our church. We walked through those doors hurting and needy, and have grown into women filled with the love of Christ and the joy of sharing that love with others we meet.

So, to move ahead in this story, many years have passed and my partner, Sharon, and I have been active members in our church. We have actively participated in any and everything we could join and become involved in. We have had Bible studies in our home, joined the worship commission, preached on Sundays, planned services, and were baptized and blessed. We are fully and completely involved in the life of our church and all that comes with being a full member. We invited our friends and family to come and see what had made us so happy, and they could all see the positive change that this church had made in our lives.

So, things had been going great with us and our church. Sharon and I decided that we really wanted to share a very important event in our lives with our church family. It's an event that is traditionally held in the church and is something that many women dream about much of their lives. We wanted to get married. Okay—not married in the traditional sense—but we wanted to have a union ceremony in our church having our pastors, Nancy and Larry Cervi, perform it for us. They had become close friends, mentors, spiritual advisers, and family to us. It was important for us to ask them to share in this ceremony and special occasion in our lives. We really had felt loved and accepted in our congregation, and were ready to take this step. This was about six or seven years ago—so, by that time, Sharon and I had been together in a committed, monogamous relationship for over fourteen years. We really did not foresee what this one request was going to do.

Nancy and Larry presented our wishes to the leaders of our congregation to gauge their reactions. Let's just say that it did not go as well as we had hoped for. There were several members of the priesthood who were absolutely, completely, and totally against this ceremony in their church and would not even consider it. We also had support and encouragement from members of our congregation who I never would have thought would support or encourage us. Needless to say, these were very hard times for Sharon and me, for our congregation, and for Nancy and Larry Cervi, our pastors.

There were many meetings and discussions. One of the things that was a sore point was to call our ceremony a *union ceremony*. There were a few people who just would not agree to that in their church. We agreed that we would call it a *commitment ceremony*, instead. Then, there were concerns about us advertising our ceremony. I had never before heard of anyone advertising a wedding, but we assured the congregation that our invitations would say, "Please join us in our commitment ceremony." And we would not be broadcasting it on the news or in the paper. It seems somewhat trivial now, but during that time, it was very personal to the people on both sides of the issue.

In the end, our congregation voted to allow us to have our commitment ceremony in the church. We lost a former pastor and his family due to that vote, and to this day I feel bad about that. He and I have spoken several times, and he is very cordial to me, but he just could not reconcile his lifelong belief that homosexuality is wrong and a sin. He didn't believe that his church should perform this commitment ceremony in the sanctuary. It's sad that the congregation lost the gifts he and his family brought to them, and I will always feel somewhat guilty for that.

Nancy and Larry Cervi, our pastors and close friends, suffered and fought for us and our ceremony during a most difficult time in their own personal lives. The sacrifice, commitment, and spirit they gave to that day is probably one of the greatest gifts anyone has ever given to Sharon and me. There will never be enough words to thank them or tell them how much they did for us and how much they mean to us.

So, we had our commitment ceremony in the church. We sent invitations to our family and friends, and we invited anyone and everyone in the congregation to join us on our special day. It was amazing. Our friends and family helped us decorate the church, and it never looked more beautiful—of course, I might be a little biased in that opinion. We had our moms walk us down the aisle and give us away. Our friends Barb and Margaret came, and their daughter was our flower girl. We asked family and friends to participate in the ceremony, and the Cervis performed it. Nancy shared words that made us both laugh and cry. In their words, they truly represented the essence of the day and of the couple that Sharon and I are. We had one point in the ceremony where we asked the people who attended to please stand, come forward, and take a cut flower, which we provided, to help us create a bouquet together to symbolize our coming together as a family on this day. We asked people to only do this if they supported our commitment to one another. Every single person came forward! I have to admit that I cried at that point. It had so much meaning for me.

Sharon and I celebrated our twenty-first anniversary on April 1, 2011. But we feel that the blessing we had in our church was the most important day of our lives together. Our congregation has made great strides, as well. We have gone through the process of becoming a welcoming church. We are open and affirming, and welcome everyone who comes to our doors. We have marched in the gay pride parade in Buffalo, New York, for several years now and have also set up a table afterward to share the story of our welcoming church. We now have a monthly dinner and a celebratory evening with several other churches in our community to celebrate being open and affirming, and to work together to help the people in our community that need it most. We now have several more gay members in our congregation. One of our members is a celebrated drag queen in Buffalo, who has raised countless amounts of money to help in the fight against AIDS. Our congregation supports the Buffalo Gay Men's Chorus, attends Gay Bingo monthly, and constantly supports Sharon and me, and all of our sisters and brothers, in our chosen careers. Sharon and I are both in the mental health field, and we ask for donations and support from our congregation throughout the year. They are always eager to share their time, talents, and resources for the causes we present.

I can't even predict what the future holds for our little congregation. We have already done such big things. When I first walked through those doors, I was a young, frightened gay woman with a family who was embarrassed and ashamed of me, churches who told me I was no good, and a real fear of being hurt by religion once again. Today, I am a strong, proud, gay woman. I have a partner who is my best friend, my strength, and my hero. I have a family who is proud of my partner and me, I have very good friends, and I have a church family filled with love and acceptance.

The truth is, without my church family, I would not be the woman I am today. They gave me the strength, support, and love I needed so desperately in my life. I only hope that if you read this story and have turned someone away from your church or from your life, you will remember where I started, and open your heart and your doors to them. It only takes one hand reaching out to change a life.

35

I Am a Whosoever!

Nathan Phillips-Frey

I grew up in a small village tucked into central New York with a population under five thousand and a name alleged to mean a "cluster of pines near still waters." It was incorporated in 1835—less idyllically described as "muck land"—and was suitable for the farming of onions. This was the historic location where I grew up.

I was next to the youngest in a family of eight children. Before I was born, one of my brothers drowned when he was only five years old. My two older brothers served in the military. Dad was physically abusive and suffered from Alzheimer's in his later years. We lived in more than one house while I was growing up and experienced fires in a couple of them. Life was not necessarily easy, but my mother did the very best she could with what she had, and she expected her children to grow up to be responsible, productive adults. Our play clothes looked very much like our Sunday clothes, but we never complained.

Looking back, hardly anyone ever left our small town. Usually, they got a job at the silversmith manufacturing company, a few miles down the road. It has since vanished along with its make-a-living-wage jobs. My younger brother was also gay, but he passed away suddenly from a heart attack before he turned forty. This is my perspective that I want to impart—that is where I came from, and that is what I left behind.

My mother made sure we attended church on a regular basis. We attended a Roman Catholic church for a time, until one day the local priest stopped by the house to visit. During the sharing time with my mother, he indicated the church had noticed that for a family as large as ours, we only gave a small amount each week in the offering. We should be able to give substantially more. (Oh my! What part of poor, large number of kids, just barely keeping clothing on their backs and food on the table, had he overlooked?) My mother escorted the priest to the door, and the next Sunday we began attending the Church of the Nazarene.

Although we moved from church to church for one reason or another, we still went to church. If one of us had told Mom that we did not want to go, her response would have been something like, "Well, at this point in time, in our home, we attend church. When you get old enough to go out on your own, you can decide which church you want to join or not join any at all. But for now, you will continue to attend, listen, and learn." This sounded so much better than, "You'll go, because I say so," that others may have heard in their homes.

Did I have a particularly tough time growing up gay in the seventies? Not any more than anyone else. Did anyone know I was gay? How could they not, considering I was a three-hundred-plus pound, baton-and-rifle-twirling member of the local high school marching band, and drum and bugle corps. My summers were spent with the corps: practicing, traveling, sleeping on gymnasium floors, performing on football fields, and getting back on the bus to travel to the next performance location. During the school year, I was one of the more popular kids, so I didn't get picked on all that much. I was determined. No way would they find me working in the muck lands, servicing the onion crops.

I was fortunate to get a scholarship that took me to a Catholic college in Buffalo—one that catered primarily to nursing students, but also offered training in elementary special education. There, I reconnected with the Catholic religion and attended services with a priest who had a unique take on services designed to get the student population to participate. After graduating and completing a master's program, I started working in the area of special education.

During the 1980s, as AIDS was recognized and people began to die from the disease, I was active as an advocate. The AIDS quilt was started in our area. Educational programs were developed that addressed the significance of participation in risky behaviors. Relationships were forged; some passed the test of time, and some never would. One of my best friends moved to Buffalo, and we shared living quarters as we each pursued our teaching careers. He became involved with someone. They adopted a son and started attending a church.

During this time, one of my friends was dying of AIDS, and one of his last wishes was that I would perform in drag. Arrangements were made for him to be brought to the venue, and I requested to be put on the schedule early, as I was somewhat nervous. Although he was there with nursing support, he seemed to be asleep in all of the hustle and bustle of activity around him. When they announced that a new drag queen was in town, who was somewhat shy and nervous about performing and to be kind to her, he woke up and seemed to sit up just a bit taller. Then, he heard her name was Gladys Over. The smile on his face through that oxygen mask was unmistakable. He was thrilled! His words after the performance were to the effect that Miss Gladys should never give up doing drag. She had the unbounded capacity to make people happy!

Since then, Miss Gladys Over has raised awareness of the continual fight against the spread of AIDS, and the tender care that those suffering from the disease and their families and friends deserve, as they struggle to support those they love. Along the way, there have been numerous fundraising events that have been directly supported by the efforts of this and many other drag personas. It is somewhat interesting that people react and interact differently to a man in drag, than if he were not. There is something almost liberating and uninhibited that goes on between "the man on the street" and a drag queen.

Much of the time, lives are lived out and intertwined with others in the community. Some are fortunate enough to find soul mates or partners, and some find there is something more they want out of life. I sensed my need for something more when I woke up one morning and said to my partner, "Let's go to church." For me, it was not necessarily going back to a church from my past; there had been a number of them in various forms, and they pretty much did not look favorably upon persons who were gay. We went to my partner's church, the one from his youth, the one I'd been to before with him. The people there seemed nice enough, but I was still not sure about them. If they hurt me, like I'd been hurt in all the other churches I'd gone to, that would be the end. It was almost like I was already looking for a reason not to attend. I wasn't sure that God even cared about me. Why should God care? I'm gay!

At first, I refused to sing the hymns during worship. No one was going to make me do anything! I certainly did not want to go out to lunch with these people after church. I could barely stand to be within the walls with them for the hour we were there. Yet, slowly, after attending a few times, I found that these people really cared about me, because I was a child of God. They were more than willing to let me grow at my own speed, while they encouraged me along the way. Slowly, I became involved in worship, volunteered to speak, and let them talk me into attending and testifying at a summer reunion. They convinced me of the importance of my sharing my story with those who didn't know anyone gay or perhaps were too afraid to acknowledge that they did. There were people out there who did not know how to begin a conversation about *our* hopes and fears—as if they were different than their own. People began to learn that we are all more similar than different, and God loves us all, just the way he created us.

Every year since we began attending the Buffalo-Clarence congregation, the people there have supported us. They march in the Buffalo Gay Pride Parade on a yearly basis. The idea came to a couple of us, as we looked at the annual parade, and thought how we might make a positive statement and impact in our community. There were a number of churches that marched, but there were never many from any one church. What if we organized an effort to get the churches together? Each congregation could wear a different colored T-shirt with their church name on it. We could all walk as a group—a network of western New York open and affirming congregations.

The power of numbers would speak to everyone along the route, straight or gay. It would send the statement that there are congregations out there that welcome everyone with open arms—just as you are when you come through their doors. There are gay people who already attend these congregations, and there are straight allies that are enthused by our participation. It would speak to the straight people in the crowds along the parade route saying, "It's okay to be supportive! It's okay to show that you really care for someone who is different from you!"

For us, marching side-by-side is still a work in progress. However, we have the vision that we will accomplish this soon, and from there, maybe we will be able to provide direction to those congregations that want to become open and affirming. Our mission, as the Network of WNY Open and Affirming Congregations, includes this statement: "We strongly believe that everyone has a place at the table and that we are called together to stand as one, so that none need stand alone!"

My journey has taken me much farther than I would have ever imaginced, and I look forward with hopc to thc futurc! My hopc is that one day Community of Christ will acknowledge us as children of God. God knows that I am gay! Why should anything else matter?

36

Does It Matter? Yes, We Are Made in God's Image

Clyde Phillips-Frey

What provides encouragement to you when you feel discouraged? A smile? A warm touch? A few words? A friend shared with me the following poem written by an anonymous high school student when I was going through my coming out process. It provided support at a time when I needed it most.

Does It Matter?

My father asked if I am gay.
I asked, "Does it matter?"
He said, "No, not really."
I said, "Yes."
He said, "Get out of my life."
I guess it mattered.

My boss asked if I am gay.

I asked, "Does it matter?"
He said, "No, not really."
I told him, "Yes."
He said, "You're fired, faggot!"
I guess it mattered.

My friend asked if I am gay.
I said, "Does it matter?"
He said, "Not really."
I told him, "Yes."
He said, "Don't call me your friend."
I guess it mattered.

My lover asked, "Do you love me?"
I asked, "Does it matter?"
He said, "Yes."
I told him, "I love you!"
He said, "Let me hold you in my arms!"
For the first time in my life something matters.

My God asked me, "Do you love yourself?"
I said, "Does it matter?"
He said, "Yes."
I said, "How can I love myself? I am gay."
He said, "That is the way I made you."
Nothing again will ever matter.

I carried a well-worn copy of this poem in my wallet. Whenever I felt disappointed, let down, unsupported, or pushed down, I took out that tattered piece of paper, read the words, and cried. It *does* matter when we are assaulted by words that hurt us, turned away by people we mistook for friends, trampled on by those who are able to give us birth but are unable to support us without reservation, turned against by people whose so-called Christian values do not allow them to think or act for themselves. I cried because I could feel the hurt in others. I've read of those who have taken their lives, because they were not strong enough to stand alone—who lacked the realization that they had support and would never need to stand alone again. Each of us has a story to share with others, a story that points to the movement of God within our own journey, and shares of the times that we have been blessed with great love.

Geographically, my physical journey has taken me from California to Iowa, then back to California, and on to Alaska, and then to New York. Moving from California to Alaska in 1957, was a challenge for my young parents with three children, especially when there was no specific employment waiting for them at the end of the Alaska Highway. I was blessed spiritually with parents who were members of the RLDS church and had raised all of their children in a rural Alaskan church. Part of our spiritual upbringing was adherence to attendance at all church services and events. On Wednesday evenings, there was a prayer service where, primarily, the same people gathered in a local home, gave prayers or testimonies (in about the same order), and sang songs. Sundays were reserved for preaching services during both morning and evening hours. Not as many people made it back for the evening services, but I don't recall missing many.

I was nine when I was baptized a member of the RLDS church. In my preteen years, I suspected that my perception of reality might well be at odds with others in society. I realized that I belonged to what others referred to as a minor denomination. One of the lessons I learned at church was "to be in the world, but not of it." Yet, I was entering the difficult teen years and knew I was different. I desired to listen to my parents, yet I wanted to be my own person.

I began working at age thirteen. I stopped going to reunions and youth camps. They were only held during the summer months when I was able to work. In my senior year in high school, I was on the yearbook staff and edited the faculty and seniors sections. I did not date or participate in any of the social activities at school.

The words "The Last Frontier" were printed on Alaska's license plates at one time, and it was an interesting fit for a developing teen who felt like a misfit. I felt like I was growing up in an odd frontier, was a member of an unusual church, and was attracted to guys. I felt that there was no place to turn and no one to turn to for advice. Sure, there was talk around the town of gym teachers who got involved with students, but that only made things worse, because it reinforced the perception that no one wanted to know and, therefore, no one should be told—ever!

After graduating high school, I made an attempt to out myself; however, the phrase was not in use at the time. Although I have long since forgotten whatever it was I wrote in that letter, to the only adult I could think of who might be willing to sit down with me and hold a confidential discussion without going ballistic, it was a moot point as the letter went unopened for months, due to unforeseen circumstances. In my estimation, since I did not receive a response, I was either incorrect in my presumption that I would find a counselor or they simply did not want to speak with me about the matter. About four years later, I discovered that the letter was in a pile of unopened mail and had finally been found, opened, and read, months after I had initially mailed it and a long time after I left for college. For this they apologized, and I assured them that things were fine.

Going away to college was a trip. It was, literally, a trip of about four thousand miles from Fairbanks, Alaska, to Graceland College in Lamoni, Iowa, and was quite a culture shock! I had been a Boy Scout and had participated in campouts in all types of weather, and attended summer and winter camps away from home. It never dawned on me that there would be buildings on campus that looked so very different than what I was used to. I was familiar with seeing natural wood, log, and cinder block homes, and now I was experiencing red brick everywhere I looked, and I found it depressing.

My determination to get a college degree was coupled with my determination to start a new life where no one knew anything about me, and I was *sure* I could become just like everyone else. Little did I know that this would be impossible, no matter how long or how hard I tried.

During my tenure on campus, I worked as business manager for the campus paper and yearbook while keeping up my studies. The cohesiveness afforded by "house" living was exactly what I needed. Dating opportunities on campus were easier than at home due to the close proximity we shared with others and with planned events and mixers available. It became apparent that in order to really fit in, one needed to become part of an exclusive couple. It also became apparent that unless one wanted to live alone, and perhaps be lonely, there needed to be the commitment afforded by marriage.

During my last semester on campus, a trip to Des Moines for possible entrance into the military was met with a permanent medical deferment, due to a burn I accidently sustained as a teenager. The selective service and the military now had no interest in me. I became engaged, and, following my senior year, I married. Two wonderful children subsequently followed.

The ensuing years were filled with making a living, raising a family, and working in our local congregation. At church, there were always things that needed attention, and I was elected treasurer. I spent many hours in that capacity with fundraising activities that helped keep our physical facility running. I was ordained a priest and several years later, an elder. Our family was close knit, even to the point that I left my job to go to work for my spouse's extended family. Every gathering, church or family, found all of us together.

I'm not sure when the breaking point was exactly, but I do recall driving home from work around one in the morning. I was whizzing down a dark carless parkway with the windows rolled down and the stereo blasting. I found myself shouting at the top of my lungs, verbalizing a feeling that I didn't even know or want to acknowledge existed. So began a long, logical thought process. I was asking, "Why?" My life was just fine—or so I'd thought—but I began questioning and taking stock of everything in my life.

The period of my self-examination took time, and it became clear that there were issues of personal health and well being that needed to be addressed for all of the parties involved. Along the journey, I decided to seek professional assistance. During this process, I was encouraged to move outside my comfort zone and take responsibility as a participant in life. I found that I became more than a mere observer standing on the sidewalk watching everything pass by.

When my psychologist requested that I at least come out to my spouse before my next visit, I knew the doors would open to everyone. The opportunity to out myself to my spouse came almost immediately upon my arrival back home. Within the next several weeks, I came out to those friends and family members that I wanted to let know. I found that those people I had considered to be my friends were still my friends and loved me for me.

The situation we found ourselves in was less than unique. The alternatives were to remain married or to divorce. I learned that most of the folks who remained married eventually ended up divorced. Clearly, the healing process for each of us could begin once our pathways parted. The opportunity to renew our lives stood a better chance of success once we moved beyond this point that had become an impasse. Although my children were primarily grown, there were still issues with timing and anger for each of us that required healing.

Divorce is never easy for children, regardless of their age. The year I came out, my daughter was engaged and planned to be married later that year. My son was completing a college degree.

Church was another matter entirely. I was asked to surrender my priesthood card (because that's what occurs in matters of separation). I was removed from the preaching schedule and relieved of financial responsibilities as local treasurer. The actions were taken in a one-on-one setting without benefit of observation on either side. I immediately stopped attending church and made no attempt to contact anyone—nor did anyone contact me. I was angry, because I felt there was no love extended from my church family. I was sad when I realized there were things about church that I dearly missed and would probably never find again. Those were lonely times, times of despair.

After my divorce, I moved to another town, rented an apartment, found a different job, met my partner, Nathan Phillips, and bought a townhouse. Later, after introducing my partner to my children, we all became a family. My children are both married now, and enjoy and appreciate my partner in their lives.

After buying our townhouse, my folks wanted to visit us. They wanted to attend church, so we attended a congregation of Community of Christ. I told my partner that I would not pretend that we went to church on a regular basis. I do not recall my folks ever asking if that was the case. They visited every couple of years, generally following world conference, and always wanted to attend church.

The folks mentioned a gay couple they'd met at world conference who attended the Buffalo-Clarence, New York, congregation. Although I knew most of the people from that congregation, I did not know them all. I was skeptical that we might receive less than a warm welcome when we attended, since the members of that congregation would have been familiar with my former spouse and her family. Actually, it was quite the opposite. The people there were warm, friendly, and genuinely gracious. I recognized it immediately. It took my partner a while longer.

I tried attending at least one other church during this time. One was filled with folks I knew were gay. I found the atmosphere to be different, although I couldn't put my finger on exactly how. People there were friendly, greeted everyone, and made small talk, but I did not sense an underlying graciousness and caring. The hymns were unfamiliar, the surroundings were full of stained glass, dark wood, and rough stone, and I just didn't feel that I belonged.

During this time, I came to the conclusion that I was who I was, and there would be no changing. God made me, knew who I was from the beginning, and still loved me! In Community of Christ, we believe that priesthood calls are of God. I used to ask people if they really believed that. After all, isn't that what we were taught? If so, then, how could God possibly be mistaken? How could God not have known from the very beginning? The resounding response was that God knew and loved me. He held me in his arms, then, as he still does now—there must be a reason I was put here to testify of his love in my life.

My partner refers to himself as a recovering Catholic, having been baptized in that faith more than once. He also was baptized a Nazarene, Lutheran, and who knows what else. One bright Sunday morning, he woke up and said to me, "Let's go to church today." I recall thinking, "Okay, I wonder which Catholic church he intends on dragging me to!" But when I asked him where he wanted to go, I was more than slightly surprised that he wanted to go to Community of Christ, where we'd gone with my folks when they visited. We got up, dressed, and made it to church on time—although, he was still not too sure if the people there were for real.

He had been hurt along the way in his various church experiences. Those other churches always wanted him to attend and participate. It didn't matter to them that he was gay—after all, they would say he could eventually change or refrain from actively participating in *that* lifestyle.

We found there were two other couples there at Community of Christ who attended regularly and participated—one was gay and one was lesbian. My partner enjoyed the music but refused to sing in the beginning. He was particularly impressed that no one person provided ministry from the pulpit. He was also impressed that not all people who ministered from the pulpit were priesthood members, and that the services were so diverse. It took us some time before he became comfortable and realized that these people loved him as a person and would not think of asking him to change in any way.

We developed a friendship with several people and began attending a casual Thursday night get together in a member's home. There my partner learned to do some basic woodworking and built a wonderfully constructed potato box as a gift for a sister. He also learned to turn a bowl from a block of wood; the bowl now has a resting place in our kitchen. He became friends with those who sincerely loved him and encouraged him to share his light. He was a pillar of support to several and was instrumental in the process that our congregation undertook to become welcoming and affirming, where all are truly welcomed. His personality had always been infectious, and he was able to extend the hand of friendship and love to everyone in attendance.

Along the way, we began providing ministry from the pulpit, and he began attending reunion where he brought his own special brand of testimony to those in the mission center. For a few years, his travels took him to SPECTACULAR on the Graceland University campus. He also began singing in the Buffalo Gay Men's Chorus. We both volunteer in the AIDS Plus Fund of WNY, which produces Buffalo Gay Bingo and operates the Serendipity Shoppe, a high-end thrift store in Buffalo, New York. I served two terms on the GALA board of directors as secretary, and we both attended GALA retreats. His alter ego, Miss Gladys Over, has entertained folks during a rendition of Gay Bingo that will be remembered for a very long time.

During the thirteen years we've been together, my partner lost his mother and his younger brother, also gay, and I lost my dad. My partner came from a family with eight children. He was next to the youngest. His oldest sister married a person of the Jehovah's Witnesses faith. He never really knew his oldest sister because of their span in age. She was already grown and gone when he was growing up. We would go to their house to visit and were always met in the driveway, where we would chat and then be on our way. We were never allowed to come into their house to visit, because we were gay, and it was against their religion.

When Ma, as we referred to Nate's mother, was in the hospital in Syracuse, my partner and most of the rest of the family were there with her. I was in Buffalo ready to fly to Winnipeg, where I would participate in a fundraiser as the Buffalo representative for a local nonprofit organization. The phone rang at my desk and it was Ma. She asked if I could come to Syracuse to be with her son to take care of him, as she was not going to be with us much longer. Nate told me that I was the only spouse that she insisted on calling, and that she loved me dearly, too. I left almost immediately and arrived less than three hours later. She passed from this life within a day or so.

During this most difficult time, when the family came together to let their mother go, they also got to know one another better. My partner's oldest sister made the comment that she never really knew him before and was impressed with what a fine gentleman he had become. He indicated that we could all have been closer in the intervening years if it were not for alleged religious restrictions that he honestly did not understand. In explaining, he said that any religion that pulled families apart, instead of encouraging them to love one another, was not a religion to which anyone should be a party. Since that time, we have all grown closer. We've visited in one another's homes, shared meals, played board games, chatted, and shared our lives. We've attended weddings and funerals, and we've grown as a loving family.

In the process of this journey, I came to the realization that the foundation my life had been built on was firm. The church, which I somewhat despised as a youth because of its seeming lack of being able to take a stand one way or another, has actually appeared to move outside of itself and is making progress. What turmoil accepting women in the priesthood has generated. Yet, to me, it was natural. My mother could have been a poster child for women in the priesthood. Also, what unrest changing the name of the church has caused. But look where we've come since then, and how calming and cohesive the name—Community of Christ—has enabled us to become.

Could LGBT people in our membership and in our priesthood be a reality? Are we ready to truly support *everyone* who walks through our doors? Or will we continue to only support those few who live a mirror image of ourselves? I found in my journey that this is where I belong—here in this church, Community of Christ. I was baptized here, grew up here, left the fellowship, and returned with a conviction that I belonged, and I would allow no person to treat me any differently. I'm back and I'm here to testify of God in my life.

We need to be together to feel the power of God's presence in the sanctuaries of our churches and to realize hope by knowing that there are hundreds of others who share faith in a God who welcomes all to the table. We need to remember that we are not alone, and we are here to testify so others need not be alone either!

If you take only one thing away from my story, please, let it be the message that God cares, and you are loved just the way you are! We are made in God's image. God has known us from the beginning and has made us. It matters that we love ourselves! Listen to others as they express the pain through which they have grown. Extend support in whatever manner you are able. Allow yourselves to be shining examples of God's love to the world!

37

Love the Unloved: The Clearwater, Florida, Congregation Story

Heather L. Dixon

When my brother-in-law, Mark Dixon, moved to Clearwater, Florida, from California, he first attended a Metropolitan Community Church (MCC). It took a while to assure him that he would be accepted as a gay man into the Clearwater congregation, Community of Christ. When he finally started attending, he was met with love and acceptance. Although the congregation was small in number, we were a loving group of people. After a few years of attending the church, I was voted in as pastor. I knew that God had great things in store for our congregation, and I always felt there was more that we could do to show others how welcoming we were.

One day, Mark approached me with the idea of becoming part of the Welcoming Community Network. Not knowing much about it, I researched and prayed about it. I felt as if God was telling me, "This is what you need to do, and this is where you need to go." I talked to my counselors, and we decided to go forward with the process of becoming a church that was part of WCN. For the most part, people were okay with it. Their general response was, "Hey, if it causes more people to have a relationship with God, then, let's go for it."

Others, however, had mixed feelings. One person in particular said, "Well, we already are accepting. Why do we have to specify lesbian, gay, bisexual, and transgender people? Won't they feel welcome here, too?" My response to this person was these individuals have been discriminated against in the past, particularly by churches which claim everyone is accepted. I said once we put the rainbow flags on our church sign, those individuals who are gay, lesbian, bisexual, and transgender will know that they can come into a worship service and actually sit next to or hold hands with their significant other, and know that no one will judge them, or ridicule them, or ask them to leave. Once it was explained in those terms, the person quickly agreed with the idea of being part of WCN.

Mark and I arranged to have the people from WCN come to our congregation and start the process with us. During all of this, there was one woman who was not very vocal about her thoughts. In fact, Mark and I thought she might show up at these meetings just to cause problems. As pastor, the last thing I wanted was disagreement over this process. I wanted us all to be on board, as I felt strongly that this was where the Lord was leading us. On the night of the first meeting, Mark and I pulled aside the WCN presenters and told them there was one woman who may voice a lack of support or acceptance, and they needed to be prepared for that possibility. They assured us that they had dealt with this before, and they would be well prepared.

When the meeting started, the two presenters went over what it meant to be part of WCN. They talked about acceptance and tolerance. You can imagine the surprise of all of us when this woman, who had held back her opinion on the issue, spoke for the first time that night. Her exact words were, "Well, why wouldn't we accept gays and lesbians? Of course we would!" All of us just sat there in stunned silence. This woman, who had not acted very accepting and loving toward others, summed it all up in one sentence: *Why wouldn't we accept gays and lesbians?* Indeed, why wouldn't we? The congregation quickly moved through the process of becoming part of WCN, and we were very excited to be one of the first—if not the first—Community of Christ congregations to hold that distinction.

Soon after the meeting, the rainbow flags went onto our church sign. As pastor, I was filled with pride over how far our congregation had come. We had gone from one gay man feeling certain no one would accept him, to opening our doors to all who are lesbian, gay, bisexual, and transgender. Not long after the flags went out, people started to come. Individuals came to test the waters to see how we would react, and we loved and accepted them. Couples wanted to see if taking Communion together would cause a stir, and we loved and accepted them.

While all of this was going on in our congregation, I was also participating in the Co-Missioned Pastor Initiative. During one of our first meetings, we were discussing our congregation mission statements. Our congregation had been struggling through this process and not getting anywhere. It was during this meeting at the Community of Christ Temple in Independence, Missouri, that I was praying about our mission statement, and the Lord spoke to me and said, "We seek to foster peace and reconciliation by being Christ in the community." When I returned to the Clearwater congregation, I presented this statement to them, and they unanimously voted to accept it as our mission statement.

And you know what? We do seek to foster that peace and reconciliation every time a person walks through our doors. Some people come and desire a deeper relationship with the Lord, but they come in fear. They come fearful of rejection. However, these individuals are healed through the love and acceptance we have shown them—the broken are made whole. The unloved are loved. The unworthy become worthy. We are Christ in the community to all who are lesbian, gay, bisexual, and transgender. And they, in turn, seek to foster peace and reconciliation with others by being Christ in the community. And our growing congregation wouldn't have it any other way!

38

The Bruised and Brokenhearted Shall Be Blessed

Lisa Meyer

I have been involved in Community of Christ my entire life. My family was always involved in the church in Michigan. I am at least a fifth-generation member, perhaps more, but that is as far back as I have been able to track. I have attended church and camps for as long as I can remember, and I spoke in front of the congregation for the first time when I was ten. I was involved in youth groups, taught Sunday school and vacation Bible school, and was in charge of the church bulletin when I was still in high school. I went to Graceland College and was very involved there. I was a chaplain, and helped plan and carry out Renaissance Week.

When I graduated from Graceland in the 1990s, I returned home to a new congregation. It was difficult to break into a new group, and

I often didn't know where I fit. I was asked to be a youth minister and was given several other responsibilities, including leading a Ventures group and Young Peacemakers, and teaching Sunday school. I was called to the priesthood office of teacher, which fit my skills, desire to serve, and where I was spiritually in my life. I have always been committed to social justice. I truly felt called, and I was strongly encouraged by the numerous people who stood up at various business meetings to confirm this call.

I had never had a serious relationship during all of this time. I dated several people for short periods of one to three months, but I never felt a true connection with any of them. I began to feel that I might always be alone. Being committed to social justice meant I had always spoken out against discrimination against homosexuals, even from the pulpit, and I had always received relatively good reception. At that point, I didn't really understand my own sexuality, but I assumed that I was heterosexual. I hadn't really had strong feelings for anyone, male or female.

I met Erin through the church. We became very close over time, and rumors began flying around the church that something inappropriate was going on between us. I addressed these rumors with the truth. I reassured everyone that our friendship was platonic and that nothing inappropriate was happening. I also encouraged Erin to do the same. The rumors continued, even though Erin was dating a young man in the church.

In the spring of 2005, Erin and I began to realize that we did have feelings for each other. We expressed our feelings one night and realized the mutual attraction. As we talked, we began to recognize other signs throughout our lives that may have pointed this out, but we had never admitted it to ourselves before.

I felt concerned when I remembered previously defending our platonic relationship. Although that was the truth at the time, I also felt I should honestly let people know that the situation had changed. I almost immediately (within a week) began to tell people in the church about this change and that Erin and I were now dating.

I think it is fair to say that I anticipated some controversy about coming out in my congregation, but it was nowhere near the amount of hurt that I ended up experiencing. Immediately following my attempts to be honest about my sexuality, every activity I had been doing and every responsibility I had held in the congregation was stripped away from me. There were people who said that, since I was a lesbian, I was not an appropriate person to be a role model for their children. There were people who said I should be banned from the congregation. There were people who told lies about Erin and me, priesthood members who violated our confidentiality, and people who refused to acknowledge that we even existed in the congregation.

After several months of this treatment, we stopped attending the church for a number of months. Not one person asked about us or contacted us to see if we were okay. I believe they were glad to be rid of us and the apparent controversy we brought to the congregation. This whole period of time was very confusing to me, as we had a gay, male member in the congregation, and he seemed, from my perspective, to be treated well. However, once I got to know him better, I realized this was not the case. Since then, he has stopped attending the congregation and has vowed that he will never return.

Erin and I finally decided to return to the congregation at the insistence of my family. At this point, I was informed that if I wanted to remain in the office of teacher, I had to cease my relationship with Erin. I was unwilling to do this—my relationship with Erin was the only thing that felt right in my life at that point. I had prayed constantly for guidance as to whether I was doing the right thing, and had received confirmation several times that my sexuality and relationship were fine from God's perspective. I was told if I refused to end the relationship and give up my priesthood card, then I would be silenced. I was overwhelmed at that point in my life, and I questioned my relationship with the church. I agreed to give up my priesthood card to avoid being silenced.

As I continued to occasionally attend the congregation, I noticed the activities that had been taken away from me began to dwindle away in the congregation. I believed the people responsible for them were not carrying them out with the same passion that I had, but did so only to fill a position. My heart was broken, as I saw the children and youth ministry programs continue to deteriorate.

At the same time, I asked our pastoral team what I could do. As far as I knew, world church policy stated only that I could no longer be a priesthood member. It appeared to be silent on any other ministry that could be carried out. Our pastoral team put me off and stated they would have to contact our mission center president. This was the case for months. Finally, when I pushed them again, they said they thought it would be okay if I cleaned the church. This broke my heart. I didn't have a problem with cleaning the church and had taken my turn doing it in the past, but I didn't feel that it was well suited to me and my gifts.

That summer at reunion, I spoke with our mission center president. He reiterated to me that world church policy didn't say there were any other restrictions on the ministry that I provided, only that I couldn't remain in my priesthood office. I spoke with my pastors concerning this; however, they restated that they were waiting to follow up with the mission center president.

The next spring we had a series of speakers who shared with our congregation and encouraged the members to get more involved in the church. Following the third sermon in a row relating to this topic, I broke down in tears during the service. I found our pastor after the service and told her that I had to know something. I couldn't continue to sit in the congregation and hear about how nothing was being done because the people weren't willing to do it. There had to be some way that I could contribute without causing problems.

The pastor suggested that I start a young adult group at the congregation. I jumped on that. Erin and I bought pizza after church the next Sunday and invited all the young adults to attend. We had approximately twenty people there and excitedly began to plan activities for the next several months.

Shortly after that meeting, I began to hear from our pastors. They were unhappy about some of the activities that the group was planning and wanted us to report back to them before we did anything. We continued to plan and carry out activities primarily for outreach into the community.

Erin and I took a vacation to Florida around this same time. We specifically looked up Community of Christ churches in the area and found that the Clearwater congregation was a welcoming congregation. We decided to attend there on the Sunday we got into town. We found the building, saw the rainbow decal on the sign, and walked into a congregation that was so unlike our own that we almost cried. We stayed after the service and talked to some of the members and leaders of the congregation, telling them about the struggles we had faced. Mark Dixon encouraged us to attend the GALA retreat coming up on Labor Day weekend.

We did attend that retreat and discovered that the LGBT community within the church was alive and well, though some members had left the church due to frustrations about not being accepted. We felt that the GALA retreat was the only place in the church where we had felt fully accepted. I think there was a change inside of me that weekend. I had become so used to being treated like a second-class citizen that I had begun to act as if I was, even though I knew that God loved me as a lesbian woman as much as he had before I had known I was one.

I went back to my congregation, and the next Sunday we were discussing priesthood in Sunday school. I brought up the issue of my own priesthood and reminded the class that God knew I was a lesbian when he called me, even if I hadn't known it at the time. I was ridiculed and told that I should leave the congregation for "promoting the gay agenda."

Several Sundays later, the young adult group led the congregation in a worship service they had planned. I stood up and gave a testimony regarding the GALA retreat. I stated how accepted I had felt and thanked God for my partner. I found out several months later that numerous members of the congregation contacted our pastors to complain about the testimony I had given. I was told that I should no longer mention GALA or anything to do with my relationship or family life from behind the pulpit.

Erin and I continued struggling with this congregation for several more years, always anticipating our return to GALA retreats for our personal, spiritual feeding. The pain and hurt we experienced caused us to fill our lives with other things outside of church. I began to look for things to fill up the time that church activities had once occupied in my life. I applied and was accepted to graduate school. Erin and I decided to go through donor insemination to start our own family. Kennedy Marie Cavanaugh was born November 16, 2009.

Throughout our struggles with the church, we had always felt some connection to the congregation we attended, mostly due to my family's connections to it. However, there is a "last straw" to every situation, and we experienced it. Before our new pastor was elected, Erin sat down with one of the potential pastors and discussed with him his feelings relating to LGBT issues. At that point, he informed her that he was opposed to the LGBT agenda and there were multiple people in the congregation who were upset with the fact that Kennedy existed. We knew then that this congregation wasn't a place for our family to be. As much as we had tried, and as much hurt as we had experienced, we weren't willing to expose our child to this discrimination and hatred.

We began to attend an alternative evening service at another congregation within Community of Christ. We felt accepted within this small group and decided to give this congregation a chance. Although we were and still are, very tentative and guarded, we are also hopeful that this will be a different and better experience for our family.

39

The Battle

Erin Cavanaugh

I HAD MANY HILLS to climb and battles to fight on my way to becoming a member of Community of Christ. As a child, I was raised in a Catholic home. It wasn't your typical, churchgoing home. We went to church until I was in fourth grade; then, for some unknown reason, my parents quit taking us. We still understood that Catholicism was important, but, for some reason, we didn't attend anymore. During this time, a good friend of mine invited me to her church's family camp. No one knew how great an impact this invitation was going to have on me. My week at camp was incredible, and I learned so much. I was even able to witness a baptism in one of Michigan's Great Lakes.

When I came home from camp, there was hell to pay when my father found out I had witnessed a baptism outside of his faith. He forbade me to go to any more church events in *that* church. My mother fought this decision and was able to get me to a few more reunions and one wilderness camp. In the end, my dad won out, and I stopped going to the church altogether.

As time passed, I grew further and further away from Christ. I didn't have a strong foundation in his teachings. The things that ended up dictating my interests were whatever was cool in the eyes of my high school peers. In the beginning, it was sports and being extremely girly—wearing makeup and dressing up. After a while, I met some different friends and began to get into a crowd that drank, smoked weed, and frequently skipped school, along with other poor choices. During this time, my parents divorced and I began to get more and more depressed—I even contemplated suicide on several occasions.

In the summer before my junior year of high school, my friend who had asked me to church as a fourth-grader extended an invitation once more. This time, my father wasn't there to say no, because I was living with my mom after their divorce. I went to reunion, which led to two more invitations to other camps that summer. I was invited to senior high camp and then to junior high camp, as a counselor in training. During these weeks at camp, God touched my life and allowed change to happen that I didn't even know was possible. I was on fire with the Spirit of Christ. I wanted to climb the mountaintops and shout of his love.

My life changed the moment I got home. I stopped making poor choices and participating in my old, bad habits. None of my friends understood, and even my family gave me grief over my change. I started going to a congregation regularly and participated in all the events I could.

I made the decision that I wanted to be baptized and confirmed a member of Community of Christ. I was sixteen at the time, so I had to have permission from my parents. I asked my mother if I could get baptized, and she, regrettably, said that I could only after telling my father. I was terrified to tell him, but my need to get baptized was greater than my fear—so I pushed ahead. I studied the Bible and prayed at great length before approaching him. He wouldn't hear any of it and told me how horrible I would be if I went ahead with this. He told me that I was being a bad child and disobeying God's commandment to "Honor your mother and father." After several months of arguments, and weeks of my father and me not speaking, I made arrangements to get baptized three days after my seventeenth birthday.

As I became an adult, I found myself taking on more and more responsibilities in the congregation—I taught a Sunday school class, assisted with Young Peacemakers Club every Wednesday night, prayed from up front, helped at dinners and moneymaking activities, and jumped at the opportunity to help at anything I could. I was developing into a young adult and had found the place where I belonged.

Through the church, I met an incredible woman who was to become my life partner. I had always known that I had feelings for women. Other than kissing one or two girls in elementary school, I had always been too scared to act on my feelings. I knew that Lisa was perfect for me. This was a relationship that was real, and I needed to pursue it.

Lisa was in the priesthood at the time. We were both very active in our congregation doing a number of youth activities. Lisa felt that she had to come out about our relationship and be truthful with the congregation.

Upon telling the pastors, Lisa was told she had to give up her priesthood card or be silenced. Lisa struggled with this and eventually turned in her card, because she was told that was better than being silenced. Following that, all activities were taken away from us. We pleaded with the pastors and asked them what we were allowed to do. All they told us was what we couldn't do. We were finally told that we could clean the church. We had no problem helping clean the church, but we wanted to do more. It was a slap in the face—saying that we were only fit to clean. We were devastated.

The stubbornness within me kept me coming to church, because this was *my* church. I knew that God had work for me to do there, and I belonged to Community of Christ. We stayed in the congregation, did what we could, and tried our best to stand up for LGBT people. We were eventually told that we could work with the young adults, and so we formed a group.

I continued to search for resources in the church. I came across a website that told me about welcoming congregations. I was so excited and hoped that there might be one close to us. There wasn't, but I did notice that there was one in Clearwater, Florida, near my grandmother's house where we were going to be visiting.

My partner and I decided we had to check out this welcoming church in Clearwater. We were scared because of how much we had been hurt, but excited to see a congregation in Community of Christ that was accepting of LGBT people. We left for church early that Sunday morning. We allowed lots of time to get there, which was fortunate, because we got lost. When we finally arrived, ten minutes into the service, we couldn't find the entrance to the sanctuary. There were several doors into the building and we walked around quietly trying to figure out how to get in and not accidentally walk out onto the rostrum. After walking around aimlessly for a while, we decided to go back outside and try another door. This time, luckily, we found our way in.

When I walked into the sanctuary of this small Clearwater church, I had no idea how great an impact it was going to have on my life. That day, we met some people who opened their hearts to us and told us about an amazing group demonstrating acceptance, love, and spiritual growth called GALA. I also felt the overwhelming love of God there, knowing that I had finally found a place where I could be accepted as a Christian and a lesbian.

The next Labor Day weekend, we went to a GALA retreat. The experience was overwhelmingly powerful. I continued to feel God's love pour out to us through my interactions with this amazing group of people. I forged friendships that I know will last a lifetime and made a promise to myself that as long as I was able, I would be at this retreat each year.

The Sunday after we returned from the GALA retreat, our young adult group provided a testimony worship service. Lisa and I gave a testimony about how God had touched our lives at GALA. Lisa was one of three people chosen to give their testimony from the pulpit before the floor opened up for everyone. It seemed to us that the service went well and that our testimonies were well received. We later found out that our stories were not so well accepted.

After a rough day in church, we were yelled at for promoting the gay agenda and told that standing up for LGBT people was like promoting alcoholism. We were told that it was not acceptable for us to mention GALA ever again from the pulpit. We were so hurt after that Sunday that we left the church. We were gone three months and were only contacted by one person. We looked for another denomination, but, ultimately, we knew that God's plan for us was in Community of Christ.

In 2008, Lisa and I set out to start our own family. Before we began our fertility treatments, we were administered to at a GALA retreat. I believe that this was my daughter's first introduction to our church. We became pregnant and delivered a beautiful little girl in 2009.

Our congregation seemed to be getting more accepting to us. They were beginning to support us and showed nothing but love for our daughter to our faces. One day, during a conversation with a man in our congregation seeking to be pastor, I was told that there were several members of the congregation who wished that our daughter, Kennedy, was never born. They didn't think it was right for two lesbians to be moms.

Nothing in my life, to this day, has ever stung so much. We left the congregation that day, knowing that we would never again return. There was no way I was going to let them hurt my baby like they hurt us. She was a gift from God, and if they could not see that, it was their loss.

Lisa and I went to several churches outside of Community of Christ trying to find a church home. Nothing felt right. But there was no way we were going back to the congregation that had hurt us so badly. God led us another way. One of my camp friends invited me to her congregation. I resisted at first but eventually gave in and went. It has been slow going, and I know that this congregation is going to have to break down a lot of the walls I've put up. But I also know that I have found a new spiritual home. I know that my wounds have at least started to heal, and this congregation has great possibilities for us.

Community of Christ is my spiritual home. I fought hard to get into this church, and I will fight hard to stay. It is my mission for LGBT people to know that God loves them, and they have a place in

God's kingdom. Community of Christ's mission statement is: "We proclaim Jesus Christ and promote communities of joy, hope, love, and peace." There is no way to genuinely do this without God's LGBT children.

40

ON MY JOURNEY TO COURAGE

Pat Danielson

COURAGE! The sound of the cowardly lion echoes in my head. How does one find courage? How does one cross the line from cowardliness to bravery? I feel like such a coward. It has been a long coming-out journey for me.

I grew up in a happy, strict, moral, Reorganized Church of Jesus Christ of Latter Day Saint home. I was naive, shy, and ignorant as to what went on in the world. I knew my parents loved me very much. They were protective and encouraging toward me—but they could be judgmental and close minded toward others. Their attitude was due, primarily, to their strong belief in the morality of the Christian principles taught to them. I believe some of my father's attitude was because he was brought up in the culturally prejudiced South. My parents believed what they believed—and they couldn't be swayed. I know they sheltered me out of love.

I didn't know what the term gay meant and can't even remember when I first heard the word homosexual. I just didn't pay attention and was happy going through life in my Pollyanna world. What I did know was that I was attracted to women, but I didn't equate it with a label. I thought most women looked at other women and appreciated their beauty. I knew that when there was a kissing scene in a movie, it was the woman I was looking at. I remember being crazy about Doris Day. I went through the regular crushes that teenagers had on guys, and I dated and had boyfriends, but I also had crushes on girls that were obsessive at times.

As a young woman, I wanted to go to Graceland College, and I was lucky enough to be able to attend. My future husband was a Graceland graduate, but we didn't meet until after finishing school there. I took marriage very seriously, and I loved him. I had always wanted to marry a church member, preferably someone in the priesthood. He was all of that.

We were engaged for about six months but were unable to agree on many things. I wanted to call the marriage off. I decided to get some guidance from an evangelist in the church. I received a meaningful evangelist blessing and many things were made known to me about my life. God revealed that "the marriage was planned." That was certainly good enough for me to go ahead with marriage plans, and we married in 1974. We were blessed with two sons, one in 1976 and the other in 1979.

At times the marriage was good, but it deteriorated as time progressed. I went to a couple of counselors about our problems and was going to leave the marriage; but, again, my parents' influence weighed heavily, and they begged me to stay in the marriage. My parents had been complimented many times on the way they had raised my sister and me, and I know they were concerned about my decision and its reflection on them.

However, there were insurmountable problems that I will not reveal out of respect for our privacy. I could not convince my husband that his issues needed to be corrected in order for the marriage to work, and he wouldn't listen to the counselor. I felt overshadowed by a domineering personality, and I became a lonely, angry person.

In 1991, I met Mary, a friend of a friend. We occasionally met over coffee and tea at restaurants or visited on the phone. We became close friends who loved to talk about spirituality, God, and our experiences in life. She was a Christian education director and a youth director for a local United Church of Christ, and filled in for the pastor—giving sermons, helping at funerals, and visiting the sick. She had been married for twenty-three years and had two sons about the ages of my sons. She was also very unhappy. Her husband gave her no support in her church work, and she, too, was very lonely. The only reason she was still with her husband was because he had threatened to take the boys if she ever left him. She didn't love him at all because of the way he treated her, and she had considered suicide many times. I highly respected Mary for her spirituality, insight, and desire to serve God and to live a good life.

Our friendship was turning into love, and we knew it. This was the first time I recognized that I must be gay. I had never had a relationship with a woman and realized that I could connect with her on an emotional and intimate level that I had never experienced before. While I was still the same person I had always been, I had difficulty understanding that I was actually gay. Mary and I said we didn't feel like lesbians. We were two people who had fallen in love with each other who just happened to be women. It was like we had to be called gay now, and we didn't relate to the term. We had our own stereotypical prejudices and associating the word gay, to us, didn't seem to fit. Looking back, I feel that because we were ignorant of the gay community and didn't have gay friends, we had trouble relating to it.

I do know that with Mary I felt fulfilled and loved as never before. Once we realized our strong feelings for each other, I knew I owed it to my husband to be honest with him. I talked to him about my feelings for Mary and that our marriage was not working after nineteen years. It was a difficult decision to break up my home, though, because of our sons, and both my husband and I served in the priesthood. If "the marriage was planned," it was not as I had hoped and expected. I still don't know what was meant by that phrase in my evangelist blessing.

In 1993, the divorce was finalized and in a very short time things began happening. I moved to a nearby apartment and lived alone, while the boys made the decision to stay with my husband. I experienced a mixture of emotions as I wanted to be with both Mary and my sons. I didn't have the courage to tell them about my relationship with her, as I felt it wasn't their business, and as teenagers, they were too young to understand. There's that word courage again.

Mary decided to divorce and move out of her home, and one of her sons moved in with her. We were still not living together, when, in February 1994, I learned she had a rare form of uterine cancer. She had surgery, and they thought they got it all.

When Mary was first diagnosed, we had gone to one of the evangelists in the church to receive a blessing. In this blessing, he told Mary that God was encouraging us to tell those around us of our love for each other—especially to tell our sons, and it would be a blessing to others. However, God also cautioned us to use wisdom in that sharing.

It was obvious to anyone who was around us that we were in love with each other, but we never expressed any physical love in front of anyone. We weren't always sure where to practice wisdom, either. Maybe we carried the wisdom part too far. I believed I couldn't tell my parents or come out to my sons. In fact, there were people close to us that I didn't tell until those few days when Mary was in hospice. Mary was always afraid that people in her church would find out. Her pastor was so against homosexuality that she was afraid she would be fired from her job.

Luckily, we had three years where we believed she was in the clear of recurring cancer and thought we had years of happiness ahead of us. We bought a home in 1995, and, at times, one of my sons lived with us as well as her older son. Where I once felt anger, now I felt peace.

In 1998, Mary developed a cough, and the doctors found a mass in her lung. She had part of her lung removed, and then, they found a mass in her kidney. So, she had one kidney removed. Then, she found a lump in her breast, and it was diagnosed as breast cancer, unrelated to the other cancers. In the fall of 1999, we went to Nashville, Tennessee, to undergo a six-week, very expensive, controversial treatment. Her church friends donated money to cover the costs of our hotel and the treatments. They were wonderful to her, and the youth adored her. They wanted so much for her to get well.

Having returned in November, hoping that the treatment was working, I unexpectedly had to take Mary to the emergency room on New Year's Day 2000. She was acting rather strangely—calling items by the wrong names. She didn't want to go to the hospital, but I insisted on driving her to the emergency room. It was discovered then, that she had a brain tumor, and she had surgery to remove it. She made one more trip back to Nashville, as the doctors thought they could try another treatment, but there were too many tumors in her body. We knew that we were coming to the end of our journey together.

We decided to both get administered to by our friends who were priesthood members in Community of Christ. Mary was very impressed with the church and particularly the sacrament of administration to the sick. After we had both been administered to, one of the priesthood members said to us, "Mary, I have to tell you that I did not hear the prayer being said over Pat, because all I heard were these words being spoken to me over and over." The words were spoken to Mary and were: "I have not yet decided where you are to serve, but know now, because of your faith in me, that you shall always have your place in my kingdom." A few days later, a card came in the mail from the high priest with the words that were spoken, so we could always refer to them. What a great gift, and what a mountaintop experience. It gave Mary comfort and still comforts me.

I was able to keep her at home and care for her until a few days before she died in May 2000. The night that Mary died, my mother told me that she would come to stay with me. I called her from hospice and gave her the news that Mary had passed. When she came to spend the night, I finally told her that Mary and I had been more than friends. She was very upset and told me that she wished I had never told her. As I've said before, maybe we carried the wisdom advice too far, but when my mother reacted as she did, I was very discouraged and hurt.

How was I to go on without Mary? We could never stand to be apart more than a few days. What was I to do? Immediately after Mary died, I didn't care about life. I knew I didn't want to be in a relationship where I couldn't openly hold hands or kiss in public, having to constantly work at editing all my words, and feeling I couldn't tell others about my relationship. So, a guy at work asked me out, and I thought, "Why not?" I'll get into a relationship where I don't have to hide. We dated for about six months. He was very good to me when I needed care and touch, and needed to get my mind off the grief. We separated friends.

When that ended, I started to go deeper into depression. One day, my brother-in-law, a high priest in the priesthood, stopped by and let me know that he had had an experience with God impressing on him that there would be another person in my life. I laughed and said, "Please, tell me it's a guy, because I don't want to be a martyr in the congregation (since no one had come out there), and I don't want to be in a relationship where I can't tell anyone." We laughed and both knew that it wouldn't be a guy. I felt expectant and hopeful again.

In 2002, I was going to my church's world conference, and I had asked my son to go with me. He decided he couldn't go. A friend, Geri, a member of our congregation, wanted to go, so I asked her if she wanted to ride out with me. She said she did. We didn't know each other well, but as we talked with each other, we learned that we were both gay. She had been in a long-term relationship with her partner, who had died in 1987 of a very sudden illness. We had in common the death of someone whom we loved very much.

Well, I had told her about the experience my brother-in-law had and that there would be someone else in my life. We both looked at each other during world conference, believing that she was that someone. We pretty much have not been apart since that week in 2002. She moved out of her apartment and into the home that Mary and I had lived in, and then, eventually, in 2004, we bought our own home. I was so grateful that God had put another wonderful person in my life to be my companion.

I decided I would be upfront with my parents about Geri and not hide, as I couldn't stand that anymore. So, the week following conference, I went over to visit with them. Needless to say, they were not happy and told me the usual arguments against it. They used the "Adam and Steve" argument, telling me it wasn't normal, and it wasn't a moral relationship as we weren't even married (of course, we couldn't marry if we wanted to). My dad begged me not to do it, as I left the house in tears. I felt that I could never be honest with them, and they would never accept me for being me. However, for once, I had the courage to tell them the truth about our relationship at the beginning. We didn't talk for a few weeks. We never really talked about that discussion after that time. My dad passed away in 2006. He was friendly with Geri, though, and I know he really liked her. He just didn't understand.

Mom was cordial to Geri. I know she liked her a lot and tried to understand. I loved my mother very much, and I wished we could have come to a closer understanding, but I knew it could never be as I wished. I never felt that she was interested in anything I had to say about gay life. She never asked too much, but at times I would tell her of my involvement with my gay friends. Mom passed away in March 2011, just over two months ago, as I write this. My cousin, Mom's caretaker during her last few weeks, told me that Mom referred to Geri as my "companion." That was wonderful, as she always referred to Geri as my "friend" when she was introducing us. That made me happy. I know she loved me and was making strides to understand.

I was lucky that I never had any confrontations within the congregation as talk of our relationship and the fact that we were living together got around. I understood that those in the congregation who were most against our relationship were my own parents. We never announced our relationship to anyone within the congregation until we had a Listening Circle in 2008. In the break before the time of sharing, I was pacing and shaking, as I knew it would be the first time after fifteen years of silence that I told my story to members of my congregation. Funny how I could share with my friends, but the last people I felt comfortable telling were the people in my congregation. It turned out to be an emotionally gratifying experience, and it felt wonderfully liberating to finally tell the small group that day.

Because Geri and I were raised in different backgrounds and brought different cultures into our lives, we have had a growing relationship with some major problems at times. Different childhood experiences have caused us to not understand each other. She had many demons to deal with, due to abuse and neglect from her mother.

Our congregation had a healing service a few months ago. A member representing the Aaronic priesthood and I prayed for Geri. Geri previously had a dream where God told her she had a choice to make of choosing him or not. While the other priesthood member was praying over her during that healing service, the exact words were given to her that had been given in her dream. She gives the credit to God for healing her, during that service, from a lot of those demons that were getting in our way. Geri has taught me to understand and respect others who are quite different from me. She has taught me understanding and patience in our differences. Our relationship has never been better, and we look forward to our future together. I love her very much.

I have had a wonderful life and appreciate so much the enriching spiritual experiences I've been blessed with. I have many friends and acquaintances who are very supportive and enjoy being around Geri and me. I have been blessed to stay actively involved in a loving congregation that allows me to fulfill my priesthood responsibilities. I became involved with GALA in 2008 and was happy to be later elected to serve on the GALA board of directors. I have never enjoyed the warmth and friendship of anyone more than those on the board and within the GALA membership.

I am excited about the future of Community of Christ and the USA National Conference now scheduled for 2013. I love this church. It took me a long time to realize that I am gay and to not be ashamed, because I was raised to think that it was wrong. I know it isn't wrong. I know I was meant to be on this wonderful path to learn to be more nonjudgmental and accepting of all people, including those who don't understand. I was there once. I didn't understand.

I know that being gay is the best thing that ever happened to me. When this church *celebrates diversity,* then we will truly become the disciples who can change the world into that peaceable kingdom. I pray that I will always stand strong and show courage and love to those I meet on this journey.

41

Lesbian and Led to Community of Christ

Geri A. Taylor

THIS IS MY STORY of living as a lesbian in a not-so-gay-friendly world. My journey began August 12, 1956, the day I was born. At the early age of six-months-old, I was baptized in the Methodist church. By the time I was five, my alcoholic father had left home, because he could no longer stand the pressures of my mentally ill mother. We then moved in with my grandparents, who both had suffered paralyzing strokes, and my grandfather quickly became my hero. My grandmother, on the other hand, was verbally and physically abusive if I got within swinging range of her cane. For whatever reason, she hated me, so I quickly learned how close or far away to stay from her. My brother was four years my senior and from our mother's first marriage. We moved into the projects when I was eight, because that was all our mother could afford, raising two kids on her own.

We lived next door to a Pentecostal minister, his wife, and their blind daughter. They begged me to come to church with them. Mrs. Carter offered me new shoes, clothes, a coat—anything I wanted just to come to church with them once. On her deathbed, I promised her I would go to church. I kept my word and at the age of eleven ended up getting baptized, for the second time, at the Tabernacle of Christ.

It was there that I met my first love, Mary. We were secretly together for five years. People began to talk, so we thought it would be best if we started to date boys. We didn't want to be found out. Back then, being "outed" would have been devastating!

I dated Mary's cousin, George, whom I ended up marrying September 14, 1974, three months after I graduated from high school. The night before the wedding I realized I was making a huge mistake. However, Mary convinced me it was too late to turn back, so I listened and went through with it—but not without a plan.

The minister who was to marry us was legally blind and wore two hearing aids, because he was also almost deaf. His son was a minister, too. He would read the vows so Elder Carter could hear them and then repeat them to George and me. My plan was to just *not* say, "I do." Well, Elder Carter did not hear that I was not responding to the question, so he went on with the wedding, presuming that I had. I cried like a baby when he said, "I now pronounce you man and wife." People who attended the wedding thought I was crying out of happiness. They had no idea.

The only good thing that came out of my eighteen-month-long marriage was my lovely daughter Lillian. By the time she was six months old, I was a single mother, trying very desperately to figure out what was wrong with me, and to be comfortable with my sexuality and desire to be physically involved with a woman. I was also fearful of my daughter being taken away from me because of my sexual orientation.

My life spiraled into a world of sex, drugs, and alcohol. I left the church and lived as a lesbian, although I was still in the closet. Some people don't understand how this could happen. Those who have lived it, know well what I am talking about. I partied long and hard for many years—fifteen, to be exact. One morning, I woke up and said, "Enough of this." It was at that moment when God began to speak to me and move in my life, although I did not recognize it as such, at the time. I became a bus driver for the handicapped and totally quit drinking, partying, and running around.

One night, I went to bed early, because I had to get up at four o'clock in the morning for my bus route. Once I fell asleep, a bright, white light appeared, and a voice began to speak to me. The voice was neither male nor female, but it was bursting with what I could only recognize as a feeling of pure love. The voice spoke to me and indicated it was time for me to return to church; there was much work for me to do. I got up and went to the restroom, and tried to fluff this off as a dream I must have been having. But as soon as I returned to bed, closed my eyes, and drifted off to sleep, I once again encountered the white light and voice. I kept waking up, and after I looked at the clock, I wondered how in the world I was going to make it because that darn light and voice would not go away.

I was told, at one point in our conversation, that I was a very opinionated person, and, sometimes, I just needed to be quiet and listen. At that point, I could feel fingers pinching my lips together. Keep in mind, though, there was nothing but love radiating from the voice. I was told what church to go to, and, also, where it was, but ultimately, the choice was mine. About that time, I thought, "My goodness, who can I tell this to that won't think I am certifiably and totally out of my mind?" Again, I asked myself, "How am I going to cope at work, because I have been up all night now with this light and voice?" It took me a week to tell my partner what had occurred. She luckily understood and told me this was something that I should not ignore.

One day on my bus route, I drove by the church I had seen in my dreams. I pulled into the parking lot and looked around. It was a nice enough looking church. I thought to myself, "Okay, this is where you say I should be?" And I still somewhat reluctantly said, "I'll try it."

I went home, and my partner and I made plans to attend a service at that church to see what it was all about. We attended the Easter service and found it to be very moving. The people were all friendly, and, although I knew nothing about the church, I knew this was where I was supposed to be. Thereafter, I became a regular at the Reorganized Church of Jesus Christ of Latter Day Saints.

My partner and I eventually split up—I had become too holy. I wanted to get baptized and spoke with Richard Cole, our minister at the time. I expressed my concern about my inability to quit smoking and my desire to become a full-fledged member of the church. He told me not to worry about it. If I waited to quit smoking, my baptism would never occur. We set a date, July 5, 1998, and he said to let God take care of the cigarettes. So, I got baptized for a third time. By October, I had thrown out my cigarettes and I have been smoke free ever since.

The gay issue was still hanging over my head, though. I didn't know what to do with or about it. Since I was now single, I resigned myself to spending the rest of my life alone. I focused my energy on living my life in a Godly manner proclaiming the love and peace of Jesus Christ. Then, the church's 2002 World Conference came about. How excited I was! My first world conference at the temple in Independence, Missouri, which I had heard so much about! I was also selected as a delegate from our congregation, and that brought with it such an overwhelming feeling of joy.

I decided to ride to conference with Pat Danielson from our congregation. Her son was also going to ride with us. I was, and still am, very shy and I had never met her son. And I wasn't sure how I felt about Pat, because I hardly knew her. I made it a point to pack my compact discs and headphones, so I could listen to them for the twelve-hour drive to Independence—that way I wouldn't have to make small talk. It turned out, though, that her son couldn't make the trip, so it was just Patti, me, and my headphones. Patti made all the reservations, because she was familiar with the area. I never pulled out my headphones, and we gabbed all the way there. I quickly realized that it was not in God's plan for me to spend the rest of my life alone, but I was to spend it with Patti, in this church, and not in the closet!

I've come to the realization that God does not make mistakes. A person's sexuality has nothing to do with their spirituality or their relationship with God—nor should it make a difference in their relationships with others. I am so glad I did not have to live my life alone and lonely. I am gay, I am a lesbian, and I am a member of Community of Christ. I will not go away, and that is okay!

42

SHARING OUR CHURCH: A DUAL PERSPECTIVE

Samuel W. Bellinger and David Caceres

OUR STORY TOGETHER starts in 2002 and is shared here from both of our perspectives. Our time together has been a wonderful, loving experience. Not everything has been a honeymoon since we met; no one in any type of relationship experiences that. We have each been the person that the other had been looking for. We bring much to each other's life. We are challenged to grow, yet allowed to feel comfortable where we are. When Dave's life was in shambles after he lost his job, I was able to help him reorganize and get things back on track. We laugh, cry, and are growing together.

Sam's church story starts like most members. He was brought up in the church and was a fifth-generation member from Michigan. During his teenage years, he moved away from being an active participant. It wasn't until 1999, when he was having personal struggles in his life, that he sought out the church again. It was at this time that he joined a small congregation in East Lansing, Michigan. In early 2001, he received a priesthood call to the office of deacon. He was ordained in September of that year in his home congregation. After his ordination, he felt the urge to be true to himself and come to terms with being a gay male. He had repressed these feelings until this time.

Then, in early 2002, he attended his first world conference as a delegate and heard Grant McMurray's sermon. Later that year, he attended his first and only GALA retreat at Camp Bountiful in southern Ohio. For a newly out church member, this experience proved to be uplifting and spiritual. It was shortly after this retreat that our story as a couple began.

Up to this point, neither of us had dated much. When we did date, we hadn't had any long-running relationships. When Sam and I met, we bonded right away as a couple. Sam remembers well that one of the first times we were together I played for him one of the songs I had written for guitar.

When I met Sam, I was not attending church, but religion had always been important to me. I have a very deep faith that has been nurtured by my parents and some special folk who have moved in and out of my life. I was searching for a place where I fit in, a place that would accept me where I was and for the person I was. I grew up Catholic and had visited many of the Catholic churches in the Lansing area, but none of them made me feel at home or comfortable.

As our relationship grew over the next couple of months, Sam's friends at church could tell there was a change for the better in his life. He was still attending church on Sunday evenings and was very active with the Journey House (church operated housing for college students) and the congregation. We chatted a lot about life and religion during our times together.

It was in late November that we attended church together for the first time, followed by the congregation's annual harvest dinner. At first, I was a bit apprehensive about attending services. The group where Sam attended church was small and intimate. They held services in the living room of the student residence that was associated with the church. But Sam and I had shared much in the area of faith with each other, and I knew his faith was deep. I knew that he came from a strong church tradition, and that he was active in his church. So I went, but I wasn't really sure what to expect.

Wow, talk about acceptance! Everyone I met there tried to make me feel at home and welcome. The best part was that it was my kind of service. We experienced lots of sharing, music, and a message based on the teachings for that week. I had rarely witnessed that kind of feeling during a service since my days in high school when I attended a high school seminary. The music that this small group of people could produce was amazing. You were lifted to a new spiritual level as you sat in the living room of the Journey House and raised your voice with everyone else.

Whenever I pray with a new group of people, I tend to keep my eyes open. If people ask me why I do this, I tell them that I am watching to see if God is present in the group. Too often, I just don't feel his presence with people who profess to be devout Christians; I don't see him in the group. I can truly say this was a group I felt comfortable enough with that I could close my eyes when I prayed, because I knew God was present. The fact this was a group that had already accepted Sam, only added to the experience. Sam was an active minister and part of the congregation.

From this point forward we regularly attended services as a couple. Over the next year, Sam included me in his planning and speaking at services. He also had me share my ministry of music with the congregation through singing, playing guitar, and sharing my own music. I have played guitar for a while, and was familiar with a good number of religious songs and hymns. During services, I played guitar by myself or with other instrumentalists. I learned a ton of new songs and shared those I knew with the congregation. I also felt moved to create new music and share that with the group. I had not written music in a long time, but the closeness I felt to my congregation and to God moved me to start writing once again.

In 2004, Sam and I attended Community of Christ World Conference. I had learned quite a bit about the church from Sam and was thinking of joining it. We spent many of our traveling hours discussing aspects of Community of Christ. But the matter of being rebaptized weighed heavily on my mind. I had been baptized and confirmed

Catholic, attended seminary, and had been very active in my church. I just didn't understand the need to be baptized again.

During conference we attended a couple of the sessions, but spent most of our time in the temple and Auditorium, learning more about the church. We attended an evening session where Prophet-President Grant McMurray addressed the assembly. After hearing his words and seeing the openness he showed towards the LGBT community, I knew I had found a home I could be a part of and I could understand why Sam was so positive about this church. When we returned home, I shared my decision with Sam, and we started talking with folks in our congregation to begin preparing for my baptism. In August 2004, I was baptized and confirmed, and one of the best parts for me, was that my parents were there to take part in this important event.

In 2006, when Sam and I had been together for almost four years, we began talking about the possibility of having a commitment ceremony. Before we had mentioned it to our friends at church, they began asking us when we were going to do something like that. Those were confirmations to us that we really needed to do something public about our relationship. So we began the process. Little did we know where that process would lead us.

We did the usual things to prepare. We picked a date, decided on how we wanted to do the food, chose announcements and those people who would stand up with us, decided what people would wear and where we would do everything, chose rings and suits, etc. But we experienced an interesting caveat we had not expected. We had to find someone to perform the ceremony, which meant we had to get the approval of the church.

It wasn't a problem finding someone who would want to be a part of our ceremony, but we had to make sure they would still be in good standing with the church after that. So, the local leadership took it to the world church. Being new to the church, I wasn't really sure how things were supposed to happen. We were told that the question went to the Council of Twelve Apostles before a decision to allow our ceremony came back. We would be allowed to have a church ceremony; however, the minister who officiated could not be an employee of the church. So, the person who was our first choice had to bow out. But our pastor at the time was more than happy to officiate for us. We met with him, did the same survey that straight couples would do before they got married, and planned our service.

Looking back, I wondered if it was worth all the hassle that occurred. Yes, it was! It was a beautiful day, and when we exchanged rings, there was not a dry eye in the place. I wasn't able to make it through the first sentence of my vows before I started crying. The feeling of love that was there was tremendous. And the feeling of support was unquestionable.

Since then, we have continued to be active members of our church and our congregation. Sam is a deacon and holds his priesthood very sacred. We have attended every world conference, either together or separate since we have been together. Although I am not allowed to be an ordained minister in our church, I have been asked to serve on the pastoral team for our congregation. I didn't even know that was possible if you weren't ordained, but it was something that folks felt strongly about. How could I not serve those who had so willingly served my needs as I grew into this church?

Is it a perfect church? No. We would like to be the same as anyone else in our church. We would like to see people be able to share their relationships in a sacred blessing in the church and serve as ordained ministers because of who they are as humans and members—not as a result of their sexual orientation. But the place where we are as a church is a good place to be. We are light years ahead of many other denominations out there, and we are in open dialog to move to where we believe God is taking us. If that doesn't happen soon or simply doesn't turn out to be what we are hoping for, will we leave? How could we? This is our church. These are our people—the people who have shared important times in our lives. They are people who have supported us, cried with us, and laughed with us. This is our family, and we are here to stay.

43

UNEXPECTED

Kevin Williams

WHEN I COME ACROSS the unexpected, I usually do one of two things: either I ignore the unforeseen force and turn the other way, or I face it head on. Of course, there are those particular moments when you don't have a choice, and the unexpected throws your entire life in a different direction. You find yourself looking in the mirror wondering, "What happened?" It was in one of those very moments, while I was pondering, that my life revealed its twists and turns.

As my high school senior year was nearing its halfway mark, I became increasingly concerned about who I was. I had decided to leave high school at the end of my first semester and prepare for college. I made the decision after discovering that high school was but a short moment in my life. After spending my childhood moving from one state to the next, I saw life differently than others. I had found that as I stepped foot into a new school, others seemed scared to meet me, to encounter the unexpected. I began to question my reasons for "being on the outside, looking in." I slowly realized that I was the unexpected, and it gave me fuel to ask the question, "Why?" So, here is my story of discovery, renewal, and affirmation.

***

I quietly left the small town of Bailey, Colorado, and traveled east toward my new home in Lamoni, Iowa. My father helped me unload the car, hugged me, and I watched as he disappeared into the gray mist. I sat in my room that evening, crying. I knew the days and years to come were going to be different and would bring on the unexpected. I also knew I had the freedom to search and explore the question that had been haunting me, "Why?"

Rather quickly in my first semester, I began the search—and got lost. I had thought freedom of choice meant I could search anywhere without judgment. I was excited, because I felt like I was beginning to discover myself, my identity. Then, I realized that you can look too deep and find limitations. I spent countless hours as I poured over books and did little praying. I knew that, as I began to ask myself the question: "Am I gay?," I would be reminded of those classmates who were scared of me. I knew I was going to be the unexpected. A huge part of me was concerned about what others, like my roommate, thought of me, but I had to share it with someone. After a disastrous confrontational encounter with my roommate, I began to shut down. I removed myself from the world, avoided activities, and only attended classes. Sadly, my first semester was one I don't recall and choose not to remember.

I spent the summer reflecting on my identity, about how God fit in my life, and why I felt the way I did. I had grown up with a strong foundation in God, so, naturally, I should have gone to God to find my answers. But, as the next two years unrolled, I meandered through life's twists and turns. As I struggled with my identity and determined how I was to fit God in my life—knowing who I was slowly becoming—I began to realize it was not a question of whether or not I was gay, but whether or not God loved me for who I was.

I began to really wonder how God could love me. How could God love me, knowing all that I was experiencing and feeling? I hated myself. I felt clouded over and grayed out. It was after a short, powerful moment at a worship service in the midst of a Community of Christ world conference, that I discovered the unconditional love God pours over us. I discovered the breadth, the affirmation, and the strength of God's love.

My coming out differed from others in that I didn't come out to the world, per se, but I came out to God. I came out being true to myself and recognizing that despite my differences, my oddities, and the unexpectedness, God loved me for who I was. I remember that moment because I was smiling, both inside and out. I had found myself and was at peace.

My coming out differed from some in that I rarely encountered resistance. I had encountered a world that accepted my unexpectedness. I was loved and respected for, as the Latin term goes, *nosce te ipsum*—knowing thyself.

As my college years came to an end, I realized that I was really focusing on who I was. I needed to confirm my identity, on many levels. One of my favorite quotes from Shakespeare's play *Hamlet* is: "To thine own self be true." I now think to myself and wonder: How can we not be true to ourselves? It is crucial that we know ourselves. Staying true to ourselves allows us to help form our identity, and it also helps us create a great support group of those with whom we surround ourselves. I had searched from within the closet, and it took me three years to run through the doorway. I knew there were questions I needed answered. I wanted change. I wanted to find the freedom to discover!

During my college career, I became increasingly involved with the Gay Straight Alliance (GSA) on the Graceland University campus. This support group provided me with guidance, as well as a shoulder to cry on. The members of the group actively advocated for domestic partner benefits and worked to build relationships in the midst of the Human Sexuality Forums. During my tenure as president of the club, the group's name briefly changed to PROUD (People Representing Our Unique Differences). We provided support and promoted awareness through the Day of Silence, working with each "house" (Graceland's housing system or social club).

While some may disagree, we all have closets. At times, we can open the door to our closet, peer in or out, and ask ourselves, "What more is there to learn about me that I don't already know?" Honestly, every individual can peer in or out and find something different. It doesn't have to be profound or unexpected, but it should make you question something. Then again, it can just be an affirmation of the work you have already been doing. The hardest part is being willing to open that door.

I shared the following words in my senior art exhibition, *Declaration*, at Graceland:

> I want to declare. I want to be able to seek my identity without being told what my identity is. I am here declaring or should I say proclaiming my identity. It is my personhood, my embodiment, and my opportunity to recognize the diversity and the value in it. Know thyself. That is what I believe! To be able to accept our own differences, those changes, and to appreciate the uniqueness there in.

Today I have recognized, while in the midst of God's beautiful work, that our identity can be shaped by those with whom we surround ourselves. My self-identity happened to come to me during a spiritual conference where I discovered God's presence among us all. It was a true affirmation of my faith and my calling as a person.

As my journey has continued, I have been met with little hesitation and unexpectedness—but rather with much love, which has allowed me to continue to stay actively involved in church life. For several years, I served as a youth minister. While I found plenty of support in that community, there were occasional bumps along the road—opportunities to learn and grow. Through my calling to serve God, I continue to look forward to opportunities to learn and share with others, even in the difficult moments when we discover that each of us come from different places. I thank God for showing me the worth of all persons and the exciting ways that servant ministry can be offered and accepted!

44

I Left

Micah Selu

I LEFT. I did. I honestly never thought I would be on this side of the horizon. I am a child of "the Church"—with a capital C. I am a fluent speaker. I am someone who grew up in the great heart of that community—whose ancestors walked the Restoration story. I have been blessed, baptized, confirmed, administered to, ordained, hokey pokeyed, "grey squirreled," snipe hunted, the whole megillah. I got my adult blessing when it was still patriarchal and then received an evangelist blessing later, both from dear men whose wisdom I still trust implicitly. None of this makes me more of a loss, but it tells you my first language.

I left—not because I was let down, although I was, but because I was lifted up elsewhere. I was awestruck by acceptance. I personally witnessed a whole denomination stand up and say at their version of world conference, "We want you." I cried, my friends cried, and a whole row of grownups and seminary graduates hugged and cried—because an official church body told us we mattered as much as anyone else. I didn't know that I had felt fundamentally different until that moment when I finally didn't.

I asked a friend to baptize me right there on the conference floor, even though she wasn't yet clergy (they don't rebaptize and I don't believe in it). She and I were both preachers' kids, though. We got it. She put water on my head three times from the central basin and spoke the baptismal formula over me. Then, we walked back to the hotel on a hot, July night in Atlanta, through a public fountain full of giggling, screaming children. I got completely soaked in all my clothes. Then, it felt right. It's the weight of the water in my clothes that always reminds me of baptism.

Out here in the wilderness, the rules are loosey-goosey like that. It's what you do when you know what you care about, but there seems to be no framework that will hold it all. When there is no one to talk to or no one safe, you start talking to yourself. Then, if you're lucky, you notice other people talking to themselves, and it ceases to matter where they came from or that they don't speak your language. You have all found yourselves in one place because of something you care deeply about, and that something matters more to you than all the blood, history, accolades, potlucks, and reunions put together. It's an extreme place, but when it matters, you'd rather be there 100 percent than live half a life.

Leaving Community of Christ was a long process for me. For a few years after that baptism, I was a member of a congregation in another denomination, but retained my Community of Christ membership and priesthood. I made other major life decisions in those few years that reflected a sea change in my identity. I added a first name to my given name, effectively changing the name I'm called without losing any part of it. And I left the doctoral program I'd wanted so much to get into. The picture I saw of myself as a New Testament professor in a high-powered research institution popped like a bubble. I cared about the stigma of failing but was relieved to stop searching for something to motivate me to be that person. I wanted to *do* ministry.

Eventually, I entered a clinical pastoral education residency program and worked full time as a hospital chaplain for a year, as part of that. It was, as you can imagine, a profoundly significant experience. That's when I got off the fence and finally saw that if I wanted to move forward into ministry and accreditation within a denomination, I had to let go of my old commitments. I put my membership and priesthood cards in the mail postmarked July 4, 2008—Independence Day.

The whole next year I felt weightless, as if I had unzipped my skin and stepped out of it. Imagine letting go of an identity you have never been without—like your gender, or your skin color, or shaving your head (for some people). Everything was without boundaries, new and raw—all nerve endings exposed. I never expected to feel that way. It was very strange. Of course, I stayed in touch with Community of Christ family and friends. Over time, I've come to understand that you can't leave part of yourself, and mailing in a card is not the same as returning one's history.

I left, and what I've noticed is how many more people today are included among my trusted family. I, of course, include my literal family, but I also include the people to whom I am spiritually kin and with whom I consider to have common cause—people at several churches, teachers, activists, ministers, PFLAG parents, the lady who owns the tea shop in town and carries fair-trade products, the older fellow going door to door raising money for the local stroke foundation, artists, denominational colleagues, kids. Good news is abundant, and, frankly, the spirit of restoration has never been limited to one movement. We all need to study well beyond Restoration history to know the source of our spiritual roots and to understand our ecumenical kin. There is so much more to know and so much that will help us in the task of restoring, healing, and connecting. I never did much of that until I ventured out into denominational hinterlands.

Since leaving, I've moved from the United States to Canada and become a full-time foster mom to two of my partner's nieces who are from Ontario. As of this writing, my partner and I have been legally married for five years, and I'm turning forty this year. The move here is new, and I can't work legally yet, so the kind of work I'll be doing is still a mystery. I'd still like to teach. I still enjoy chaplaincy. I attend a United Church of Canada congregation and could probably serve a

United Church in a year or two. I did stop in at a local Community of Christ congregation one Sunday and introduce myself. I met some lovely people, some of whom remain friends. I'm absorbing a tremendous amount of new information right now: a new country, a new town, a new family, a new home—a new everything. We live way out in the country near Lake Huron, ten miles from the nearest town. I've always wanted kids, and I'm learning a lot raising an eleven- and twelve-year-old who have had little church background. My partner and I are teaching meditation in the evenings at the library in the small town where we live.

I don't presume not to need a spiritual home, but I have learned a wider language and now really have no single place to return to. There are things I miss everywhere and things I love everywhere. I'm a nomadic appointee kid and have never really had a hometown, anyway. I am beginning to see that all my scattered experiences do eventually coalesce into useful constellations. And right now, that's what's important for me out here in the wilderness. I try to take what comes as it comes. Grace and peace to you all.

45

Yearning for Something Sacred

Mike McFall

My experience in Community of Christ is probably different than most, but I suppose no one's story is the same. I have never been to a church camp, a reunion, or world conference. I was never a guide at a historic site, and I've never read the Book of Mormon. These things are all relatively new to me. I wasn't even baptized in the church, and I was just recently confirmed as a member. I was born into the church but not raised in it.

My immediate family was never very church oriented. I can barely recall attending Sunday services as a child, but I know we did a few times. Why we stopped, I don't really know. We would attend weddings and an occasional Christmas service but that was about it. Yet, I have always, for as long as I can remember, yearned for something sacred.

My spiritual journey has been long and varied with its ups and downs. I've studied Islam, Buddhism, and many Christian denominations. But I've never felt the Spirit like I do at Community of Christ. I've made my way back to what I feel is my home. I've always struggled with my beliefs—not only because I'm gay—but, because I seek the truth. I seek to feel whole. Somewhere along the journey I lost my way.

Like many gay men, alcohol played a huge role in my life as I struggled with coming out and entering the gay scene. Bars were the only place I knew where I could meet people I felt I could relate to. Ultimately, I discovered that we had nothing in common, other than alcohol and the next party—which eventually caught up with me, causing my life to spin out of control in a downward spiral.

I was able to land on my feet because of an angel. That angel is my aunt. She asked me to attend church with her one Sunday. I did and immediately felt at home. The people of the Troy Oaks congregation welcomed me with open arms and have never made me feel otherwise. But, I must confess that I've never officially come out of the closet to the congregation. I've never felt like I had to. Many of them know—but not all of them. And those who do know have never made me feel anything but accepted. Two positive experiences stand out.

My first experience was on a Saturday, not long after I began to attend Troy Oaks. I went to a class on the Old Testament that was well attended. The topic, of course, touched on the often-quoted passages used to denounce gay people. During the discussion, one of the older members of the congregation raised his hand and spoke with a voice choked with emotion. He began to explain how he believed that God, in all his great wisdom and love, would not have created his own child, who is gay, for him to be ostracized and condemned. At that moment, I knew I was where I needed to be.

The second experience happened the day I was confirmed. My partner, who does not attend church with me (he is originally from Malaysia and is Buddhist), attended this very important day alongside my family. Everyone at Troy Oaks was extremely warm and genuinely welcoming. The one person who stood out the most was

Talitha Pennington, our pastor and dear friend. I was so touched by how she spent a great deal of time conversing with my partner and making him feel comfortable. He, of course, had no idea what to expect from a church he had never attended but was grateful for her kindness and hospitality.

Attending and becoming a member of Community of Christ has been a very positive experience for me. I believe God has a plan for me—one that has brought me back home.

46

Committed to This Community

Stephen Donahoe

Sisters and brothers, I rise in support of this counsel. Brothers and sisters, I need you to know who I am. I was a homosexual man,

When I accepted God's call to the priesthood at the age of sixteen,

When I baptized Luke in McArthur, Ohio,

When I prayed over the sick in Orissa, India,

When I preached in Chingola, Zambia,

When I helped church members rebuild after Hurricane Katrina, and

When I accepted the job of representing the church and Outreach International in Washington, DC.

And I will always be a homosexual man. I understand that cultural differences prevent my sisters and brothers in some cultures from accepting my sexual orientation. This brings me great sadness, but I understand the complexity of this issue. However, I need all of you to know who I am. I, also, need you to know that I have many things that prevent me from fulfilling my full potential as a priest, but my loving, committed relationship with my partner is not one of these. I love him the way you love your spouse. Can you look me in the eye and tell me I don't deserve to be who I am? Will you look me in the eye and tell me I'm not worth it?

THIS IS THE STATEMENT I made at the 2010 Community of Christ World Conference to the assembly in the Auditorium as they discussed Doctrine and Covenants, section 164, allowing individual countries to decide on gay ordination and gay marriage. When I found out we would be discussing this issue at world conference, I knew what I was called to do. I knew that if I shared this piece of myself with the body of the church, there would be personal consequences, but I also knew this would shift some people's opinions. I knew there were many people around the world, who I had served in ministry with, who didn't know they were serving with a gay man. I thought that some of these people would change their opinion on gay ordination (and maybe gay marriage) if they knew I was gay. This was a risk I decided was worth taking. So, I got up and gave my testimony.

I believe that if we want church members to support changing the policy on gay ordination and gay marriage in the near future, it's necessary for people to come out, and not just in congregations that are welcoming but to people who disagree. We have to be willing to share our story. This is my story.

In 2001, at the age of sixteen, I received a priesthood calling to the office of priest. I was conflicted about accepting this call, not because I was aware of my sexual orientation and thought this would prevent me from being accepted in the priesthood, but because I didn't know if I wanted to stay in this church for the rest of my life. However, I received very strong confirmation of my calling from God and from other members, so I accepted it.

Since then, a lot has changed in my life. Like many Christians, I have gone through phases of seriously questioning my faith, but I have always decided to continue as a minister in this church. In this capacity, I baptized Luke, prayed over the sick, served communion countless times, preached in many congregations, and performed two weddings. I attended Graceland University and got very involved in Campus Ministries and Outreach International. I served a two-month World Service Corps assignment in India. I ministered in church congregations in Colombia, Nicaragua, India, Zambia, and South Africa, as I traveled during college.

In the fall of my senior year at Graceland (2007), I finally realized a major part of who I am—I am gay. I was worried that coming out would jeopardize my priesthood; however, I knew that I couldn't live a double life. I craved to live authentically—so I did. Soon after this realization, I came out to my parents and my closest friends. In the early spring of 2008, I came out publicly at an event at Graceland where we were sharing stories of discrimination. In some ways, it would have been easier for me to be silent about this major part of my life. However, I believe deeply that my sharing this piece of myself with the world can play a significant role in changing people's attitudes and prejudices—and indeed it has. For example, soon after I shared publicly at Graceland, guys on my hall virtually stopped using homophobic language.

During my sophomore year of college, I remember telling Dave and Dustee Heinze, Graceland University campus ministers, that I would never get married, because I felt a relationship with a significant other would take away from my ability to minister to people. I felt like my calling was much more important than my personal happiness.

In my evangelist blessing, right before I graduated from college, I received the affirmation that if I was able to love myself more fully, I would be able to accept the complete love of another person and enter into a loving, committed relationship. I am so happy that in January 2009, I met the man who helped me to do that. I learned to love myself, not in a prideful way but in an accepting way. I learned that it is okay for me to love another person completely. My partner and I started dating immediately and got engaged July 4, 2010.

Throughout our relationship, we have had to deal with a great deal of discrimination. The most painful is the discriminatory immigration laws of the US government. My partner is an Indian citizen. He came to the United States to get his PhD in economics and was teaching economics at a small, liberal arts college when I met him. However, his contract wasn't renewed in the spring of 2010. This was devastating, because he was relying on his job for his work visa. This jeopardized his ability to stay in the United States legally. Thankfully, after several months of tremendous stress, my partner was able to switch to a student visa to finish his dissertation. Now, his student visa is expiring soon, and he has to find a job to sponsor his work visa again, or he will have to leave. Because of the uncertainty of this situation, we have applied for Canadian residency, although neither of us wants to leave the United States.

The most frustrating part of this whole process is that if we were an opposite sex couple, we could get married, and he could become a US resident. We can legally get married in Washington, DC, where we live, but because the federal government doesn't recognize gay marriage, it wouldn't help my partner's visa situation.

Because I am dealing with this painful discrimination from the federal government, it makes the discrimination from Community of Christ much worse. I crave a community where I have the same rights and privileges that everyone else has. I crave complete acceptance of who I am. At times, I am tempted to leave Community of Christ to join a more accepting community. However, I feel a strong calling here, and I'm committed to this group of people. I want to help Community of Christ truly live out our principle of accepting the worth of all persons, and I hope that my story helps move our community toward this direction.

Afterword

Allan C. Fiscus

The Bible is a historic compilation of stories involving people, their cultures, and their relationships with God. An important part of present-day history consists of shared narratives of our own journeys through life. We grow up attending prayer and testimony services—listening to people share stories of their spiritual experiences with the living God, and we glean insight from these stories. We grow in the understanding that each person has a unique sojourn in life and relationship with the Divine. We see the living God in the lives of others, and we become filled with the Spirit.

We take time in the GALA community to share our stories. We see each person's joy, pain, laughter and tears. We see hope, love, and how the living spirit of Christ touches the life of that person and others. We see that we are not alone in our journey with Christ.

Since coming out to church leadership in the late 1970s, my journey within my faith community has been a rollercoaster ride of amazing mountaintop experiences and very low, dark valleys. Yet, when I hear the testimonies and stories of the members of this faith, my spiritual cup is filled to overflowing. Revived, I have the strength to venture forth to share my own story.

Putting ourselves out in the forefront of LGBT issues in our religion can be painful. We never know if our stories will make a difference. But, we step out in faith, anyway, believing that they will. In the thirty-plus-years I have shared my story and life journey with the faith community—in workshops, classes, reunion, retreats—I have been met with anger, suspicion, threats, laughter, and scorn. Leaving those settings feeling tarred and feathered can be very disheartening and painful. But, every once in a while, someone will come up to me and say, "If it hadn't been for you and your story, I wouldn't be here today." Then, they tell me how my story has impacted their lives. It's in those moments that the pain I've felt and the struggle I've had sharing my story is gone. I again step out in faith—believing.

In this present day and time, many people have shared their stories on the Internet in the format of "It Gets Better"—offering hope and encouragement to young people struggling with self-identity issues, bullying, loneliness, despair and even suicidal thoughts. People share deeply and passionately of themselves in the hope they can make a difference. That is what we do here. By sharing these stories, we desire to give insight, hope, and understanding of a people struggling to find a place in a faith community. In faith we open ourselves to the world—believing, desiring to serve a community of faith, as active full members, in Christ's mission of love, hope, joy and peace.

GALA IN PHOTOGRAPHS

GALA Retreat 1987, at Camp Manitou, in Michigan.
This is the first event that GALA was allowed to use church campgrounds.

Vinnie's Baptism at Deerhaven Campground in Florida.

GALA Booth at World Conference 2000.

GALA's largest retreat held at Camp Bountiful in Ohio.
Guest Ministry: President Grant McMurray.

GALA travels to Kirtland.

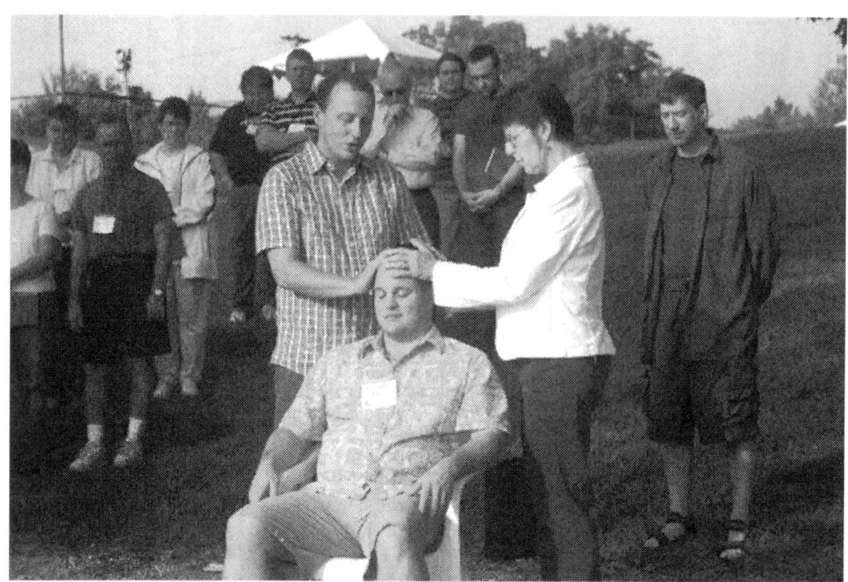

Kris's Confirmation, Camp Doniphan in Missouri.

Blessing of a Child and her family.

At San Francisco Gay Pride Event.

GALA worships in the temple in Independence.

Appendix: Definitions

Apostle: An apostle in Community of Christ is a high priest who has been set apart to be a member of the Council of Twelve and is assigned to administrate a particular field area (e.g., Apostle Bunda Chibwe administratively supervises the African Mission Field). An apostle is one who is sent to act on the authority of another—to be a representative witness. There are twelve people in the Quorum of Twelve Apostles who administer the church throughout the world.

Delegate conference: Community of Christ holds delegate conferences to make legislative decisions related to church policy and procedures. These conferences do not include full representation by every member; but, rather, local jurisdictions elect delegates to represent them in making these decisions. These conferences include *world conference*, *national conferences*, and *mission center conferences.*

GALA (Gay and Lesbian Acceptance): The GALA organization is made up of gay, lesbian, bisexual, transgender persons, and allies, who are, or have been associated with Community of Christ. The purpose of GALA is to affirm the dignity and worth of all persons without regard to gender, race, sexual orientation, or religious affiliation.

IYF (International Youth Forum): The International Youth Forum is a youth ministry experience where youth from various nations meet to learn about Christ and discuss important issues related to the church.

LGBT (Lesbian, Gay, Bisexual, and Transgender): *LGBT* is a term that refers to the collective group of persons who do not identify with the heterosexual norm. The LGBT term in this book is also used to refer to people who identify as *queer* (unconventional sexuality), *questioning* (unsure of their sexuality), *intersexed* (experiencing elements of both sexes), or *asexual* (not attracted to another person).

A *lesbian* is a woman who is attracted to other women. *Gay* refers to people who are attracted to a member of the same sex, mostly used when referring to men. *Bisexual* refers to people who are attracted to both sexes. *Transgender and transsexual*: It's interesting to note that definitions for these terms are in flux and are continuing to evolve. Often these terms are used interchangeably, as noted in "Be Yourself: Questions & Answers for Gay, Lesbian, Bisexual, and Transgendered Youth," © PFLAG (Parents, Families, and Friends of Lesbians and Gays, Inc.), 1999, 2002. "When a person's gender identity or expression differs from conventional expectations for their physical sex, they may identify as being *transgender.* The term transgender is used to describe several distinct but related groups of people who use a variety of other terms to self-identify. Transgender people can include *transsexuals* (people who change, or plan to change, their sex through surgery).... Like other people, transgendered people can be straight, gay, lesbian, or bisexual."

Member: The office of member in Community of Christ is the base unit of belonging to the church. A person becomes a member of the denomination through baptism and confirmation.

Priesthood: The Community of Christ denomination is administered through a priesthood system. The two orders of priesthood in Community of Christ are the *Aaronic* and *Melchisedec orders*. The *Melchisedec order* includes the offices of *high priest* and *elder*, as well as *evangelist, seventy, bishop, apostle,* and *president of the church*. The *Aaronic order* includes the offices of *deacon, teacher,* and *priest*. The priesthood of Community of Christ conducts the sacraments, provides order to the denomination, and provides ministry to members and each other. Almost all of the local priesthood members in Community of Christ are *lay* priesthood, meaning they receive no compensation and usually have full-time jobs elsewhere. There has recently been a move toward retaining paid pastors, but local resources determine the extent. LGBT persons in relationships are presently not eligible for priesthood. This policy has recently been extended to *all* LGBT persons, unofficially, in light of the issue being front and center in the church. Many LGBT persons serve in priesthood capacities throughout congregations who accept them fully, minus the ability to perform ordinances.

Priesthood offices: These offices are the various stations noted in priesthood (see previous definition for a more complete explanation). The offices include deacon, teacher, priest, elder, high priest, seventy, evangelist, bishop, apostle, and president.

Prophet-president: The leader of Community of Christ internationally is the prophet-president. The prophet-president has two counselors; together they make up the First Presidency. The First Presidency has the responsibility of setting broad vision for the denomination and providing primary leadership for the church. Periodically, prophetic counsel is brought to the church through the prophet-president.

Silencing: A priesthood member of Community of Christ may be silenced (or released from priesthood service) when the administrative officers of a jurisdiction determine the member is no longer fulfilling the duties of their office or when they are not meeting the expectations held for their office. Silencing is an involuntary, administrative procedure. It does not affect membership status.

SPECTACULAR: Graceland SPECTACULAR is a youth camp focused on sports, fine arts, and leadership. Sponsored by the Community of Christ, it is held at Graceland University in Lamoni, Iowa, and provides a week of programming for youth leaving grades ten through twelve. This annual camp also offers youth an opportunity to explore the possibility of attending Graceland University.

Welcoming Community Network (WCN): Welcoming Community Network is an international grassroots organization that exists to enable full participation of persons of all sexual orientations and gender identities in the life and ministry of Community of Christ, both in policy and practice (*WCN Mission Statement*). Congregations can joint this network by following the procedure given at *welcomingcommunitynetwork.org* or by contacting Welcoming Community Network, P.O. Box 1601, Independence, MO 64055.

Welcoming congregation: A welcoming congregation is defined as a congregation where LGBT persons are invited into full membership in the community and are treated as such. A congregation goes through a discernment process creating a mission statement before becoming a welcoming congregation.

Welcoming process: The welcoming process is the procedure a congregation or other organization goes through to become a welcoming congregation. This process may involve meetings, surveys, creating a welcoming statement, and other means to acquaint the membership with the needs of LGBT and other persons, as well as increasing awareness of issues related to social justice.

World Conference: World Conference (also known as International Conference) is a delegate conference that is presently held every three years in Independence, Missouri.

16647860R00146

Made in the USA
Charleston, SC
04 January 2013